A Beginner's Guide
to
Nietzsche's *Beyond Good and Evil*

For Mam and Dad,
without whom this book would not have been possible – literally.

All my love

A Beginner's Guide
to
Nietzsche's *Beyond Good and Evil*

by

Gareth Southwell

A John Wiley & Sons, Ltd., Publication

This edition first published 2009

Blackwell Publishing was acquired by John Wiley & Sons in February 2007. Blackwell's publishing programme has been merged with Wiley's global Scientific, Technical, and Medical business to form Wiley-Blackwell.

Registered Office
John Wiley & Sons Ltd, The Atrium, Southern Gate, Chichester, West Sussex, PO19 8SQ, United Kingdom

Editorial Offices
350 Main Street, Malden, MA 02148-5020, USA
9600 Garsington Road, Oxford, OX4 2DQ, UK
The Atrium, Southern Gate, Chichester, West Sussex, PO19 8SQ, UK

For details of our global editorial offices, for customer services, and for information about how to apply for permission to reuse the copyright material in this book please see our website at www.wiley.com/wiley-blackwell.

Library of Congress Cataloging-in-Publication Data

Southwell, Gareth.
  A beginner's guide to Nietzsche's Beyond good and evil / by Gareth Southwell.
    p. cm.
  Includes bibliographical references (p. 206) and index.
  ISBN 978-1-4051-6004-9 (hardcover : alk. paper) – ISBN 978-1-4051-6005-6 (pbk. : alk. paper)
1. Nietzsche, Friedrich Wilhelm, 1844–1900. Jenseits von Gut und Böse. 2. Ethics. I. Title.
  B3313.J44S68 2009
  193–dc22
                              2008026531

A catalogue record for this book is available from the British Library.

Set in 10 on 12.5 pt Minion
by SNP Best-set Typesetter Ltd., Hong Kong
Printed in Singapore by Utopia Press Pte Ltd

1   2009

Contents

List of Illustrations   vii
Acknowledgements   viii
Introduction   x

Chapter 1:   Background   1
  Life of Nietzsche   1
  Nineteenth-century Europe   8
  Romanticism and German Idealism   9
  Pessimism   9
  German Politics   11
  The Text   12

Chapter 2:   Explanation and Summary of the Main Arguments   14
  Introduction   14
  Preface   14
  Part One: On the Prejudices of Philosophers   16
  Part Two: The Free Spirit   34
  Part Three: The Religious Nature   44
  Part Four: Maxims and Interludes   52
  Part Five: On the Natural History of Morals   55
  Part Six: We Scholars   63
  Part Seven: Our Virtues   68
  Part Eight: Peoples and Fatherlands   81
  Part Nine: What is Noble?   88
  From High Mountains: Epode   103

Chapter 3:   Critical Themes   **105**
  Introduction   105
  Reality, Truth and Philosophical Prejudice   106
    Philosophical prejudices   106
      1. The will to truth   108
      2. Faith in antithetical values   110
      3. Distinction between appearance and reality   112
      4. Atomism   115
      5. Teleological explanation   120
      6. Immediate certainty   124
      7. *Causa sui*   129
      8. Reification   133
    Nietzsche's anti-realism   135
  God, Religion and the Saint   137
    The question of God's existence   137
    Religious neurosis and the saint   142
    Beyond pessimism: the *Übermensch* and the eternal return   144
  Morality, *Ressentiment* and the Will to Power   149
    Ethical naturalism   149
    A natural history of morality   151
    Ressentiment   152
    Will to power   155

Appendix: Overview of *Beyond Good and Evil*   161

Notes   169

Glossary   181

Bibliography and Suggested Reading   206

Index   210

Illustrations

1. Friedrich Nietzsche   2
2. Arthur Schopenhauer   10
3. Nietzsche as sphinx   17
4. Antithetical values   18
5. The philosopher's ass   22
6. Nietzsche's refutation of idealism   27
7. The problem of free will   30
8. Immanuel Kant   49
9. Jean-Baptiste Lamarck   69
10. Richard Wagner   82
11. Representative realism   113
12. Rutherford's model of the atom   117
13. Aristotle's four causes   121
14. Darwin's two islands   122
15. The duck–rabbit illusion   128
16. Sigmund Freud   139

Acknowledgements

To adapt an old and much-used saying, books are never finished, their editor merely gets fed up with waiting. Thankfully, this was not the case with this book, and so my first debt of gratitude is to Nick Bellorini, whose patience in waiting for this particular manuscript has been more than exemplary. I only hope that the result has merited the wait. Thanks also, of course, to everyone at Wiley-Blackwell who was involved in the production of the book, to Valery Rose, for cracking the whip (good luck with your studies!), and Caroline Richards, for euthanizing my commas (amongst other things).

Once again, as regards the development of the manuscript, I am grateful to everyone who read and provided their opinion on it. Chief of those I must thank is Professor Duncan Large, whose Nietzsche-seasoned eye was invaluable in diagnosing and remedying a host of deficiencies, and – I think it is safe to say – improving the whole immeasurably; nevertheless, of course, those flaws which remain are all my own. Thanks also to George McWilliams (once again) and to James Christopher, whose helpful and supportive comments provided a key input at an important stage of writing. To all the other teachers whom I approached and who agreed to read the manuscript, please accept my apologies that I did not take you up on your kind offers; in the end, deadlines proved much tighter than I thought they would be, and there was not time. However, there should be other opportunities to lend a hand, and I still hope to take advantage of your generosity at some point in the near future.

As regards family and friends, there are many whose support, encouragement, friendship and advice mean a lot to me, but especial thanks go to the following (in no particular order): Dr Mark, for his early-morning Nietzsche vigils, and his historical nous (I'm waiting for your version of 'Voodoo Child (Eternal Return)'); Dad, for his text-message proofreading service (you may have started something there); Robi Wan, for his inspirational anecdote, and his complete apathy regarding anything I ever do (which has allowed me frequent holidays from my daily mental toil); Mike, for revisiting Zarathustra, and for 'Rawhide' (which, unfortunately, didn't make it to the final draft, but made it to my wall); and lastly (but not small-ly), to Phill, for taking the time out to read it, and to both him and Carol for putting up with me for all these years ('sarcasm' is just 'love' with some letters added and others taken away).

Of course, no writer could hope to complete his task without the loving support of his spouse and offspring. No man is an island, and few resemble any sort of land mass at all. It is with quiet astonishment, therefore, that I found myself washed, dressed, fed, and pointed at the computer on an almost daily basis; without this assistance, and the quiet industry with which she set about her daily chores (watering the cat, hoovering the children, or whatever arcane female mysteries constitute her 'lady-day') nothing at all could have been achieved. So, to Jo, with all my love: thank you. Also adding to the general ambience of my working day, punctuating it with sometimes alarming noises and requests for intervention, I must of course mention my children (they are taller now, and of different sexes, so I must refer to them separately): to Eliot, whose inspirational lack of industry or urge to do anything which doesn't involve some sort of plank has taught me the real meaning of the phrase 'watching paint dry'; to Tesni, who rarely gives me a moment's peace, and who has taught me that, if you really want something, you must bug it incessantly until it gives in out of fear of going insane. Thank you both. It is in these twin spirits of coma-like patience and psychotic determination that I have approached the writing of this book. I think it shows.

Finally, please forgive me if I have not yet mastered the delicate political science of acknowledgement. No one has been deliberately excluded from my gratitude, and I would hate to think that you thought to find yourself here but have not. However, if this is the case, then there is obviously something you're not doing that you should be. Please remedy this immediately.

Introduction

A friend recently confided to me that, when he was 13 or so, he built a small fire in his back garden, and there, in a little ritual, burnt a copy of *Beyond Good and Evil*. It was consigned to the flames purely on the reputation of the author – he had something to do with Nazism, apparently – and, perhaps, because it had the word 'evil' in the title. Therefore, the action took on more significance than simply providing a more entertaining means of clearing his room.

Aside from the ironic fact that the Nazis themselves were quite fond of book burning, what might we have said to have saved poor Nietzsche from this fiery fate? The bad press surrounding Nietzsche has been around for some time, but it began in earnest around the time of the First World War, as a contribution by British intellectuals to the war effort, and continued with the Second World War, as part of the anti-Nazi propaganda of the Allies. Before that, his ideas had already been distorted by his anti-Semitic sister into a form that was to appeal to the young Adolf Hitler. So, whilst his reputation among serious thinkers is well established, you can usually still find those who will happily trot out the old accusations: he was a proto-Nazi who inspired Hitler; he was a racist who hated Jews; he was a sexist who hated women; he was an atheist who proclaimed that 'God is dead', and himself to be the 'Anti-Christ'; he was an amoralist who believed that 'might is right', and that all morality is just 'will to power'; he believed in a 'Master Race' of 'Supermen', whose destiny it was to rule over the genetically weak members of the 'Slave Race'; his works stem from a deranged mind, and he wrote most of them whilst in the process of going insane.

Like any good slurs, all of these accusations have a grain of truth in them – but only enough to make the untruths plausible. I will, at various points in this book, address each of these claims, and – while attempting to be as unbiased as possible – try to show what is myth, what is lie, and what has grounds for debate. In all of this, however, I will be very *biased* in trying to convince you that, whether you agree with him or not, whether you *like* him or not, Nietzsche is one of the great philosophers, and deserves to be studied seriously.

It is in contrast to this distorted image that I intend to draw a different portrait of Nietzsche. The difference between the two can be nicely illustrated if we consider that one of his books, *Twilight of the Idols*, is subtitled 'How to Philosophise with a Hammer'. Now, given the demonic caricature, it is tempting to imagine that the hammer is used to smash, to illustrate the fact that 'might is right', and that the frantic, wild-eyed madman with the huge moustache who is wielding it is set on destroying everything we hold dear. But the hammer is in fact very small and delicate – like one that an archaeologist might use with a small chisel to gently tap away the strata of years surrounding an artefact. Furthermore, the 'madman' is in fact quite still, and his head is lowered and turned to one side, as if intent on listening. But what does he hear?

> to pose questions here with a *hammer* and perhaps to receive for answer that famous hollow sound which speaks of inflated bowels – what a delight for one who has ears behind his ears – for an old psychologist and pied piper like me, in presence of whom precisely that which would like to stay silent *has to become audible* . . .[1]

But what are these hollow things? Why is it necessary to have especially acute hearing ("ears behind one's ears") to discover them? For Nietzsche, the things in question are the great, imposing 'idols' of Western culture, and there are many of them – the metaphysical systems of the philosophers, the conventional justifications of morality, the prescriptions of religious doctrine – and, in line with the old proverb that 'empty vessels make most noise', it is his job to 'sound them out', to find out not only which ones are just 'full of air', but also – as an "old psychologist" – to determine *why* they have come about, and what secret purposes they hide.

But if all these ideas, systems and beliefs are hollow, then what does that leave us with? Nothing? If, for argument's sake, you discovered that there were no God, that there were no such thing as objective truth, or 'good' or 'evil', how would you live? What would be your purpose in life? Would *anything* be permissible? Here, then, is Nietzsche's great task: faced with such assumptions, how do we move forward? What, in fact, does moving 'forward' mean? If we question our own values – *all* our values – what do we question them in relation *to*?

Philosophically speaking, these are extremely subtle and deep questions, because – ultimately – they question the nature and role of philosophy itself. Can philosophy question itself? A person who uses tools to measure things must rely on the accuracy of those tools, but what happens when we call their accuracy into question? What can we measure their accuracy with? Other tools? And the accuracy of *those* tools . . .? In a similar way, Nietzsche is seeking to understand the basis of such notions as 'truth', 'certainty', 'the Good', etc. Do we 'discover' them?

Are they fixed and unchanging? Do we create them? Nietzsche therefore represents a key influence in the history of philosophy, and is arguably the first philosopher to turn his 'philosophical microscope' upon these issues. He is also the first to question the role of the *personality* of the philosopher in his own philosophy – foreshadowing the work, some years later, of the father of psychoanalysis, Sigmund Freud (though both, undoubtedly, owe a debt to Schopenhauer). More fundamentally, he tries to show that what we think of as 'truth' is really only 'human truth', and furthermore that any other kind would be of no use to us!

The questions that Nietzsche is interested in are very difficult and subtle ones, and for this reason alone he may be considered a difficult philosopher. However, he may also be considered difficult for other reasons; chief amongst these is his style. Nietzsche was very fond of short passages of text, sometimes no more than a few lines, and rarely more than a few pages. Some of these are deliberately brief *aphorisms*, consisting generally of one or two sentences that are meant to be somewhat enigmatic, thus forcing the reader to dwell more on their possible meaning (a whole section of these can be found in Part Four of *Beyond Good and Evil*, 'Maxims and Interludes'). However, even in the parts containing long passages of text, a further problem lies in the fact that sections sometimes share the same topic or theme, but at other times go off on a tangent, take a different focus on the same problem, or discuss a seemingly unrelated issue. Therefore, the problem here for the student – and especially for the commentator – is that it is difficult to get a sense of the overall position being argued. In one sense, this is deliberate, and Nietzsche is in part reacting against the previous tendency of philosophers to arrange their philosophical views in tight, logically ordered systems. Nietzsche's method may be considered both more true to life (thoughts and observations do not tend to form themselves naturally into a coherent system), and an expression of 'anti-systematisation'. If we want to make a clear, unambiguous account of Nietzsche's thought, it is very difficult to condense the views expressed in these short, sometimes unconnected passages into a coherent whole. Furthermore, in reading Nietzsche, one gets the feeling that the opinion expressed in one particular place is only what he thought *at the time*; he is less concerned with being tied down to one opinion or another, and is more honest than a great many philosophers in admitting his own fallibility and changeability. Concerning his ideas, it is as if he is saying that they are only temporary resting places on his journey to a greater understanding:

> For me they were steps, I have climbed up upon them – therefore I had to pass over them. But they thought I wanted to settle down on them . . .[2]

Another aspect of Nietzsche's style that makes him difficult is his tone, or the way in which he expresses himself. So, quite often you may find the use of rhetorical question, direct address to the reader, irony, humour, word play, veiled reference, etc. These are all, properly speaking, literary devices, and accordingly it is no surprise to find that Nietzsche has always had a great appeal for writers, artists, and other creatively minded non-philosophers. Nevertheless, for those *studying* Nietzsche, whilst this approach may increase the literary enjoyment of the text, it can also make philosophical understanding more difficult. Let's face it: reading philosophy can be difficult enough when the writer is *trying* to make himself understood; where the author is not primarily concerned with those who might otherwise find it difficult to 'get' him, then the task of understanding can be very difficult indeed. This is not to say that Nietzsche aimed at being deliberately obscure, merely that he is writing for a particular sort of well-read, cultured and serious reader – a high standard that few of us can live up to completely.

Finally, the other aspect of Nietzsche's writing which deserves mention is its wide-ranging subject matter, and use of reference and allusion. Firstly, a great number of things are discussed with which the average reader may or may not be familiar. These range from philosophers (such as Kant, Schelling, Spinoza, Schopenhauer and Descartes) and philosophies (such as utilitarianism, stoicism and idealism), to religious, political and scientific movements (such as the Jesuits, the Enlightenment, and positivism). Allusions are also made to contemporary and historical events, which, without some sort of glossary, will more than likely render the sense of the text incomprehensible.

One of the main purposes of this book is to remove the obstacles to understanding Nietzsche that these issues represent. I have provided as full an explanation of those events, people, ideas, movements, etc. as are needed for a sound understanding of the text. Also, where ideas are expressed somewhat cryptically, I have done my best to expand on them so as to make them clear. Finally, for ease of study, I have grouped what I think are Nietzsche's main ideas under topics which make for easier relation to traditional areas of philosophy. So, in the 'Critical Themes' chapter, you will find sections on 'Reality, Truth and Philosophical Prejudice' (epistemology, or theory of knowledge), 'God, Religion and the Saint' (philosophy of religion), and 'Morality, *Ressentiment* and the Will to Power' (moral philosophy, or ethics).

I should also say a word or two about what I consider to be the best way to use this book. I am assuming that the reader will either be on a course of study where *Beyond Good and Evil* is a set text, or else that he or she is making some serious attempt to work through the book for some other purpose (e.g. for interest's sake), and requires a guide. So, whilst the book *can* be read as a general introduction to Nietzsche's philosophy, it is actually more designed as a companion to Nietzsche's text – though, of course, since *Beyond Good and Evil* may be considered a central work in Nietzsche's philosophy, the ultimate goal is also to familiarise the reader with his ideas in general. For those working through *Beyond Good and Evil*, the best method is probably, having first read the background material in Chapter 1, to then work through a section of Nietzsche's book at a time, checking understanding against the summaries in Chapter 2. After the summary of certain sections I have also made a list of the key concepts introduced in that section; these can then be looked up in the glossary (along with all other references to philosophers, philosophies, movements, ideas, etc.). On reaching the end of the text, or the sections that you have been directed to study, you can begin to work through the analyses in Chapter 3. However, this said, some readers may find it easier to start by reading Chapter 3, thus giving them an overview of Nietzsche's ideas, before actually tackling the text. Obviously, readers will use the book as they see fit, but I think it is important – for students especially – to try to get an understanding of Nietzsche's text in his own words, because the way in which he conveys his ideas is also key to understanding his philosophy.

Regarding the text itself, all quotations come from R. J. Hollingdale's Penguin translation, and page numbers refer only to this edition. However, since there are many other good translations which readers may use, and page numbers will obviously differ, I have also included the section number in all references to aid in tracking down the place of origin. I have followed this procedure for other works in translation and works that may exist in a number of editions (e.g. Descartes). Finally, for direct quotations from texts, I use "double quotes"; 'single quotes' are used for chapter or essay titles ('How the "Real World" at last Became a Myth'), to identify terms under discussion ('will to power'), or to imply that the term is not being used literally ('war') or that the traditional meaning is under question ('reality'). *Italics* are used for book titles (*Beyond Good and Evil*), to identify a technical term used for the first time (*idealism, perspectivism*), for foreign words (*cogito, a priori*), and for emphasis (you *can't* do that!).

You can find more Nietzsche study material on my website, www.philosophyonline.co.uk, including a version of the text itself. Also, if you have any comments, suggestions or questions about the book, wish to purchase copies of this or other texts, then you can contact me through the website.

It is a tricky thing to write a commentary such as this. As Nietzsche scholar Walter Kaufmann points out:

> The extent of such a commentary poses insoluble problems: if there is too little of it, students may feel that they get no help where they need it; if there is too much, it becomes an affront to the reader's knowledge and intelligence and a monument of pedantry. No mean can possibly be right for all.[3]

I have tried at all times to avoid both pitfalls. However, if I have erred, then it is probably on the side of too much, which – given that my purpose is not pedantry but the comprehension of the widest readership – I hope will be forgiven. Nietzsche would no doubt have disapproved of such an approach, which is perhaps a central reason why such a book as this is needed.

Chapter 1

Background

Life of Nietzsche[1]

Friedrich Wilhelm Nietzsche was born on 15 October 1844 in Röcken,[2] a small village just outside the town of Lützen, not far from the city of Leipzig, in what is now mid-eastern Germany. However, at the time of Nietzsche's birth, the area (the province of Saxony) was part of the Kingdom of Prussia, which at that time was the largest and most powerful of the many independent sovereign states that made up the German Confederation.[3] The nineteenth century was a time of great political upheaval in much of Europe, and as he grew up the young Nietzsche could not help but have been aware of the political and social turmoil that surrounded him.[4]

Friedrich was the first child of Carl and Franziska Nietzsche, and was followed by two other children: his sister Elisabeth, in 1846, and his brother Ludwig Joseph, two years after that. Carl was a Lutheran pastor – that is, a Christian Protestant minister who followed the teachings of Martin Luther – and was himself the son of a minister. Franziska's father had also been a minister, and so we can see that the young philosopher would have grown up amidst an atmosphere of sincere religious devotion.

In 1848, Carl Nietzsche suffered a sudden and severe deterioration into illness, and died a year later. This was probably not, as was later claimed by Nietzsche's sister, due to "becoming seriously ill as the result of a fall", but most likely due to some sort of degenerative mental illness.[5] Sadly for the Nietzsche family, this was not the last tragedy they were to face at this time, and in 1850 the youngest child, Ludwig, died (according to his mother) from "cramps while teething", which may possibly have been epilepsy.[6]

Shortly after, what remained of the Nietzsche family moved to the nearby town of Naumburg. Here, for the next eight years, Nietzsche lived as the only male in a household which consisted of his mother, his sister, his father's mother, and

Friedrich Nietzsche

two unmarried aunts (his father's sisters). As a result, he seems to have grown up in quite a cloistered environment, fussed over by his female relatives, and protected from the outside world. He appears not to have mixed well with other boys, and even at this age showed signs of the aloofness and firm adherence to personal ideals that was characteristic of him in later years.

In 1858, at the age of 14, he entered the boys' boarding school, five miles away at Pforta, on a scholarship. During the six years he spent there, he excelled in the study of religion, German literature and Latin, was good at Greek, and satisfactory in French, history, geography and the natural sciences. However, he showed little skill in mathematics and drawing.[7]

Even at this early stage there are signs of the health problems that were to dog his later life, and the school medical records indicate that he was "shortsighted and often plagued by migraine headaches".[8] The records also make the connection between Friedrich's health and the circumstances of his father's death, noting that a close eye should be kept on the son for signs of his father's illness. However, modern opinion does not generally agree with there being a connection between the condition which killed Carl and his son's later mental collapse, and most experts now agree that neither condition was a hereditary one.[9]

On graduating from Pforta in 1864, Nietzsche enrolled at the University of Bonn, where he studied theology and philosophy. At first, he made an effort to engage in the type of activity expected of the average German student. Traditionally, this included drinking, singing, the passionate discussion of serious issues, and chasing girls. Whilst at first he seems to have partaken in all of these activities, Nietzsche quickly tired of what he termed – in a letter home – the "coarse, Philistine spirit, reared in the excess of drinking, of rowdyism, of running into debt".[10] (It is good to see that today's student has shaken off these tendencies.) After a year, his disillusion with the atmosphere of Bonn was complete, and he left to take up studies at the University of Leipzig. Here, he was much happier, and he quickly settled down to his studies, which he now changed to philology.

Philology is no longer a subject studied in modern universities – at least, not by that name. Traditionally, it consists in the study of language through an analysis of written texts – usually Greek and Latin literature. Professionally, then, Nietzsche was never a philosopher (in the academic sense), and he often, half-jokingly, refers to himself as an "old philologist".[11] However, there is a serious aspect to this self-description, and it highlights an important difference between Nietzsche's approach and that of the traditional philosopher. Nietzsche, as a mature thinker, was more interested in the role that the personality of the philosopher played in his own philosophy than he was in finding answers to the traditional philosophical questions. As such, it might be said that his training in philology helped him to analyse the *way* in which the philosophical ideas were expressed, and the significance of that for understanding *how* such ideas had originated. So, whilst he does eventually have something to say about many traditional philosophical problems, he frequently gets there by his own brand of character analysis.

It was whilst at Leipzig that Nietzsche's academic career took off. His ability quickly made him a favourite of one of his teachers, a Professor Ritschl, and Nietzsche's studies flourished under his guidance. The high point of this period came in 1868 when, whilst he was working towards his doctorate, he was offered a chair in philology at the University of Basle, in northwest Switzerland. For a young man of 24, this was an exceptional achievement, but whilst this testifies to the high academic regard that Nietzsche was held in, his appointment to the position may have been in large part due to the sponsorship of his professor. On his move to Basle, Nietzsche renounced his Prussian citizenship, and for the rest of his life he was, in official terms, 'stateless'.

Whilst he initially made an attempt at fitting in – and despite the fact that it was here that he formed what was to be a lifelong friendship with Franz Overbeck, a professor of theology – his pickiness about company, and his deeply ingrained love of solitude, gradually started to exert themselves, and the friendly invitations from his fellow professors for walks and meals were mostly politely declined in favour of his own company.

Unfortunately, his teaching duties were interrupted quite early on by the outbreak of the Franco-Prussian war (1870–71). Initially aloof to the whole affair, his patriotic feelings were eventually roused (as was the case with much of the youth of the country), and he volunteered on the Prussian side as a medical orderly. However, his illusions about the glory and nobility of war were quickly shattered, and his miserable experience was compounded by, firstly, contracting both diphtheria and dysentery, and later by a bad riding accident, which saw him 'invalided' out of the service. On returning to Basle, he appears to have shared in the general good feeling at the eventual German victory, but he ultimately began to become sceptical about its value, and his abandonment of patriotism and its motives may be traced from here.

It was at this time that Nietzsche's intense and short-lived friendship with the composer Richard Wagner began to develop. The two had already met briefly in 1868, though now Wagner had moved with his wife Cosima to the Lucerne suburb of Tribschen in central Switzerland, and Nietzsche took advantage of this proximity to call on them. Nietzsche was a great admirer of Wagner's music, and possessed no little musical knowledge and ability himself (he played the piano very well, wrote his own compositions, and was generally a keen student of contemporary and classical music). The Wagners admired young Professor Nietzsche also, being drawn to his obvious learning and passion, and he quickly became a member of their close circle of intimate friends.

This friendship was ultimately to influence Nietzsche's first published work, *The Birth of Tragedy out of the Spirit of Music*, published in 1872. In it, he sets out his conception of the two competing forces at work both in art and life, the *Apollonian* and the *Dionysian*, and argues that the greatest art – such as ancient Greek tragic drama – is a synthesis of both these powers. The Apollonian (after the Greek god Apollo) symbolises the rational desire to order and control experience, and so it represents reality through forms or ideas; the Dionysian (after the Greek god Dionysus) represents a non-rational desire to go *beyond* these forms, and to directly experience reality in its raw state. In this way, the two forces are directly opposed, and constantly war with one another for dominance. Thus, Nietzsche sees his purpose as to try to bring these two forces back into balance by championing the Dionysian in what is otherwise – he considers – a rationalist age.[12]

Whilst the Wagners greatly admired the book (it was, after all, written with Wagner in mind as the great example of the perfect artist), Nietzsche's fellow professors did not view it so highly. It was, for them, insufficiently scholarly for an academic work (they considered its main arguments to be unsubstantiated conjecture), and its poor reception marks a turning point in Nietzsche's ambitions. From this point on, he began more and more to dedicate himself to his own writing, and to neglect traditional scholarly studies. Between 1873 and 1876, Nietzsche wrote four essays on contemporary German culture, which were published together as *Untimely Meditations*.[13] At this time, Nietzsche was still heavily influenced by the views of Wagner, and the ideas of German pessimistic philosopher Arthur Schopenhauer. However, two events were to begin to turn the tide in his philosophical life: the first of these was a friendship with the German author and philosopher Paul Rée, whose influence caused Nietzsche to question and ultimately abandon the pessimistic attitude he shared with Schopenhauer (and Wagner); the second was the Bayreuth Festival of 1876, which Wagner had created to showcase his music, but in which Nietzsche began to finally recognise those elements in Wagner's music and character which led him to abandon the friendship. This departure from both influences was apparent in the publication of *Human, All Too Human*, in 1878, which set out, in the form of aphorisms (short observations),[14] Nietzsche's views on a wide range of topics.

The combined factors of the reception of his published books, a related drop in the number of students choosing his courses, the attitude of his fellow professors, increased ill health, and a growing feeling that he didn't belong in academia, caused Nietzsche to withdraw further and further from university life. He took long holidays, had few teaching responsibilities, and generally gave every sign that he no longer wished to be a part of the institution. The institution itself, when, in 1879, it finally recognised this, accepted his resignation on the grounds of ill health, and for the rest of his life he was financially dependent upon its teaching pension.

Freed from his academic duties, the next ten years see Nietzsche produce his greatest and most influential works, living the life of a wandering philosopher as he moved between towns and cities in France, Italy and Switzerland, and occasionally making visits back home to see family. During this period, he maintained the habit of isolation that had been growing throughout his time at Basle, keeping contact with his few friends through regular correspondence and occasional meetings. A new friendship developed with an ex-student, Peter Gast, who aided Nietzsche in a secretarial capacity, and who, together with Franz Overbeck, remained a loyal friend of the philosopher until his death. Generally, though, whilst his many physical complaints were still present, his health generally improved at this time – though it is difficult to say how much of this was due to the freedom to constantly change his surroundings, the release from his teaching duties, or the various self-prescribed medicines, diets and treatments that he increasingly followed.

The next major work to come from Nietzsche's pen was *The Gay Science*,[15] in which he sets out his vision of the ideal life whereby the search for knowledge is tempered by a positive passion for living. At this time, he also becomes involved with Lou Salomé, whom we know him to have sought romantic involvement with. She was undoubtedly an intellectual, and though Nietzsche eventually came to see her as a prospective student rather than an equal, he obviously felt her to be enough of a kindred spirit to be his wife, delivering a proposal of marriage to her through their mutual friend, Paul Rée. However, she turned him down, and there is some suggestion that she even for a time became involved with Rée himself (though this is still open to debate). From this point on, the idea of marriage, or even female companionship, seems to disappear from Nietzsche's mind.[16]

Following the emotional upheaval caused by the peculiar situation between himself, Rée and Salomé, and amidst quarrels with his sister and mother over his involvement, Nietzsche appears to have suffered a nervous and emotional crisis. However, this was to lead to a breakthrough in his philosophy, and in the winter of 1883 he completed the first part of his great work, *Thus Spoke Zarathustra*, in only ten days. The work, which he was to complete over the next two years, represents an embodiment of Nietzsche's philosophical ideals in the person of Zarathustra, or, as he is also sometimes called, Zoroaster, a Persian mystic and founder of Zoroastrianism.[17] However, Nietzsche's Zarathustra is his own invention, and he is rather a symbol and vehicle for Nietzsche's thought than a portrait of the historical figure. Written in poetic form, *Zarathustra* sets out Nietzsche's ideas in a series of parables, sermons, and other forms of prose traditional to religious literature, strongly echoing on a grander scale Nietzsche's own conception of himself and his mission: he is the philosophical prophet of the age, come down from his hermetic isolation on the mountain to expound the truth to his fellow man.

In 1886, Nietzsche fell out with his publisher, E. W. Fritzsch, because of his publication of anti-Semitic material. From this point on, he bore his own publishing costs, and entrusted the publication to C. G. Naumann, whom Fritzsch had used as a printer; Naumann was eventually to become responsible for the printing, publication and distribution of Nietzsche's books. The first book to appear after the break with Fritzsch was *Beyond Good and Evil*, followed by second editions of some of his earlier works. This year also saw the marriage of his sister Elisabeth to the anti-Semite Bernhard Förster, an event which caused friction between them. Förster's attitudes were, in many ways, a fore-echo of Nazism, and together the couple were eventually to leave for Paraguay, where they hoped to form a racially 'pure' Germanic colony.

Towards the end of this decade, Nietzsche's output speeds up even further: 1887 saw the *Genealogy of Morals*, followed in 1888 by *Twilight of the Idols*, *The Antichrist*, *The Wagner Case* and *Ecce Homo*, a sort of philosophical biography. Some commentators have claimed that there are growing signs of Nietzsche's imminent mental collapse in these last four books – one going so far as to say that they are, "as all but a few of the most extreme Nietzscheans admit, the work of a madman"[18] (though few modern commentators now share this view). By this time, his long-term ill health, as well as the strain of his mental exertions, had begun to take their toll. On 3 January 1889, in Turin, Italy, he was arrested by the police after causing a public disturbance. The exact events are unknown, but legend has it that, seeing a man whipping a horse about the eyes, he ran to protect it by throwing his arms around its neck, after which he collapsed.

From this point on, Nietzsche's descent into madness was swift. He wrote letters to various friends, acquaintances, and even the then King of Italy, containing cryptic and half-sensical statements of his grandiose plans to save Europe. Realising what had happened, his remaining friends and family quickly came to his aid. He was first transferred to a clinic, where various treatments failed to cure him, and ultimately was brought back to live with his mother. Here he lived, for the next ten years, in a state that the medical experts of the day termed "incurable insanity",[19] paralysed down the right side of his body, and looked after by his relatives. The traditional view as to what caused Nietzsche's madness is that it was brought on by syphilis contracted from a prostitute during his student days, though there is still debate about this. Some modern research suggests that this is just part of the long smear campaign against the philosopher, and that other diagnoses – e.g., a brain tumour – provide a better fit to the evidence.[20]

On the death of her husband in Paraguay, and despite the great rift that had grown between her and her brother in the latter years, Nietzsche's sister now returned to look after him. Ultimately, it was Elisabeth's control of her brother's legacy, and her manipulation of his writing for her own anti-Semitic and nationalistic ends, that distorted his message into a form that was to appeal to such warped minds as that of Adolf Hitler.

Finally, on 25 August 1900, Nietzsche died after contracting pneumonia. He was buried at the Church in Röcken according to his sister's wishes.

Nineteenth-century Europe

In understanding Nietzsche, it is important to be familiar with some of the intellectual and social forces that would have influenced him. We may take as our starting point the end of the eighteenth century, which is generally considered to be the end of the so-called *Age of Enlightenment*, during which there was an increased emphasis on the importance of rational principles as the primary basis for government and the formation of law. During this period, key thinkers in America and Europe questioned the authority of Church and State, attacking what they saw as elitism and privilege. In America (1776) and France (1789), the ideas of figures such as Thomas Paine, Voltaire and Jean Jacques Rousseau ultimately led to revolution and the overthrow of the previous regime, and to the establishment of democratic republics. In science and philosophy, the *empiricist* ideas of John Locke and David Hume embodied a new desire to get away from the abstract metaphysical theorising associated with such *rationalist* philosophers as René Descartes and Baruch de Spinoza, and the discoveries of Sir Isaac Newton continued to inspire a new generation of scientists to account for the workings of the universe in mathematical terms.

At the beginning of the nineteenth century, other forces began to exert an influence. As war and conflict continued to redraw the map of Europe, over-throwing monarchies and reshaping nations, a gradual *Industrial Revolution* began to sweep through Europe and America, as developments in science and technology allowed many labour-intensive manual processes to be replaced by faster, more efficient mechanical ones. Industrialisation led to *urbanisation*, as a growing population formed through the expansion of towns and cities as rural workers left the country to look for better-paid factory work. In some countries (such as the UK), concerns regarding the conditions of workers and their living conditions etc. led to the formation of the first trade unions. This in turn led to the demand for social reforms and equal rights, and strike action by the workers in major industries was a major factor in – for example – the establishment of *universal suffrage*, whereby all male adults were accorded the right to vote (all of Europe did not grant women equal voting rights until the twentieth century, some not until its last quarter – e.g. Portugal in 1976 and Lichtenstein in 1984). In philosophy, this democratic, scientific and rational spirit was embodied by the English *utilitarians* Jeremy Bentham and John Stuart Mill, who tried to show that happiness could be reduced to a simple calculation involving pleasure. In such a way, the growth of democracy, industry, business, philosophy and science can be seen to have gone hand in hand.

Romanticism and German Idealism

At this time in Germany, two further important movements can be identified: *Romanticism* and *idealism*. The first of these can be seen as a response to the rationalism of the Age of Enlightenment, and a reaction against what many saw as the dehumanising effect of the Industrial Revolution. Romanticism spans the end of the eighteenth century and the beginning of the next, and can be characterised by an appeal to the emotions over reason, and a desire to return to a direct experience of nature (as opposed to a scientific understanding of it). Such attitudes were embodied by, for example, the poetry of William Wordsworth, Samuel Taylor Coleridge and Lord Byron (England), and the writing of Johann Wolfgang von Goethe (Germany); the music of Ludwig van Beethoven (Germany) and Hector Berlioz (France); the paintings of J. M. W. Turner and John Constable (England), Eugene Delacroix (France), and Caspar David Friedrich (Germany); and the philosophy of Jean Jacques Rousseau (France) and Joseph Schelling (Germany). Romantics also explored the darker side of human emotion, and the birth of the *Gothic* movement in art, literature and music can be traced from here.

German idealism stems from the writings of Immanuel Kant, whose philosophy is often termed *transcendental idealism*. Kant believed that human beings could only experience *phenomena*, and that the real objects of experience (which he termed *noumena*) could not be directly known. So, for instance, human beings experience the world in terms of sound, colour, sensation etc., but we cannot know what the world is *actually* like independent of these sense impressions. Following Kant, many philosophers took up his ideas and adapted them to their own ends. So, figures such as Johann Gottlieb Fichte, Friedrich Schelling and Georg Wilhelm Friedrich Hegel all used Kant's ideas to talk about *exactly those things* that Kant considered to be beyond experience. In this way, their ideas became *metaphysical* in that they took it upon themselves to talk about the true nature of such things as God, the soul, free will, and other issues which Kant himself had considered unknowable. In *Beyond Good and Evil*, Nietzsche is critical not only of Kant (for setting up these philosophical distinctions), but also his followers (for making their own metaphysical truths using Kant's ideas).

Pessimism

Besides Kant, the other great philosophical influence in nineteenth-century Germany was Arthur Schopenhauer, whose ideas were very popular at the time, heavily influencing not only philosophers (such as the young Nietzsche himself), but also artists

Arthur Schopenhauer

and musicians (such as Richard Wagner). Schopenhauer is traditionally associated with *pessimism*, or the philosophical view that existence has a negative value. However, rather than presenting this as a mere attitude or opinion, Schopenhauer presented arguments to show that this was logically the case. For instance, if the orbit of the earth were to shift minutely, the temperature of the earth were to change by a few degrees, or other similarly small changes were to take place, then life as we know it would end. So, in this sense, we are already living a mere step away from total extinction, and therefore in what he termed 'the worst of all possible worlds' (in direct opposition to Leibniz, who had made popular the idea that we are living in 'the best of all possible worlds').

Another key feature of Schopenhauer's pessimism is his contention that the most powerful source of human behaviour is not *intellect*, but *will*. By *will*, Schopenhauer here means the basic instinctive drives of the human being, such as the need to reproduce, to eat, to find shelter and security, to defend oneself and preserve one's life, and so on. It was these drives, Schopenhauer argued, that underlie all our motives to thought and action, and not any spiritual or moral motivation. So, for Schopenhauer, humans were closer to animals than Plato or Kant would care to admit.

As is apparent from *Beyond Good and Evil*, Nietzsche is in accord with many of these ideas: he points out the basic drives ('prejudices') motivating many philosophers, and his idea of *will to power* is quite close to Schopenhauer's conception of the will. However, Nietzsche diverges from Schopenhauer in the conclusions that he draws from these ideas. For Schopenhauer, the fact that we are driven by our basic instincts is the source of misery, because such desires are ultimately selfish, and apart from being the source of constant frustration, also produce conflict as we strive to achieve our own goals at the expense of others. In this sense, Schopenhauer's pessimism is close to *Buddhism* (which he was very influenced by) in that desire is seen as the cause of suffering, and happiness (or *enlightenment*) is considered to arise from freedom from desire. Conversely, for Nietzsche, even to give life a negative value is to make a choice, and so if we *do* have a choice, then it is better to make a positive one, and in so doing choose the highest values possible. But these values must be based on a clear acceptance of the sometimes unpleasant truths about life, and not a set of pleasant lies. Furthermore, rather than seeing the dominance of the will in the human personality as a bad thing, Nietzsche viewed it as the source of all possible happiness, and the development of stronger and more refined expressions of will (through his own enlightened brand of philosophy) as the goal of life; in this way, the temptation to falsify life – even to paint it negatively – could be overcome.

German Politics

Many of Nietzsche's comments regarding Germany in *Beyond Good and Evil* can only be fully understood against the backdrop of great political upheaval that took place from the end of the eighteenth century and through the next hundred years or so. Up until the Napoleonic wars in 1806, Germany, as it is now called, was merely part of a large collection of states in Western and Central Europe which made up the Holy Roman Empire. It was created by the great warrior-king Charlemagne who, through conquest, had expanded his initial rule over the kingdom of the Franks. After his conquest of Rome, Charlemagne considered his achievements fitting of the title of Emperor, and he was so crowned by Pope Leo III in AD 800. At its height, the Empire comprised not only Germany, but also Austria, Belgium, the Czech Republic, Liechtenstein, Luxembourg, the Netherlands, Slovenia, Switzerland, and parts of France, Italy and Poland. By the time it came to be broken up in 1806, the Empire had lasted over 1,000 years, though during this time it had undergone many internal changes, and many of its member states governed themselves.

In 1815, following the Napoleonic wars, during which Emperor Napoleon of France sought to unify much of Europe under his rule, the German Confederation was formed, combining 39 sovereign states into a loose union pledging to defend one another from outside aggressors. In 1848, revolution in Paris inspired popular revolt in various states in the Confederation as, fuelled by the ideals of Romanticism, people expressed their discontent at aristocratic rule and lack of democratic freedom. These events caused many of the states to give way and implement constitutional reform. Underlying this was a popular call for national unity, held back by a constant struggle for dominance between the member states – particularly the two strongest, Austria and Prussia, who feared that unity would require one state to be dominant (a supremacy which they both desired for themselves).

This situation continued until, in the 1860s, the Prussian Prime Minister, Otto von Bismarck, began to exert an influence towards founding a Prussian-dominated, unified Germany that excluded Austria. Bismarck's attitude embodied a new approach to politics, using both diplomacy and military might in a manner that was not driven by ideologies or belief systems, but rather by a clear, pragmatic focus on what needed to be achieved; this became known as *Realpolitik*. The situation ultimately resulted in three wars: the Danish–Prussian war (1864), the Austro-Prussian war (1866), and the Franco-Prussian War (1870–71) – Nietzsche himself served as a medical orderly in the latter. Unification was achieved in 1871, and, from this date to the end of the First World War, the German Empire (or the *Second Reich*, as it is sometimes known), was ruled by Wilhelm I (formerly King of Prussia), with Bismarck as its First Chancellor (equivalent to the British Prime Minister).

Nietzsche's attitude to these events underlies much of Part Eight of *Beyond Good and Evil* ('Peoples and Fatherlands'). Reading between the lines, we can see that he appears to have been caught up in the romantic patriotism behind the German wars of unification, but to have quickly got over it following his disillusioning experiences in the last of these wars. His opinion of Bismarck is therefore of someone who, whilst strong (he was nicknamed the 'Iron Chancellor'), lacked the ideals of previous conquering heroes (such as Charlemagne, or even Napoleon). However, he also realised that the future of Germany lay in moving *forward*, rather than in harking back to the days of the Holy Roman Empire, or in looking to a falsely romantic nationalism, the only purpose of which was the increased political power of a unified Germany.[21]

The Text

Before progressing to an analysis of the text itself, it is perhaps useful to consider some of its history. *Beyond Good and Evil* (hereafter *BGE*) was originally intended by Nietzsche to form part of a larger work which he had provisionally entitled *The Will to Power*,[22] and later *The Revaluation of All Values* (initially the book's subtitle). However, whilst this work never materialised, it is still useful to consider *BGE* as fulfilling a definite purpose in this overall project.

Nietzsche began collecting material for the *Will to Power* project after *Thus Spoke Zarathustra*, and at least as early as 1885, but did not announce his intention to write such a work until the publication of the *Genealogy of Morals* in 1886. As such, he drafted a number of different plans as to the project's organisation, and it looks as if his central purpose was to organise his philosophy into a comprehensive whole. From this point of view, *BGE* can be seen partly as an elaboration of the ideas presented in *Zarathustra* in poetic form, but also as a selection from the material that Nietzsche had amassed toward the larger work. In *Ecce Homo*, published in 1888, Nietzsche describes *BGE* as "an attack on modernity", and we can view one of the central purposes of the book as providing a critique of contemporary values and philosophies. Therefore, *BGE* may have formed part of the 'negative phase' of the *Will to Power* project; a destruction of false foundations before the building stage – the 'revaluation of all values' – which was to follow. However, these plans were all ultimately abandoned. *The Anti-Christ*, published in 1888, originally bore the subtitle 'Book One of the Revaluation of All Values', but even this was removed from later editions. Some see this as a suggestion that, rather than being a future work that Nietzsche never completed, the *Will to Power/Revaluation of All Values* project was actually complete, and that with the publication of *The Anti-Christ*, Nietzsche had actually reached the conclusion of the project.[23] If this is so, then *The Will to Power* would begin with *BGE* and contain all Nietzsche's publications from there on, up to and including *The Anti-Christ*.

As for *BGE* itself, it was begun in the summer of 1885 and finished sometime around the spring of 1886, being published in August of that year. As noted above, *BGE* was the first of his books to be published at his own expense, but it sold poorly and he was unable even to cover his publishing costs. This was largely the case with all Nietzsche's books from *Human, All Too Human* onwards, and, as a result, *BGE* went largely unread.[24]

However, this began to change following Nietzsche's breakdown in 1889. There were three editions of *BGE* in the early 1890s, and it has never been out of print since that time. More generally, Nietzsche's philosophical stock also began to rise, and – whilst his ideas were not ignored during his lifetime – his influence and recognition continued to increase. With the exception of his appropriation by the Nazis as the 'Aryan philosopher', and the anti-Nietzsche propaganda arising from the two world wars, Nietzsche's standing has continued to grow, and his influence upon modern philosophers – such as Sartre, Heidegger, Derrida and Foucault – is unquestioned, as is his place amongst the most influential thinkers of modern times. As such, *BGE* may now genuinely be considered "one of the greatest books by a very great thinker".[25]

Chapter 2

Explanation and Summary of the Main Arguments

Introduction

What follows is a section-by-section guide to *Beyond Good and Evil (BGE)*. I haven't tried to summarise and paraphrase every point that Nietzsche makes, or to explain every difficult phrase that occurs, but rather to follow and explain the main arguments as they arise. Sometimes, summaries of short sections take up a fair bit of space, because they contain important ideas; at other times, longer sections of Nietzsche's text can be summarised quite briefly, because they contain ideas that have already by that stage been dealt with.

To aid understanding, I have listed key concepts at the end of the section in which they first occur; these can then be looked up in the Glossary. I do not list them in later sections where they reoccur, but the main sections in which each key concept is discussed are listed next to each term in the glossary. I also identify and number the philosophical prejudices of Part One as they arise, but please bear in mind that this list is not definitive, that other commentators may disagree as to the number of prejudices, and that Nietzsche himself did not number them in this way.

Finally, in terms of my attitude to the material, I do not at this stage present any criticisms of Nietzsche's ideas. This is mainly because I want you to treat the ideas with as much sympathy as possible in order to fully understand them. A full critical analysis of Nietzsche's ideas follows in Chapter 3, 'Critical Themes'.

Preface

The preface to *BGE* briefly introduces many of the themes and topics that Nietzsche will cover. He begins humorously by pointing out that, if Truth may be symbolised as a woman, then most philosophers – with their serious attitude and clumsy urgency to get answers – wouldn't get very far with her! The views that such philosophers profess are merely *dogmatic*, based on unfounded beliefs (philosophical prejudices), and – warns Nietzsche – the day when such attitudes must come to an end is close at hand. However, if we view such philosophical opinions as humanity's first attempts – i.e. as childhood playthings to be discarded as we progress – then we can begin to develop new and better ideas. The conception of truth which Nietzsche proposes here is one which is not fixed and absolute, but rather admits the fact that each one of us has a different *perspective* on truth (he will develop this idea of *perspectivism* later in more detail).

Nietzsche then lists examples of such dogmatic ideas (the idea of the soul, the notion of pure spirit, the 'Good'), and suggests that we should even be grateful to these philosophical errors for allowing us to build up our strength in seeking to recognise, learn from, and overcome them. Such ideas (e.g. Christianity and Platonism) have created a false picture of reality, and in turn this has created a great tension in society; science and reason, for instance, has had to fight against the dominance of the Catholic Church in order to establish itself and gain freedom for its ideas. The determination and effort involved in battling such errors are very useful qualities for a philosopher to possess – a *new* philosopher, that is, or 'free spirit', such as Nietzsche is himself.

There are two final points worth noting here. Nietzsche mentions two instances where certain movements in society have sought to relieve this tension and struggle between reason and belief (or dogmatism). The first of these is *Jesuitism*, which was a religious movement within Catholicism that approached moral questions by allowing people to 'bend' the moral law to suit their own purposes. In an age that was becoming increasingly secular (and turning away from religion), it sought to avoid direct confrontation between new, more liberal values, and traditional Christian doctrines. Jesuitism may also be interpreted here as justifying illusory beliefs: if an individual has lost their faith, a Jesuit approach would be to carry on 'going through the motions' in the hope that they would regain it; thus, religious belief becomes divorced from reason, but faith persists. Jesuitism as a whole therefore sought to relax the tension between reason and belief (which had been at odds with one another in Europe for centuries).

The other movement mentioned is democracy, which seeks to relax the social tension by giving the illusion of equality to the common man. The example that Nietzsche uses is the printing press, which, by making information freely available, creates the illusion that all people live in an open and free society. Whilst it appears that this new society is non-dogmatic, and that there are no unfounded beliefs, in reality the dogmas which the democratic man has to live by are simply more subtle. (In other words, simply because morality does not spring from God,

King and Church, it does not mean that there aren't *new* powers that impose their own values.)

It may surprise you here that, in criticising the effect of Jesuitism and democracy, Nietzsche appears to be in favour of the tension caused by the struggle against dogmatism and illusion. This is the first example of his complex attitude towards truth; it is more important to him that a would-be philosopher is given the opportunity to develop his own strength, than it is that he is trained in 'correct' opinions. This is because the philosopher of the future is one who will question all values, and will need all the strength he can muster to go beyond traditional prejudices and dogmas (i.e. beyond what most people consider to be 'good' and 'evil').

Key Concepts:　　*dogmatism*
　　　　　　　　　philosophical prejudice

Part One: On the Prejudices of Philosophers

Section 1

Here Nietzsche introduces the idea of what he calls the "will to truth". By this he means the central impulse that has driven most philosophers to date in search of philosophical truths that they see as being completely objective, and which can therefore be 'discovered' impartially.[1] However, Nietzsche asks, where does this supposedly impartial desire for truth spring from? Why do we seek truth, and not, for instance, some more convenient alternative (such as ignorance, which – he implies – may at times be more pleasant, or even in some ways more useful)? This question of what value 'truth' holds for us is one, he says, which has not been asked before, and it is almost as if in doing this (to use the metaphor of the ancient Greek myth), the Sphinx has taught *us* to ask questions of *it*.[2]

Key Concept:　　*will to truth* (the 1st philosophical prejudice)

Section 2

Nietzsche begins to explore the relationship between things which we generally hold to be opposites of one another (truth and error, selflessness and self-interest, etc.). In certain cases, he argues, where we value one thing over its opposite (e.g. 'good' over 'evil'), we generally find that philosophers have attempted to show that there is no relation between the two ideas (they are *antithetical*), and that the valued one (e.g. 'good') must have arisen from a completely different source from its opposite, and must be completely different in nature. So, for instance, certain

Nietzsche as Sphinx

philosophers (such as Kant) see immoral or 'bad' acts as based in self-interest. However, in order to be different, moral or 'good' acts *cannot* then be based on – for instance – a different *degree* of self-interest (i.e. be simply *less* selfish), but must not involve any self-interest *at all*. For instance, it might be argued that if I say 'stealing is wrong', then it is merely another way of saying, 'I do not want to be stolen from, therefore no one should steal.' This would make the law against stealing an extension of my own desire to safeguard my own possessions. But the type of philosophers Nietzsche is criticising here would not accept such an explanation, because it would mean that people do not do good *for its own sake*, but rather out of *an extension of their own self-interest*.

Nietzsche is asking two questions here: firstly, whether such a view is in fact possible (whether, for instance, an 'absolute good', separate from all personal motivations, can in fact exist); secondly, whether the majority of philosophers and theologians up until now have not just been deluding themselves as to the separate origins of such ideas, and that there is in fact a close relationship between them. This "faith in antithetical values" (as he calls it) is a very important target for Nietzsche, and the central focus of the whole of Part One is the identification and analysis of the reasons for such 'prejudices'.

Key Concept: *faith in antithetical values* (the 2nd philosophical prejudice)

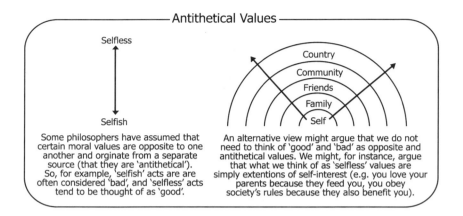

Antithetical Values

Selfless

↕

Selfish

Country
Community
Friends
Family
Self

Some philosophers have assumed that certain moral values are opposite to one another and orginate from a separate source (that they are 'antithetical'). So, for example, 'selfish' acts are are often considered 'bad', and 'selfless' acts tend to be thought of as 'good'.

An alternative view might argue that we do not need to think of 'good' and 'bad' as opposite and antithetical values. We might, for instance, argue that what we think of as 'selfless' values are simply extentions of self-interest (e.g. you love your parents because they feed you, you obey society's rules because they also benefit you).

Section 3

Continuing his attack on the notion of antithetical values, Nietzsche asserts that conscious thought is more closely related to – and more heavily influenced by – the instincts than has been previously thought. In proposing this, Nietzsche is foreshadowing the doctrines of certain schools of psychology (especially psycho-analysis) and the notion of the *unconscious mind*. Consciousness, he argues, plays no greater role in thinking than the act of being born does in the passing on and development of genetic traits – that is, none at all. In other words, conscious thought, rather than being responsible for a philosopher's freely chosen rational opinions via pure logic (as most philosophers thought up to that time), is actually "secretly directed and compelled into definite channels by his instincts".[3] But what are these instincts, and what is their purpose? They are, Nietzsche says, "physio-logical demands for the preservation of a certain species of life".[4]

Over the forthcoming sections, Nietzsche will explain in more detail what he means by this view, but it is enough to understand at this point that he is making a definite connection between *what* a philosopher thinks (his philosophy), and the philosopher himself (that is, his personality, his physical constitution, his upbringing, his environment, etc.). All these factors, Nietzsche argues, play an important part in determining what the philosopher thinks, and – more impor-tantly – what *values* he promotes via his philosophy.

Notice also that he refers to the preservation of "a certain species" of life, and not simply the 'preservation of life'; this is an important distinction, because Nietzsche will eventually argue that each philosophy (and, indeed, each philoso-pher) embodies a particular set of values and approach to life. In criticising phi-losophers/philosophies, Nietzsche is *not* merely pointing out that they are driven by their instincts (whereas *he* is not), but rather, as he will later argue, that *it may be impossible not to be driven by the instincts*, and that, in developing a philosophy, we must attempt to consciously embody only the best and most life-affirming of these instincts.

One last thing to notice in this short – but important – section is the link that all these observations have with the notion of 'truth'. In the previous section, Nietzsche refers to the possibility that our notion of truth, far from being an objective one, is in some way linked to its opposite – i.e. the *subjective*, individual, instinctive view of the world that all individuals begin with. Ultimately, he is arguing that there is no such thing as objective truth, but merely an extension of *subjective* truth (this is Nietzsche's doctrine of *perspectivism*). What has happened with the majority of philosophers is that they have tried to convince others that their own subjective truth (based on their own instinctive set of values) is *objective*, and that others *must* share or abide by those same values. Of course, they do not consciously think of themselves as doing that – but Nietzsche does!

Key Concepts: *perspectivism*
                  unconscious mind

Section 4

Nietzsche expands upon the points made in the previous section by arguing that we must "recognise untruth as a condition of life", and that "to renounce false judgements would be to renounce life".[5] What an extraordinary thing to say! Most philosophers have traditionally sought to avoid error and to find ways of guaranteeing truth, but here Nietzsche has turned the whole enterprise on its head: in seeking to establish and guarantee truth, he argues, we are in fact *falsifying* life. More importantly, in doing so we are creating conditions whereby the central concerns of life – and of human beings especially – are preserved and advanced. 'falsification', in this sense, would seem to be an unavoidable and yet vital process.

At this point, it is debatable as to what Nietzsche is actually implying. On the one hand, we may interpret him as arguing that no absolutely objective truth exists, and that all our attempts to 'know it' are only really extensions of what we would like to be the case. Additionally, we might also interpret him as arguing that, even if it were possible to arrive at an objective truth, *it would be of no use to us*. In other words, human beings falsify and simplify life in order to survive: we group separate things into convenient wholes; we attribute specific cause-and-effect relationships between things, whereas – in 'reality' – such convenient groupings may not 'actually' exist. For instance, what we think of as 'sound' is a concept relative to the human ability to hear (it would be, and is, different for a dog, or a bat, for instance). You might argue that, even so, we can still describe sound in terms of the motions of particles and waves and the laws of physics.

However, even here we are dealing with concepts evolved by human beings in order to explain certain events. For instance, the very idea of a 'thing' – a separate physical object – is, on one level, a convenient one, for if energy connects us all at some level, then we might 'actually' say that there is no such thing as a 'separate object'.[6] Furthermore, he concludes, it is in analysing our treasured values and concepts in this way that we ourselves progress 'beyond good and evil' – or, in other words, beyond the conventional value judgements which form our outlook on life, knowledge and morality.

Section 5

Picking up again on the role played by the personality of philosophers in the development of their philosophy, Nietzsche emphasises the average philosopher's complete lack of awareness of this. They are "innocent", and generally assume that they have 'discovered' truth by objective means, whereas in reality what has happened is that their philosophy springs from "a desire of the heart sifted and made abstract". For instance, if we look at Spinoza's philosophy, we can see that the mathematical form in which he set out his philosophical propositions actually reveals the "personal timidity and vulnerability . . . of a sick recluse". In other words, Spinoza's attempt to reinforce his philosophical system with such tight, mathematical reasoning is actually a sign of his own physical timidity in life. A *psychoanalyst* might ask, 'In doing this, what is he *compensating* for?' The extreme lengths he went to in order to make his philosophy appear rigorous and robust merely betray the extent to which Spinoza himself relied on its support as consolation and compensation for his own personal deficiencies and misfortunes in life.

Key Concept: *psychoanalysis*

Section 6

Nietzsche sees each individual as being made up of different "drives" or motivations – e.g. a particular type of emotion, a physical need. Each of these drives attempts to "philosophise" – in other words, it attempts to be dominant and to establish a world view based upon its own values. As such, then, there is no one "drive to knowledge" (or "will to truth", as he also calls it), but rather a great number of competing drives which seek dominance over the others (as he says, "every drive is tyrannical" – i.e. would play the 'tyrant', and seek to rule over all). What a philosopher thinks of as an objective "drive to knowledge" is really only one of these instinctive drives in disguise.

The only exception to this – and the only possible way in which a sort of 'objectivity' may be achievable – is where an individual's main interests lie elsewhere in life (in family or politics, for instance), and where their scholarly pursuits run on like "some little independent clockwork", free from the interference of any of their instinctive drives (which are preoccupied with other interests). However, Nietzsche implies, such an attitude will not be found in philosophy (where "there is nothing whatsoever impersonal"), and may only be useful for impartial observation and collection of data (such as the activities of "a specialist in fungus or a chemist").

Section 7

Nietzsche makes occasional references to the Greek philosopher Epicurus through-out his writings. Where these are not merely passing references, they are mostly favourable comments, and Nietzsche may have recognised in Epicurus an example of a sceptical philosopher who did not unwittingly falsify the nature of the world in order to achieve happiness, but rather promoted a moderate enjoyment of simple pleasures.[7] In contrast to this, Nietzsche sees Plato as the prime example of the type of philosopher who tries to argue that his moral views are objectively correct, and, in consequence, that their truth must be accepted by everyone. In Epicurus we can therefore see a parallel to Nietzsche: both philosophers are scepti-cal about the nature of knowledge, but nonetheless advocate a positive attitude to life – whereas Plato and his followers, who fabricate a false picture of life, are merely "playactors".[8]

Section 8

Continuing the analogy with the theatre, Nietzsche compares the "conviction" of the philosopher (i.e. the instinctive drive on which his philosophy is based), to the ass that arrived on stage during the medieval Mystery play,[9] ready to carry Jesus. Whilst there are a number of other associations here, the main point is that the ass is traditionally an unglamorous 'beast of burden', and that its appearance is somewhat comical. As a metaphor for the philosopher's basic view of the world, Nietzsche is saying that no matter how impressive and sophisticated the philoso-phy appears, at the bottom of it lies a humble and simple conviction (the 'ass'), which reveals the philosopher's basic drives (the fundamental attitudes and values upon which his philosophy is built). In this sense, every philosophical 'perfor-mance' must have its 'ass'.

Section 9

Nietzsche criticises Stoicism for saying that we should live "according to nature". But, he argues, to do this we would have to misrepresent nature (imagining it to be an ordered and harmonious force, embodying principles which human

The Philosopher's Ass

beings may adopt). However, Nietzsche's view of nature is rather different. It is, he says,

> prodigal beyond measure, indifferent beyond measure, without aims or intentions, without mercy or justice, at once fruitful and barren and uncertain.[10]

This wasteful, bountiful, amoral and purposeless force is fundamentally *indifferent* to human affairs. It does not care what happens to any one living creature, but is a totally *unconscious* power. This view of nature is closer to that of Darwin and may be contrasted with certain religious perspectives, which ascribe some purpose or order to nature. Traditionally, this has been a problem for religious believers (i.e. why, if 'God is love', and He created nature, do the members of the animal kingdom insist on tearing one another apart?). Some traditions propose that the reason for this is that we currently exist in a 'fallen state' (due to the 'Original Sin' of Adam and Eve), and that when a new heaven is made on Earth, "the wolf shall dwell with the lamb" (i.e. the creatures of the natural world will coexist in harmony).[11] Of course, naturalists will point out that there *is* a harmony and balance in the natural world, it is just an amoral one (what might be called 'the law of the jungle' or 'the survival of the fittest').

But for Stoics, the problem is not a religious one. Rather, it stems from the idea that somehow the correct moral action or attitude can be arrived at by trying to live in harmony with nature. However, as Nietzsche points out, to do so would not be to live *morally*. Therefore, the Stoic is actually creating an image of nature according to their own ideal – in a similar fashion to the way that, according to Nietzsche, Plato creates a metaphysical world of ideas (the *forms*) which act as a basis for our moral actions and judgements. Underlying most philosophies is always this attempt to create the world 'in its own image'. This, he argues, is the most sophisticated form of what he calls the "will to power" – that is, the drive to dominate and control others (this idea is central to Nietzsche's philosophy, and we will return to it in later sections – e.g. 13, 18–19, and 22).

Key Concepts: *stoicism*
           will to power

Section 10

It is an old problem in philosophy that 'what you see' is not always 'what you get'. The Sun 'rises', but in fact it is the Earth which turns; the straight stick half-submerged in water appears crooked, but it is light which is bent; the stars shine down on us, but in reality they are in a different position – or may even have died and disappeared altogether. Such standard examples suggest that 'appearance' is different from 'reality', and that if we are to arrive at the truth then some work is needed. The idea that such a reality exists 'behind' surface appearances goes back to Plato, who believed that to ultimately understand the world we must arrive at the true ideas or 'forms' of things (as he called them). But Platonism is not the only philosophy to paint this type of picture, and Nietzsche observes that different examples of this philosophical prejudice are widespread in the Europe of his time – for example, in the philosophy of Kant and his followers (who, although he is not mentioned in this passage, is certainly intended).

Nietzsche also observes that this prejudice can be used for different ends. Some, he says, have used it to try to guarantee absolute certainty – even where this results in a belief in the meaninglessness and absurdity of life (*nihilism* – e.g. the philosophy of Schopenhauer). Others, on the other hand, have used it to try to provide arguments for the existence of the soul (which at least, Nietzsche says, is an attempt to replace the emptiness of "modern ideas" with something by which we can live "more vigorously and joyfully").

But what are these "modern ideas"? Nietzsche mentions "so-called positivism", which we may take as a reference to the influence of the growth of scientific thinking, and the empiricist idea that true knowledge can only be based on the evidence of the senses allied to scientific method. As Nietzsche points out, however, positivism can itself lead to nihilism (to the belief in 'nothing' – i.e. no God or moral values, and consequently, no *inherent* meaning to life).

Key Concepts: *appearance and reality* (the 3rd philosophical prejudice)
modern ideas
nihilism
positivism

Section 11

In this section, Nietzsche focuses in more detail on the contribution of Kant to German philosophy. For Nietzsche, Kant's achievement lay in 'discovering' a new way in which certain types of judgement can be guaranteed as true. To understand Nietzsche's criticism of Kant fully, it will eventually be necessary to delve more deeply into Kant's idea that there are such things as 'synthetic *a priori*' judgements – something which I shall do later.[12] But for now, it is enough to understand that – for Nietzsche – Kant is guilty of the same type of philosophical prejudice as many philosophers to date. In this case, Nietzsche argues, Kant tries to argue that the reason we can be objective about certain types of value judgements (e.g. moral ones regarding how we should act), is that human reason itself contains within it the basis for distinguishing right from wrong (in other words, we are already fitted with a 'moral faculty'). Here, Nietzsche mockingly asks,

> But is that – an answer? An explanation? Or is it not rather merely a repetition of the question?[13]

24

In other words, Kant's argument is circular: How are moral judgements possible? By means of a moral-judgement-making faculty. It is like asking how the drug opium induces sleep, and receiving the answer, 'by a sleep-making power contained in the drug' – in other words, the answer tells us nothing (it is no answer at all). To which Nietzsche adds, "answers like that belong in comedy".

Nietzsche argues that the question here should not be 'how?' but 'why?' – that is, given that such 'faculties' cannot truly be said to exist, why did Kant and his followers (such as Schelling) – and German philosophy and culture itself – feel the need to invent ('discover') them? The answer, Nietzsche argues, lies in the role that such 'false beliefs' play in furthering the desire to promote certain values over others – in this case, the need of certain groups of people to find a basis for a morality which resisted the "overwhelming sensualism which had overflowed out of the previous century" (i.e. materialistic science).[14]

Key Concepts: *sensualism*
                    synthetic a priori

Section 12

In the same way as Copernicus first taught us to distrust the evidence of our senses regarding the position of the earth in the universe, so – Nietzsche argues – such thinkers as the eighteenth-century physicist Roger Joseph Boscovich have shown that even the idea of there being a final material basis to the universe (the atom) is an illusion, or merely a convenient way of talking. Modern science, especially quantum physics, whilst it may or may not agree with this, would certainly agree that the search for an ultimate picture of the universe at the smallest scale remains an elusive quest.

However, Nietzsche argues, the significance of this does not end there, because 'atomistic thinking' (as it may be called) "still goes on living a dangerous after-life in regions where no one suspects it". Nietzsche points out that we find the "atomistic need" being expressed, for instance, in the Christian doctrine of the soul. But whilst we may reject this picture as yet another philosophical prejudice (i.e. that there must be a centre to things – or, in this case, to human consciousness and personality), the idea itself need not die. Here, scientists (who are "clumsy naturalists") cannot "touch 'the soul' without losing it" – that is, they look for a tangible, physical reality and, not finding one, reject the idea totally. However, the concept of 'the soul' may live on in other ways. For instance, we may use it to describe the collection of socially constructed "drives and emotions" which the human being consists of. In this way, Nietzsche is hoping to avoid the dogmatic 'atomism' that, ironically, is the basis of the religious view of the self *and* the reason why science rejects the very idea of the soul (i.e. because it finds no 'atom'). (See also sections 17, 20, 32 and 34.)

Key Concept: *atomism* (the 4th philosophical prejudice)

Section 13

Nietzsche is arguing here that self-preservation is not the ultimate drive (as certain biologists and evolutionists – such as Darwin – would maintain), but merely an expression of the deeper "will to power". The ultimate drive, for Nietzsche, is the desire of each thing "to *vent* its strength". We must be careful here not to interpret Nietzsche merely as saying that the most powerful survive (that 'might is right'). Rather, he is saying that the life force simply wants to express ("vent") itself and that it has no ultimate purpose ("teleological principles") beyond that. However, in expressing itself, the life force gives rise to what *appear* to be drives with a specific goal (e.g. self-preservation), and it is these that biologists have latched onto. In this sense, the desire to attribute a purpose to life is yet another example of a philosophical prejudice.[15]

Key Concept: *teleological explanation* (the 5th philosophical prejudice)

Section 14

This fascinating section sums up Nietzsche's approach to science. On the one hand, as we have seen from previous sections, he is critical of attempts by certain philosophers – such as Plato and Kant – to establish a *metaphysical* basis for morality and truth. But, as can be seen from his comments here, he is also equally critical of the opposite attempt – that is, a positivistic, scientific view of the world that attempts to explain everything purely in terms of "that which can be seen and felt". The problem, Nietzsche argues, is that physics – and science in general – has "the eyes and the hands on its side", and therefore appeals more strongly to the senses. At least, he points out, philosophers such as Plato had a "*noble* mode of thinking" and did not let the "mob of the senses" overwhelm their reason.[16]

Nietzsche's underlying suggestion here is that we should understand science as simply a means of interpreting the world, and *not* as an explanation. In this sense, it is only another metaphor, and we must not let ourselves be trapped into a view of the world dictated by this metaphor, because *we control and choose the metaphors*. Obviously, this is not a suggestion that would sit very well with many modern scientists, but it would have a certain following from those who see our world view as 'socially constructed'.[17] In this sense, Nietzsche argues, we may view the current emphasis on scientific positivism simply as a way of facilitating technological progress (the work of "machinists and bridge builders").

Key Concept: *metaphysics*

Section 15

For the biological sciences ("physiology") to progress, we must reject the *idealist* notion that the physical world is merely an illusion or 'appearance' brought about by the senses. This distinction between the 'real' and merely 'apparent' world – one that goes back to Plato and can be found again in Kant – is based on a view of the senses as untrustworthy, and that true knowledge somehow exists separately from sense experience in a world of pure 'ideas' (hence *idealism*). However, if we follow this argument through, we end up with a *reductio ad absurdum* (or

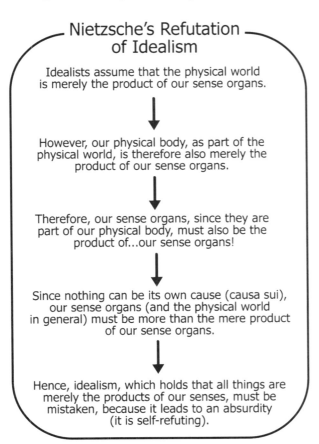

Nietzsche's Refutation of Idealism

Idealists assume that the physical world is merely the product of our sense organs.

↓

However, our physical body, as part of the physical world, is therefore also merely the product of our sense organs.

↓

Therefore, our sense organs, since they are part of our physical body, must also be the product of...our sense organs!

↓

Since nothing can be its own cause (causa sui), our sense organs (and the physical world in general) must be more than the mere product of our sense organs.

↓

Hence, idealism, which holds that all things are merely the products of our senses, must be mistaken, because it leads to an absurdity (it is self-refuting).

'reduction to the absurd', showing that the consequences of the argument lead to an absurdity – i.e. a logical contradiction).

So, if we accept idealism, then we are forced to conclude that the sense organs must be their own creation – an obvious absurdity. Idealism must therefore be wrong: the world as we see it is more than just the creation of the senses. So, we cannot base science on a philosophy that treats the world as mere appearance (as idealism does) – we must give the evidence of the senses *some* credit. On the other hand (as he argues in the previous section), we should not subscribe to "sensualism" (i.e. the notion that the only truth is that which is based on the evidence of the senses). So, we must use the evidence of the senses, but not get trapped in a world view which seems to be dictated by that evidence.

Key Concept: *idealism*

Sections 16 and 17

In these two sections Nietzsche attacks the tendency of certain philosophers to believe in "immediate certainties". The main example he discusses here is that of Descartes and his famous assertion that while he is aware of himself as thinking, it must at least be certain that he exists (for thinking things must exist, even if *that which they are thinking* is false). This is the meaning of the famous phrase, "I think, therefore I am", and the argument is generally referred to as the *Cogito*. In this case, the main purpose of the *Cogito* is to provide Descartes with an absolute certainty which can be used as a foundation for other aspects of knowledge, and so act as a guarantee of the certainty of wider-reaching assertions. In other words, it might look like an obvious thing to claim that I am certain of my own existence, but as Descartes shows,[18] there can be any number of reasons for doubting all manner of things which – at first sight – appear obviously true. What is really needed is the type of truth which cannot be doubted, and which does not itself rely on the truth of other observations – that is, an 'immediate certainty' (such as the *Cogito* claims to be).

Nietzsche argues that we may criticise Descartes's argument on a number of fronts. Firstly, why must we assume that there is a separate and distinct 'I' which thinks, or even "that it has to be something at all which thinks". Why, because there is thought, must there exist something (i.e. a self) which causes it? By arguing in this way, isn't Descartes *already* assuming that he knows what thinking is (i.e. that it involves a cause-and-effect relationship between 'self' and 'thought')? Furthermore, Nietzsche points out, there is nothing particularly immediate about any of these 'certainties'. The thought process involved in the *Cogito* uses all manner of assumptions, previous beliefs and 'knowledge' to arrive at its conclusion, and so any certainty arrived at is far from immediate, but is rather tied into things which are themselves questionable (such as the nature of self, of cause and effect, etc.).[19] To call this knowledge "intuitive" is to beg the question as to where these 'intuitions' come from. They do not, Nietzsche argues, come from the fact that such 'truths' are immediately certain, but rather from the desire of the philosopher concerned to guarantee his own version of truth and to see the world in a certain way. Descartes is therefore not alone in this, and the belief that we may arrive at certain types of knowledge which are absolutely certain is itself another example of a philosophical prejudice. It is a mistake, Nietzsche argues, based on the analysis of language (that there is a subject, 'I', and a predicate, 'think'), whereas this has no bearing on reality. Furthermore, the temptation to think of the 'I' or 'cause' is simply another example of the psychological need to think of something as having a centre or 'atom'.

Key Concepts: *the Cogito*
                    immediate certainties (the 6th philosophical prejudice)

Sections 18 and 19

These two sections concentrate on the long-running philosophical controversy concerning the notion of *free will*. Traditionally, the problem comes about through the conflict between, on the one hand, the scientific desire to explain everything in terms of cause and effect (*determinism*) and, on the other, the personal experience that each of us appears to be free to choose (*libertarianism*). From a scientific point of view, each action must have a cause, and that cause in turn must be the effect of another cause. However, this chain of causation would never have an end (or a beginning), and this results in a problem for the idea of free will: if all our actions are determined by other causes, then none of them can be said to be freely chosen (we would be, in a sense, merely robots who possess the illusion of choice).

Here, Nietzsche analyses the problem in a different way. Why, he asks, do philosophers assume that the will is a *single* thing? Acts of will are very complicated things, consisting of a number of different aspects which exist together – sensations, thoughts, desires, etc. – and which cannot be conveniently arranged into a simple cause-and-effect relationship. Furthermore, what we think of as 'the will', he says, is also the feeling of power that accompanies successful actions, and it is this feeling of dominance that we come to think of as the will itself.

'Freedom of will' – is the expression for that complex condition of pleasure of the person who wills, who commands and at the same time identifies himself with the executor of the command – who as such also enjoys the triumph over

──────The Problem of Free Will──────

In any situation we have what may be termed a 'chain of causation'.

So, in the above diagram, we may see that **A** causes **B**, and **B** causes **C**, and so on, so that each event is the next step in a chain. For example, **A** might represent a thought (I want to read), **B** a set of neurons firing in your brain telling your arm to move, **C** the muscles in your hand and arm reaching for a book, and so on.

However, we have a problem: what causes **A**? If we think of it as a free choice, then (some argue) it cannot have a cause; however, if we think of it as having a cause, then (others argue) it is not free. So, either we admit that there are some things that are self-caused (causa sui), which would appear to go against the scientific understanding of the world, or - it may be argued - we must admit that there is no such thing as free will.

resistances involved but who thinks it was his will itself which overcame these resistances.[20]

The point of these comments on 'will' – as well as Nietzsche's earlier comments on the 'I' or self – is to show how such things are far more complicated in reality than even philosophers have supposed. In fact, what is happening here is that philosophers have simply "taken up a *popular prejudice* and exaggerated it" (which, Nietzsche argues, is "what philosophers in general are given to doing").[21] In other words, philosophers have taken these commonly held beliefs (i.e. that we have a single self, that it is this self that wills things, etc.), and applied them uncritically in a philosophical context. But Nietzsche's approach is to avoid these traditional problems by asking a different type of question. So, instead of asking, 'Do human beings possess freedom of the will?', he asks, 'What is this thing that we call "the will"?' In doing this, he arrives at a different picture of the self as "a social structure composed of many 'souls'". In other words, the many different things that are taking place in the act of willing actually reflect the different competing 'drives' ("souls") that make up the individual. This picture ultimately reflects Nietzsche's doctrine of 'will to power', in that it is the most dominant drive which claims responsibility for the act of will (just as, in a society, "the ruling class identifies itself with the success of the commonwealth"[22]).

Key Concepts: *determinism*
             libertarianism

Section 20

Here Nietzsche argues that new philosophies are mostly 'reincarnations' of older philosophies, as if there were only a certain number of possible ideas that were available. Whether a philosopher is a sceptic or a system builder, Nietzsche argues, it is as if "something in them leads them, something drives them" to follow a certain philosophical path, and their philosophy is "not so much a discovering as a recognising, a remembering". But why should this be so? Nietzsche argues that it is because of the grammar of the language in which these philosophers must express themselves. Just as in previous sections he has argued that notions of 'self' and 'cause and effect' are ideas which are determined by language, so – more generally – he is arguing here that whole philosophies are limited by the way in which we are able to express ourselves. For instance, he suggests, perhaps in languages not related to our family of languages (e.g. the "Ural–Altaic languages"[23]), it may be possible to have a different view of the world because the *grammar* is different, and would allow different thoughts to exist (such as a different notion of the 'subject' or self). Each philosophy is therefore – at least in part – an expression of the racial and cultural heritage which is contained and passed on in the structure of the language used to express it.[24]

Section 21

The basis of the concept of 'free will' is the idea that a thing may be *causa sui* – literally (from the Latin), the 'cause of itself'. As I have already mentioned, the traditional problem of free will stems from the difficulty we have in imagining such a thing as an 'uncaused cause', since a scientific understanding of the world would argue that all things have causes. Here, Nietzsche is particularly scathing about the "peasant simplicity" of the idea of *causa sui*, arguing that if we were to accept its possibility, then we would also have to reject the whole notion of cause and effect (since we can't have both).

However, whilst Nietzsche is critical of this unscientific way of thinking, he is also critical of the scientist's tendency to "naturalise" these concepts (i.e. to think of them as physical things – what I shall term the prejudice of *reification*). For example, we may think of one object striking another, and think of one being the 'cause' of what happens to the other (e.g. motion). However, Nietzsche argues, 'cause' and 'effect' are not physical things, but *ways of explaining* the world. They are purely abstract concepts, and as such should not be confused with the events that they are used to describe. This is an important and yet subtle point, the main significance of which is that human beings use concepts to explain and control the world, but those concepts are not *in* the world. In other words, we *make* the concepts, we do not *discover* them:

> It is *we* alone who have fabricated causes, succession, reciprocity, relativity, compulsion, number, law, freedom, motive, purpose; and when we falsely introduce this world of symbols into things and mingle it with them as though this symbol-world were 'in itself', we once more behave as we have always behaved, namely *mythologically*.[25]

Thus, when scientists behave as if 'cause' and 'effect' were physical things in the world, they mistake the "symbol-world" (the world of concepts which we have created), with the real one (the world "in itself", as it exists independently of human understanding).[26] When we make this mistake, it is as if we are creating a 'myth' or story as to how the world is (rather than a properly scientific attitude, which should, Nietzsche argues, see these concepts as created and chosen to fulfil deeper purposes that we have).

But not only is *causa sui* a myth, so is "unfree will" (or determinism), and it is these two 'myths' which reflect different psychological tendencies. For example, the strong-willed type will see his actions as being under his control, whilst the weak-willed type will see his actions and those of others as being determined largely by things outside of his control (such as environment, biology, etc.). As you may guess, Nietzsche's sympathy is with the strong-willed type (what he later terms the 'Master' mentality), and (for example) he views the tendency to forgive and explain criminality by reference to social factors, upbringing, etc. as an evasion of responsibility for one's own actions (which he will later associate with the 'Slave' mentality).

Key Concepts: *causa sui* (the 7th philosophical prejudice)
reification (the 8th philosophical prejudice)

Section 22

Nietzsche here makes an important connection between the scientific tendency of 'reification' and the political doctrine of equality (or democracy). Both, he argues, are based on the 'Slave' mentality's need to reject everything "privileged and autocratic" – that is, things that embody a special status and power. The link here is between the scientist's desire to explain nature in terms of uniform rules and laws, and the democrat's desire to see every person as of equal importance and worth. However, he argues, "this is interpretation, not text" – in other words, to view nature or human beings in this way is a deliberate act based on a desire for uniformity and equality, and not simply an 'explanation' of how things really are. The opposite 'interpretation', Nietzsche says, would be one which saw the world in terms of different "wills" in constant competition for dominance over one another (his doctrine of the 'will to power'). Of course, he points out, "this too is only interpretation" – so, is he implying that all that exist are competing 'interpretations'? If so, then will to power is not so much a law or governing principle, but rather the state of things when "all laws are absolutely *lacking*". From this perspective, even science would only appear to be a battleground for different versions of 'the truth'.

Section 23

"For psychology is now once again the road to the fundamental problems."[27] This final sentence of this section – and indeed of Part One – sums up Nietzsche's approach so far. What he has concentrated on in this chapter are the ways in which philosophers fool themselves as to the nature of truth, being largely ignorant of the part played by their own temperament, upbringing, culture, etc. in the formation of their ideas. Analysing this, Nietzsche argues, is a job for "psychology", by which he means the study of *why* people hold beliefs. But Nietzsche's 'psychology' goes even deeper than this in that it wants to question *why* people have the moral values they do – why, in fact, *each one of us* has the values that we do (for we cannot take our own objectivity for granted). In this sense, psychology to date has "remained anchored to moral prejudices and timidities", and has failed to investigate the basis for its own values. This is understandable, for such a thing is very difficult – "it has the 'heart' against it" (i.e. our emotions and habits). For instance,

> Supposing, however, that someone goes so far as to regard the emotions of hatred, envy, covetousness, and lust for domination as life-conditioning emotions, as something which must fundamentally and essentially be present in the total economy of life, consequently must be heightened further if life is to be heightened further – he suffers from such a judgement as from seasickness.[28]

This, essentially, is what Nietzsche is doing; he *is* that "someone". This is not to say that he is embracing those 'negative' emotions as 'good', but rather he is analysing their worth – their role, in fact, in those things that we *do* consider 'good'. Nor is it to be supposed that such an endeavour is enjoyable (it may initially make him "seasick"); it is simply a process that will lead to deeper understanding and growth. The very meaning of the phrase 'beyond good and evil' is a summary of this approach. Up until now, he argues, the values which have acted as a basis for not only our morality, but also our philosophical and scientific enterprises, have gone *unexamined*. Furthermore, this has led philosophers, time and time again, into making the *same kind of mistakes* based on their ignorance of their own prejudices. Therefore, it is the job of the new philosopher – the 'free spirit' – (of which Nietzsche is the forerunner), to examine these prejudices, and to analyse his own and others' motives and values. But what sort of person is this 'free spirit'? This is the subject of the next chapter.

Key Concept: *the free spirit*

Part Two: The Free Spirit

Section 24

In this section, Nietzsche once again argues that all our knowledge is based on a "falsification" and "simplification" of the world (a "will to non-knowledge", or what might be called a "will to ignorance" – see also section 230). For, he argues, without such a basis, we could not truly "enjoy life". The basis of this argument is that if we could view the world independently of our 'filters' (i.e. our human-centred perspective), then it would be a very different world indeed. We have already seen, in his discussion of the prejudices of philosophers in Part One, how he has argued that many of the ideas that philosophers hold to be absolutely certain and objectively true are in fact nothing of the sort, and that furthermore they rely upon any number of assumptions (prejudices). However, in this section, Nietzsche makes clear that it is these very assumptions that have served important purposes in the development of human thought and culture; without these "false conclusions" we would not have come this far. Nevertheless, it is one thing to recognise the role played by these ideas, but quite another to hold them as being objectively certain and true (as many philosophers do). What is needed is a sort of detachment from these ideas, and an analysis of their role and future usefulness – which is a job for the philosophical 'free spirit'.

Key Concept: *will to ignorance*

Section 25

Nietzsche criticises what he sees as the temptation to become a "martyr" for the truth. There are those philosophers, he says, who take the search for truth – and themselves – so seriously that they treat it as a matter of life and death. All such "moral indignation [. . .] is in the philosopher an unfailing sign that he has lost his philosophical sense of humour". However, there is more worth, he argues, in "every little question-mark placed after your favourite words and favourite theories (and occasionally after yourselves) than in all your solemn gesticulations and smart answers". In other words, most philosophers who do not question their own philosophical prejudices (and end up merely defending them, thinking that they are 'the truth'), would better serve the genuine search for truth by questioning their own attitudes and assumptions.

Nietzsche therefore advises us to retire from this 'battleground' of truth, and strive for a more useful detachment. This detachment is not that of such recluses as Spinoza and Giordano Bruno (whose philosophies were a type of 'revenge' upon a world that had not accepted them and their ideas), but rather of someone who realises that, rather than seeing it as a tragic and heroic battle, there is actually an element of farce in this brave defence of truth. As he points out, with this realisation "the long tragedy has come to an end", for why should we die for the sake of truth when we are only, in reality, *defending our own prejudices*?

Underlying these ideas is Nietzsche's conception of the tragic. What is tragic to one individual is not necessarily so to another, and the increased 'distance' that the free spirit may ascend to may make even tragedy lose its edge (see section 30). Unlike Schopenhauer, Nietzsche does not have a pessimistic view of life and, in this sense, his philosophy seeks to go 'beyond' the tragic. But there is also a sense in which tragedy is a necessary thing: the isolation of the true philosopher and his misunderstanding by the common man is a tragic necessity – they *cannot* understand him, and nor can he share in their experiences. In this way, the application of the terms may even be reversed: he may appear a comic figure to them, whilst the naivety and self-deceit which allows them to enjoy life displays tragic ignorance. It is in relation to these concepts that Nietzsche's concept of masks should be understood: just as in ancient Greek drama, where each actor adopts a persona that allows him to fulfil his role in the drama, so each person adopts a social 'mask' that both allows their participation in society, and conceals their true nature (see also section 40).

There is also a suggestion that the philosopher may reach a point where life takes on almost a *comic* or farcical aspect (see section 150). In this sense, Nietzsche may be seen as fore-echoing existentialism and the notion of the *absurd*: since life has no inherent purpose, our search for meaning takes on the form of a bizarre game – with arbitrary, self-imposed rules, and no ultimate goal. In this sense, our life *is* tragic, but a total acceptance of life – the rational *and* the irrational – may allow us to develop a new insight (this, in effect, is what Nietzsche's doctrine of the *eternal return* is based on – which I shall come back to later – see section 56).

Key Concepts: *masks*
                    tragedy and comedy

Section 26

Every "superior human being" (of which Nietzsche considers the philosopher is generally an example) desires to set himself apart from the crowd. Many are tempted to seclude themselves, to live alone and by their own rules. But as philosophers we should not give in to this temptation; we must "go *down*" from our high vantage point and seek to understand humanity – however "unpleasant and malodorous" an experience this is. A useful way of speeding up the process of understanding is to observe "so-called cynics" who, whilst they share the appetites and concerns of the general person, also possess a "refined exceptional understanding". This then allows them to speak truthfully of the nature of human beings – for instance, by pointing out how apparently moral motives actually arise from more selfish desires (e.g. for sexual pleasure, for social status, and so on). Such people, whilst they point out the 'bad' side of human beings, do not do it out of any desire to improve them morally, but simply from a desire to speak the truth as they see it – which is what makes them useful to the philosopher who, whilst he may not ultimately agree with the cynic's world view, is similarly seeking to understand true human nature.

Key Concept: *cynicism*

Sections 27 and 28

In these two sections, Nietzsche again makes the connection between the language in which a philosopher writes and the structure and pace of his thought. This fact makes Nietzsche himself – who is trying to write and think 'at a different tempo' – difficult for even his friends to understand. German writers tend to be slow and ponderous, whereas the Greek, Italian and French languages tend to lend themselves more naturally to speed and ease of thought. Nietzsche uses this connection between language, life and thought to argue that perhaps Plato's attitude to life was not in fact the same one as portrayed in his writings (i.e. "Platonic") – that, in other words, he adopted a much lighter and freer approach to living than his philosophy suggests. For Nietzsche, this is suggested by the fact that a copy of the poet Aristophanes' works was discovered under the pillow of his deathbed; perhaps, then, Plato kept this attitude hidden ("under the pillow"), whilst publicly preaching a different philosophy (Platonism).

Section 29

Here Nietzsche argues that the path of the true philosopher or 'free spirit' is a very lonely one, and that such a person – by stepping aside from the shared values of society in order to examine and understand them – can no longer partake so freely in common social life, or be understood by society. He lives by his own rules and values.

Section 30

Nietzsche once again highlights the difference between the free spirit, philosopher, or "higher type of man", and the ordinary person. The view of the "common man" is "from below", and he cannot detach himself from life in order to see it more objectively (to view it "*from above*" – as the higher type of man does). Conversely, from a 'higher' view the world may appear very differently, and what is considered "tragic" from the lower perspective might not appear so from the higher one. Throughout this section, Nietzsche is attacking the idea that there is only one way of seeing things, and that it is possible to arrive at an ultimate viewpoint that will suit everybody. On the contrary, he argues, a person's viewpoint is linked to his or her upbringing, environment, temperament, etc. A more 'refined' individual would find the pleasures and virtues of the "common man" to be unattractive or even repugnant. That is not to say that such values are not important for the common man's way of life – they obviously are, but equally the higher type of man requires different goals and standards. It is almost as if Nietzsche is describing different plants that need different conditions to grow; to impose one way of life, one morality, etc. upon everyone is not only inappropriate, it is harmful. (For more differences between the higher and common man, see Part Nine, especially sections 257–67.)

Section 31

The young person sees things in terms of 'black' and 'white', "Yes" and "No". But as he grows older, he realises that life cannot be viewed in this way, and that such a simple, aggressive attitude towards truth has only led to his own disappointment and disillusion. However, even this angry reaction *against* the attitudes of youth is still itself *an aspect of the attitudes of youth*! In other words, the individual has not changed, but has simply redirected his rash youthful attitude against himself and his former naive opinions.

The implication here is that similar processes are at work in the realm of philosophy: the rejection of a philosophy that falsifies and simplifies life (as do the attitudes of youth) can give rise to general nihilism and scepticism (the attitude of maturity). Ultimately, both these attitudes are foolish, because what is needed is a third stage where the individual is more detached and can review all such beliefs without emotion. In other words, Nietzsche is asking us to guard against over-reaction, and against letting our disillusion and disappointment trick us into making different, but equally misguided choices.

Section 32

This important section first introduces Nietzsche's concept of the development of morality through three stages: the pre-moral, the moral and the extra-moral.[29] In the first stage, which stems from prehistoric times up to around 10,000 years ago, an action has value (is 'good' or 'bad') according to its success or failure in achieving certain goals. If I kill someone, that act is not 'good' or 'bad' *in itself*, but only in so far as it leads to 'good' or 'bad' consequences. For instance (to illustrate Nietzsche's point), in a tribal situation, if I kill a skilled craftsman, then it might be 'bad' if the tribe require his skills in the future. Therefore, at the pre-moral stage, it is the consequences of the act which are important.

As society evolved, and certain individuals were valued above others (i.e. the aristocracy), then the origin of an action became more important than its consequences. So, from a moral point of view, an action itself was not 'good' or 'bad', but rather the intention that lay behind it. From this point of view, an act such as killing may be considered 'wrong' in that it springs from a 'bad' *intention*. This development is also related to the growth of the concept of the self, and can be linked back to Nietzsche's earlier comments about 'atomism' and the need to imagine that each action has a source (i.e. the self).

This second phase, which Nietzsche calls the *moral stage*, is the one that we are still in. But, just as in the previous section, where Nietzsche has outlined the way in which the attitudes of youth, and a more mature reaction to them, can both be considered to be *merely stages of development* – so, can't we apply a similar understanding to morality? Having had the pre-moral and moral stages, is it not possible to imagine an *extra-moral* stage, where a deeper understanding of morality is achieved and applied? Nietzsche argues that what we think of as the conscious intention behind a moral act is actually only a "surface and skin", and that we must treat it as "a sign and symptom that needs interpreting" (as if we, the new philosophers, are doctors). It is the purpose of the free spirit to 'overcome' this morality, and to create a new, extra-moral phase by going 'beyond good and evil' (i.e. finding new moral standards by analysing the current ones).

Key Concepts: *pre-moral, moral and extra-moral*
self-overcoming

Section 33

We, the new philosophers, have a duty to analyse the current moral notions of self-sacrifice, selflessness and charity. Nietzsche argues that we should be suspicious about moral actions which claim to have no personal motive, as well as philosophical viewpoints which claim to be "disinterested" or objective. He asks, isn't there a subtle pleasure being obtained by these actions?

Section 34

The world we think we live in is almost certainly *not* the world we *actually* live in. Scientifically speaking, there are numerous examples which would illustrate Nietzsche's point: the Sun appears to go around the Earth, but in fact, the opposite is true; matter appears solid, but in fact is made up of minute flickers of pure energy, between which there are vast amounts of space; light appears to reach our eyes immediately, and yet many of the stars that we see at night time are actually greatly changed or even dead. In fact, we are mistaken so frequently about the nature of things that you might almost think that there is some force in nature that deliberately sets out to mislead us. However, the more rational alternative explanation is that *we* are actually responsible for the errors, and that it is the limitations of our own understanding which result in these mistakes. In light of this, it might be tempting to distrust our mental capacities altogether.

Many philosophers and thinkers are naive in this sense. They assume that things can be investigated without taking into account this tendency to be deceived. Furthermore, such philosophers have employed their own assumptions – such as the notion of "immediate certainties" – in the belief that such things are possible (and not, as Nietzsche is pointing out, merely a creation of our own). The true philosopher therefore needs to be distrustful and suspicious – in other words, to develop those qualities that would make most of normal society consider him a "bad character".

In the last part of this important but difficult section, Nietzsche renews his attack on the belief in opposite values – especially, that the truth is more valuable than appearance. For, he argues, "there would be no life if not on the basis of perspective evaluations and appearances" (recalling a point made earlier in section 4). In other words, these 'false judgements' may actually be vitally important ways in which human beings simplify life in order to exist and thrive. So, he argues, even if we *could* get rid of 'appearances' and valuations which are only true from our own perspective, we would be left with nothing (because 'truth' would have disappeared also). One of the reasons for this is that it would seem to be impossible to clearly distinguish between what is 'true', and what is merely 'true for us' (i.e. an appearance). So, 'truth' may perhaps always be at least in part tailored to fit our own human perspective (as things appear to *us*). So, instead of simply picturing things as either 'true' or 'false', we might propose a whole range of grades of truth (dependent upon the degree to which we can realise that something is only as it appears to us). From this point of view, there would appear to be no such thing as 'absolute truth', because there is always a sense in which we are choosing or applying the 'truth' in a way that is more or less 'useful' to us and our survival.

Nietzsche's very last point once again concerns atomism, for it might be tempting, he argues, for someone to point out that, if 'I' create reality, then isn't it at least true that 'I exist' (which is more or less Descartes's point)? But why should this have to be so? Do we have to let our "belief in grammar" influence our philosophical opinions? In other words, because we use the *word* 'I', it does not necessarily mean that there is *actually* such an 'I' (or self). (Descartes's atomism was discussed earlier in Part One – see sections 16–17.)

Section 35

The quote here is from Voltaire: "He seeks the true only so as to do the good."[30] Nietzsche's point here is that such an attitude as Voltaire's is naive; why should truth and moral goodness be the same? The attitude is yet another philosophical prejudice (one, incidentally, which Nietzsche sees Voltaire as sharing with Plato and Kant).

Section 36

Here, for the first time, Nietzsche sets out his argument for proposing the *will to power* as the fundamental drive of all life. Firstly, he argues, what is best known about cause and effect is our own experience of it – in other words, the action of our own will. Since we can observe the action of these competing "drives" (that is, the dominance of one passion or instinct over another), then it makes sense to ask whether this type of causation is the same as the one that is responsible for causation in the material world. So, when we look at biological life, or even the actions of inorganic matter , before supposing that there are at least two types of causation (that of the will, and that of physical cause and effect), we should at least try to see if one explanation won't do for both.

To fully understand what Nietzsche is proposing here, it should be noted that most of modern science in fact advocates the opposite view. In other words, modern science is mostly materialistic (i.e. it believes only physical matter exists), and tries to explain everything in terms of physical cause and effect. But Nietzsche goes the other way: he wants to argue that the laws of cause and effect as we see them in the physical world *are actually better understood in terms of acts of will*. Now, what does he mean by this? He means that all the processes that we see at work in the physical world ("nourishment, excretion, metabolism") may be considered as "a kind of instinctual life" in that when one thing *causes* another, what we are actually seeing is the dominant effect of one will over another. For instance, the process of digesting food involves the breaking down of organic matter (food) by various chemical processes; one process (digestion) is battling to exert itself over another (the 'will' of the organic matter to maintain its structure and not be broken down). Nietzsche's view sees one will acting upon another, as opposed to will acting on matter (as Descartes imagined consciousness to act on the physical brain – somehow), or matter acting on matter (in accordance with the mechanical laws of the universe). From this perspective, each process has a vitality and purpose of its own, and the whole world can be seen as a huge battleground of competing wills.

Nietzsche is also careful here to distinguish between this concept of 'will to power', and previous attempts – such as those of Berkeley and Schopenhauer – to say that we only experience our own ideas of the world (*idealism*).[31] He is not saying, as idealists have, that we cannot experience the 'real' world, but merely our own experience of it – or even that the 'real' world does not exist, in some sense – but rather that there is one principle which can be used to explain causation in the organic, inorganic and conscious realms alike: the principle of 'will to power'. (For more on the will to power see sections 51, 211, 230 and 259.)

Section 37

Here, Nietzsche anticipates the horrified reaction of contemporary (scientific) thinkers to what he has just proposed. By arguing that all life is will to power, Nietzsche has rejected the scientific notion of causation (the "God" of scientific progress), but kept the notion of 'will' (the human element – the "devil" – that science would wish to 'refute' by explaining in terms of mere physical causation). However, by speaking "vulgarly", such a reaction is seen for what it really is (i.e. a view born from the same prejudices that the scientist shares with the common man – the same types of philosophical prejudice that he is trying to help us to escape from). But, he says, why should we "speak vulgarly" (i.e. why should we share these common prejudices)?

Section 38

This short section deals with the idea of history, especially where it is viewed as progress. For his example, Nietzsche considers the French Revolution, and the common interpretation of the event as a progressive step away from tyrannical monarchy and towards rationalism and equality. But, Nietzsche says, isn't this just an interpretation that helps us to think of history as progressive, and that humanity is slowly developing? In reality this is simply yet another falsification of life that helps us to deal with it. Furthermore, once we realise this, shouldn't the temptation to interpret history progressively be "done with"? Later on, Nietzsche will outline an alternative to progress in his notion of the 'eternal return' (see section 56).

Section 39

There is no necessary relation between truth and happiness, Nietzsche argues. The truth might just as well make you unhappy, and there may even be things which it is dangerous to know. The strength of an individual's mind is to be measured by how much 'unadulterated' truth they can stand. Furthermore, being moral or happy are also not necessarily helpful qualities for a person to have as regards knowing certain parts of truth – the immoral or unhappy man may even be better placed to understand certain things. The free spirit or new philosopher may therefore need to develop certain qualities which are not in themselves 'good' – such as "severity and cunning". Finally, Nietzsche quotes Stendhal, saying that the "good philosopher" must be "dry, clear, without illusion"[32] – in other words, detached enough to overcome the philosophical prejudices of the past.

Section 40

Just as, in the previous section, Nietzsche considered that there were degrees of truth that individuals could stand, so here he considers the part played by psychological 'masks' in covering an individual's true nature. Firstly, he points out, masks are not necessarily there to hide the shame of bad deeds, for an individual may also be ashamed to reveal the most beautiful and sensitive aspects of himself. Furthermore, masks may not only hide shameful or sensitive things from *others*, but, by falsifying one's own memory, from *oneself*. However, even if an individual did *not* want to live with a mask, one develops anyway – and, ultimately, the deeper and more profound an individual is, the more likely people are to misinterpret him.

The comments here echo Nietzsche's general views of truth – i.e. that it is something that few can bear, and that we generally prefer 'untruth'. They also fill out the picture of the true philosopher as one who is isolated and misunderstood by most people, and cannot but choose to hide behind a mask, for he has no choice as to how other people understand him. (For more on 'masks' and the philosopher's relation to common people, see also sections 223, 244, 270, 278–9, 283–4 and 288–90.)

Section 41

Nietzsche continues to list the qualities of the ideal philosopher, and warns of the various 'traps' that one might fall into and thus lose the clarity and detachment necessary for philosophy. These include: affection for certain individuals ("every person is a prison"); allegiance to a "fatherland" (patriotism); pity for someone, even "higher men" (like the philosopher himself); the discoveries of science (which might make us favour theories of practical benefit); detachment itself (for its own sake); our own virtues (where certain positive qualities may, in excess, become a vice).

Sections 42 and 43

Nietzsche terms these new philosophers "*attempters*" (because, supposedly, they will attempt new modes of thinking which go beyond the philosophies of the past). As we might expect with Nietzsche, there is a play on words here: the original German word, *Versucher*, also has associations with 'tempter' and 'experimenter'. The suggestion here is not only that these new philosophers will be the first to try such things, but also that their 'attempts' may be viewed by traditional morality as immoral ('temptation').

In their search for truth, such philosophers will not be dogmatic (looking for the *ultimate* truth), nor will they search for a universal truth ("for everyman"). Also, they will not be concerned with being popular, or serving the "common good", for "what can be common has ever but little value". Here, Nietzsche emphasises his elitist view of philosophy: it is the pursuit of a few, rare individuals, not the occupation of the common masses.

Section 44

In this final section of Part Two, Nietzsche distinguishes between his notion of the philosophical "free spirit", and the sort of 'free thinker' – common at the time – who is interested in increased political freedom, democracy and equality ("modern ideas"). These latter types he calls "levellers", because they attribute all human ills to social injustice and inequality, and try to address them by changing society, sharing out wealth, giving everyone equal rights, etc. (i.e. seeking to 'level' the social conditions of life). The ultimate goal of such people, he argues, is to abolish suffering. However, the best examples of humanity have grown up in conditions ('soil') where life was most difficult, and suffering has played an integral part in making the "plant" vigorous.

Nietzsche's "free spirits" are almost the complete opposite to the free-thinking modern man; the final part of this section is then devoted to an evocative description of some of the qualities of the new philosophers that differentiate them from the "levellers": they are "full of malice towards the lures of dependence", "curious to the point of vice", "grateful even to distressful change and illness", and so on. The list, whilst it also contains some traditional philosophical virtues (they must be "collectors and arrangers", "thrifty in learning and forgetting"), is intended to show how the new philosopher will be shaped by hardship and discipline, and will not be afraid to ask difficult or uncomfortable questions; he will be non-dogmatic, variable and flexible in nature (but hard when he needs to be), and his search for truth will be a dynamic one, where the question of what 'truth' itself is will not go unasked. Nietzsche will return to the qualities of the new philosopher in later sections, especially Part Six ('We Scholars'), Part Seven ('Our Virtues') and Part Nine ('What is Noble?').

Part Three: The Religious Nature

Section 45

The religious nature is a fascinating and complex area of investigation for a "psychologist" such as Nietzsche. His use of this word here – as elsewhere (e.g. section 196) – is meant to emphasise his approach to philosophy and distinguish it from that of others. So, in his analysis of religion – just as with philosophers and their philosophies – Nietzsche is primarily concerned with *why* someone holds the beliefs they do, and what the link is between the person and the beliefs themselves. Whilst the richness and variation of subject matter for study is so vast that it makes it a difficult task for one person, there are too few people who would be willing or capable of adopting this approach, and so he must take on the work alone.

Section 46

Straight away, Nietzsche distinguishes between different types of religious faith based on environment and culture. For example, the simple religious attitude of northern Europeans – such as Cromwell and Luther – is very different from those who have been influenced by the culture of Greece and Rome, where there is a strong tradition of rational debate and liberal education. For Christianity to be dominant in this intellectually richer, southern culture is therefore much more difficult. In light of this, a religious attitude such as that of the French philosopher Blaise Pascal represents almost a "suicide of reason". We can best understand this, Nietzsche argues, once we see that the basis of Christianity is sacrifice:

> sacrifice of all freedom, all pride, all self-confidence of the spirit, at the same time enslavement and self-mockery, self-mutilation.[33]

Pascal, having made some important contributions to mathematics at a young age, gave up its study for the rest of his life out of fear that his intellectual pursuits would lead him to question his faith, or be a source of undue pride. Thus Nietzsche sees Pascal as having *sacrificed* his own intellect for the sake of his religious faith.

In this section, Nietzsche also first begins to set out his picture of how Christianity has tried to 'invert' all that was up until then considered 'good'. The image of 'god on the cross', which forms the central focus of Christianity, would have been – for the noble, aristocratic pagans – a 'paradoxical formula'. In other words, to the noble mind, a 'god' represented the highest ideal of strength, power, wisdom, etc., and so to see such a being suffering and powerless would have been unthinkable (a paradox). From Nietzsche's point of view, this turning upside down of the 'antique values' of the Greeks and Romans was the means whereby the people whom they had enslaved could revenge themselves on their masters.

This point is very important: Nietzsche sees Christianity (among other things) as a "slave revolt" in morality. The ruling classes in the Roman-occupied world (where Christianity began) traditionally held such things as power, wealth, courage, etc. as 'good', and weakness, poverty and cowardice as 'bad'. But, Nietzsche argues, what Christianity does is to take these values and *invert* them. So now, for Christians, worldly power, wealth, etc. are seen as 'evil', and meekness, humility, submission, as 'good'. This, Nietzsche argues, is a morality devised by the powerless as a means of being 'better' than their masters. In other words, they cannot be more powerful *in an earthly sense*, so they must be more powerful *in a spiritual sense*. This, Nietzsche implies, is the first time that 'spiritual' has been used in this way – i.e. as compensation for lack of worldly power (see section 195).

This "slave" morality, as he calls it, is a reaction to – and direct opposite of – the "master" morality. The "slave" hates what he sees in his "master" as arrogance, pride, lack of faith, frivolousness, "scepticism towards suffering", so in turn he values humility, absolute faith, compassion and pity.

Nietzsche investigates these ideas in more detail in his subsequent work, *The Genealogy of Morals*, in the first essay, '"Good and Evil," "Good and Bad"', where he traces the very meanings of moral terms to their origin as designations of class (so, 'good' originally meant 'noble' and 'bad' meant 'common' – see, e.g., sections 5–7 and 10 of the essay). He also emphasises how the noble morality defines its own values, whereas the slave morality must rely on noble valuations in order to *react* against them (i.e. in valuing their opposite). For a more detailed discussion of this, see especially section 260 of *BGE*.

Key Concepts: *master morality*
slave morality
slave revolt in morals

Section 47

In this section (and later, in section 51), Nietzsche begins his analysis of a certain type of religious attitude that he calls "the religious neurosis", immediately suggesting that he considers it a type of disease or mental illness. This type of attitude, he says, is most often associated with three types of self-denial: solitude, fasting and sexual abstinence.

Firstly, he says, the problem of understanding this situation is based on our difficulty in understanding how the "saint" (the person who undertakes this self-denial) can deny the "will" (i.e. turn his back on those instincts which are so fundamental to human nature).

Secondly, through this means, a sort of 'miracle' seems to take place, in that we see a "bad man" suddenly 'repent' and become a "good man" – i.e. the process of religious conversion. But what can explain this sudden and "miraculous" change? Up until now, he argues, those who have tried to understand this process have failed because they have not understood the true connection between 'sinner' and 'saint', and hence consider the conversion inexplicable by normal means (and therefore, "miraculous"). But this misunderstanding is due in fact to a belief in 'antithetical moral values' – in other words, the belief that something 'good' *cannot* arise out of something 'bad' (see also sections 2 and 3). But if we abandon this idea, it is possible to begin to understand the connection between the 'bad' and 'good' character, and – Nietzsche implies – how those things which motivated the sinner are equally present in the character of the saint.

Key Concepts: *religious neurosis*
the saint

Section 48

As with section 46 (and section 50 below), Nietzsche again points out the difference in religious attitudes between southern and northern Europe: "We northerners" (apart from the Celts) have "*little*" talent" for true religious emotion and faith, whereas the "Latin races" (e.g. Italy, Spain, Portugal, etc.) possess a temperament more naturally suited to it. This is why, he argues, "unbelief" (atheism) is more natural to northern races, whereas to southern races it is completely *unnatural*. Nietzsche goes on to consider some 'southern' thinkers, pointing out that even where they are apparently sceptical in their approach, there remains an underlying religious *type* of emotion. The general contrast in terms of religion is between northern 'coolness' (intellectual detachment) and southern 'heatedness' (instinct and emotion). Notice that, once again, Nietzsche is pointing out the influence of environment and geography on thought and belief.

Section 49

Nietzsche contrasts the religious attitude of the early Greeks, who felt "gratitude" for everything in life, with that of the later Greeks (and, afterwards, the Christians), which – he argues – was based on fear. Once again, there is also an implied contrast here between the "noble" attitude of the aristocracy (which is courageous and life-affirming) and the negative, fear-based attitude of the "rabble" (the common people).

Section 50

Different temperaments worship God in different ways: a simple, humble and level-headed attitude, like Martin Luther; an ecstatic yet unrefined yearning, like St Augustine; or even a kind of sensual longing, as evidenced by many female saints (e.g. Madame de Guyon). Nietzsche's point is that, once again – just as with philosophers and their philosophies in Part One – the attitudes reflect the personality, temperament, environment and upbringing of the person in question.

Section 51

Many great and powerful rulers in the past have been impressed by the figure of the saint, mainly – Nietzsche argues – because they sensed in him some secret power which they did not understand. In this sense, the saint represents a paradox: on the one hand, he embodies everything that is weak and powerless (he has a "fragile and miserable appearance"); but, on the other hand, there is something about him which suggests that, through turning his back on his own most basic instincts, he has achieved some secret goal. Therefore, the saint has something in common with these powerful rulers: they are both examples of a dominant will to power. Whilst the rulers are dominant in respect of their worldly power, their physical strength, their wealth and influence, etc., the saint is dominant only over his own desires and instincts. This makes the rulers both suspicious and wondering; they respect the force of his will, but wonder why anyone would undertake such a life-negating process. Is there, perhaps – they wonder – some secret that the saint knows and they do not?

Section 52

Nietzsche respects the Jewish Old Testament as a rich document of life and thought in ancient Asia. So, whilst he may not agree with the outlook on life that it embodies, he can recognise that it is a profound literature that has been formed by deep experience. In relation to this, the literature of Greece and India, as well as the New Testament itself, is shallow in comparison. Therefore, to make one book of the Old and New Testaments is – to use a modern analogy – like sticking a PVC conservatory onto an Elizabethan manor house. Modern Christianity, and the attitudes of modern Europe in general, represent a much less profound reaction to life. (For other views on the Jews and Jewish culture, see sections 194–5 and 248–51.)

Section 53

Modern religious belief has rejected traditional approaches to God ("The father", "the judge", "the rewarder"). This has left people with a vague and unsatisfying picture of God (which is a central reason why religious belief is in decline). Ironically, however, the religious *instinct* (by which he means 'the religious neurosis') is in "vigorous growth".

Nietzsche's point here is that we can separate a consciously held religious belief from an unconscious religious attitude. So, whilst the former is in decline, the latter – which consists of a certain attitude to life, truth, etc. – is growing. He will come back to this point again and again (e.g. section 55), showing how it explains attitudes in science, philosophy and politics.

Section 54

In attacking the philosophy of Descartes (to whom mind and soul were the same thing),[34] modern philosophy has concentrated on attacking the idea at the basis of Christianity: the concept of the soul. But whilst modern philosophy might be considered "*anti-Christian*", it is "by no means anti-religious". For instance, Kant tried to prove that the subject (the 'I' or soul), although it exists, cannot be known (it is 'transcendent', or is by definition beyond our experience). However, Nietzsche argues that even Kant glimpsed the possibility that the soul may only possess an "*apparent existence*", and not *really* exist at all (this is similar to the Vedanta school of Hindu philosophy, which combines a religious approach to life whilst also proposing that the soul is merely an illusion).

Section 55

Developing the theme from the previous section, Nietzsche argues that the religious *instinct* demands a constant sacrifice. In historical terms, this takes three stages: (1) in ancient times, one sacrificed one's prized possessions to God (even, in the case of human sacrifice, the most important people – e.g. the king); (2) in more modern times, the sacrifice took the form embodied by the life of the saint

— Immanuel Kant —

– i.e. self-denial; (3) however, the religious instinct demands ever greater sacrifices – but, having sacrificed most things, what else remains? The idea of God Himself, Nietzsche says, is the only thing left. So, just as modern philosophy has sacrificed the idea of the soul, modern thinking in general has begun to sacrifice "everything comforting, holy, healing, all hope, all faith in a concealed harmony, in a future bliss and justice", and instead worships "stone, stupidity, gravity, fate, nothingness". Science and philosophy, in their search for ultimate truth and certainty, will end up sacrificing meaning itself.

Key Concept: *the ladder of sacrifice*

Section 56

If we take *pessimism* (the negative view of existence) to its logical conclusion, Nietzsche says, then we must go further than thinkers such as Buddha and Schopenhauer have gone. Such previous pessimists have still hung on to a *moral* view of the world, but to do so is still to 'falsify' life – to create a false ideal in order to make the 'nothingness' of the world easier to deal with.

It must be noted at this point that Nietzsche is not a pessimist, but that he does take pessimism as the starting point of his philosophy. In other words, he accepts the inherent meaninglessness of life, the absence of spiritual consolation, and the fact that there can be no external basis for any system of morality. But having accepted this view, he seeks to go *beyond* it. He does this by asking himself what would be "the ideal of the most exuberant, most living and most world-affirming man" – in other words, the extreme optimist who did not falsify life, but rather accepted it in all its positive and negative aspects. His answer is that such a person would ask to have his life "again *as it was and is* to all eternity". This is Nietzsche's doctrine of the *eternal return* (or *eternal recurrence*), which is based upon an older idea (which can be found – among other places – in Hindu, Buddhist and Greek thought) that the events of the world recur in an eternal cycle, where each is exactly the same as the last. However, Nietzsche's ideal is not based on the assertion that this theory is literally true (or not necessarily so), but is rather a thought experiment which asks, 'What if this *were* true?'

Key Concepts: *eternal return*
pessimism

Section 57

Nietzsche suggests that the great concepts of the past – such as the notions of "God" and "sin" – may one day be viewed as intellectual 'toys' that humanity played with as a 'child'. Perhaps, he continues, in the future, different 'toys' will be needed. In other words, Nietzsche is pointing out that philosophical and religious enquiry still involve growth and learning, and that part of this growth is to be able to look back on the great and profound ideas of the past as being simpler and less significant than we thought them at the time. (This notion of intellectual growth is also a feature of Nietzsche's own attitude to his own philosophy – see, for instance, the final section – 296.)

Section 58

A life of industry and business is, in many respects, antagonistic to the spirit of true religious reflection. Most modern people either do not possess the sort of leisure time required for genuine "prayer", or else do not see the purpose of such activity. This is also true of academic scholars, who in the main feel a general superiority towards religious believers – though they nonetheless display 'tolerance' towards them in the spirit of academic detachment. Nietzsche's purpose here is to make a connection between scholars, with their "modern ideas" (as he calls them), and the attitude of the working classes: both, he argues, do not really see any point in religion, but whilst the working classes are willing to 'go along with it' (for the sake of social convention), academics can be more frank in their lack of interest. The reason for the connection is that both types come from the same source, the common man, who does not see the point in anything which does not have a direct and practical purpose. This may be contrasted with the attitude of the aristocratic type, who does not have to work, and who is not solely governed by whether actions are useful or not (or by feeling guilty for 'not doing anything' – i.e. having abstract, philosophical thoughts which may have no practical value).

Section 59

The need to falsify life and to create a comforting image of it is born out of a fear that the truth would be too harsh to deal with. The degree to which a view falsifies life is an indication of strength of character: the less the falsification, the stronger the individual (see also section 39). The religious view has, historically, involved the greatest deal of falsification (the greatest 'artistry'), and religious piety may be considered "the subtlest and ultimate product of the *fear* of truth". It should be noted here that this is not just a charge against religion; Nietzsche has other targets (science among them).

Section 60

Carrying on the theme of religious falsification of the world, Nietzsche considers the notion of loving mankind for the sake of God (i.e. trying to see the 'divine spark' in everyone). This, he says, is the furthest that the religious impulse to falsify life has gone, and it is based on a fear that – without divine assistance (loving mankind for God's sake) – it might prove impossible. In other words, it is based on a fear that mankind is not lovable for its own sake (that, like the world, the truth of the matter – of man's real nature – is too difficult to take).

Section 61

The philosopher, as Nietzsche sees him, has a duty for the evolution of mankind, and he can and should use religion in realising those goals. In this respect, religion has four main uses:

1   It provides a means of social control and rulership.
2   It allows those members of the ruling classes (or natures of "noble decent") to seek a meditative life of withdrawal and solitude, if they wish it.
3   It allows a route of progression and refinement ("ennobling") for the "rabble", and thereby provides a means for future rulers to be bred and trained.
4   It provides the lower classes with meaning and purpose, and helps to justify the drudgery of their existence.

Section 62

When these uses of religion are forgotten – when religion exists for its own sake and as an end in itself – then we have such a situation as we have now, where all the "unsuccessful cases" in life are kept alive out of pity and compassion. The consequence of this is that such religions have "preserved too much of that *which ought to perish*", and thus held back the evolution of humanity.

This is one of the more controversial aspects of Nietzsche's philosophy, and has been labelled *social Darwinism* after Charles Darwin's theory of *natural selection* (where everything which is not suited for survival becomes extinct) as applied to society. Nietzsche's view – which is often misunderstood as the notion that 'might is right' (i.e. morality is determined by the powerful, and that which obtains and maintains power is 'right') – is actually more subtle than this. As we have seen, Nietzsche considers one of the uses of religion to be as a tool in the hands of the new philosopher to bring about a 'higher type' of man. However, by venerating those who suffer, modern religions (especially Christianity) have turned moral values upside down:

> they maintain that all those who suffer from life as from an illness are in the right, and would like every other feeling of life to be counted false and become impossible.

This, then, is the so-called 'slave revolt in morals'. All the values that were once held as good – "all the instincts proper to the highest and most successful type 'man'" – are now seen as 'bad'. These, in turn, have been replaced with "uncertainty, remorse of conscience, self-destruction" in order to produce a "shrunken, almost ludicrous species, a herd animal". This, then, is the state of modern Europe after 1,500 years of Christian rule.

Key Concepts: *natural selection*
                      social Darwinism

Part Four: Maxims and Interludes

Sections 63–185[35]

All the sections in this chapter consist of short aphorisms (or sayings), the longest of which amounts to a short paragraph, but the majority of which are one sentence long. As regards their content, they mostly range through topics already covered in other sections, or to be covered later – for instance (section 177):

Perhaps no one has ever been sufficiently truthful about what 'truthfulness' is.

Obviously, such a comment fits in well with Nietzsche's observations so far on 'will to truth' and the prejudices of philosophers mentioned in Part One.

At other times, the comments are more cryptic, or may represent Nietzsche's thoughts on a topic not considered elsewhere; this makes them difficult to interpret and categorise – for example (section 157):

The thought of suicide is a powerful solace: by means of it one gets through many a bad night.

This might be a joking reference to the way in which certain philosophers adopt a pessimistic attitude, without actually following it through to the conclusion (i.e. 'The world is a terrible place; therefore, I should commit suicide'). This would fit in well with Nietzsche's later comments on Schopenhauer (section 186). However, given the brevity of the aphorism, it is difficult to say that this is definitely what it refers to, and so, at the end of the day, my interpretation would only be one possibility (others might occur to you).

It might have been possible – given enough space – to explain and interpret most of these aphorisms, but it is probably better for you to work through them on your own. Study of them will lead to a deeper understanding of Nietzsche's central ideas, but some of the more difficult ones will also force you to make connections of your own – which is probably what Nietzsche intended. What I have done, therefore, is simply to suggest the range of topics covered, and to collect together the aphorisms under certain themes. In this way, you can get a general idea of Nietzsche's interests, allowing you to relate his comments to those in other sections. However, please note: this is not an exact science; occasionally, consecutive sections will follow the same theme, but mostly they skip about from topic to topic. Furthermore, the themes identified are only loose groupings; occasionally, there may be an overlap where an aphorism will refer to one or more topics, in which case I have included it in both places. Finally, in relating the aphorisms to other themes, the reader is encouraged to make use of the glossary at the back of the book.

1 *Philosophical and moral prejudices* (64, 68, 70, 75, 77–8, 80–1, 97, 108, 117, 132, 138, 141, 143, 149, 157–8, 174, 177, 182, 185). A number of aphorisms repeat and expand upon the theme of philosophical prejudice introduced in Part One. Some of them deal with the subtle self-deceit involved in the search for knowledge (64, 81, 138, 157, 177), including self-knowledge (68, 78, 80), whilst others simply highlight the main drives and processes involved in the development of any philosophy or morality (70, 75, 77, 97, 141, 155). Some aphorisms

deal more explicitly with morality: with Nietzsche's view of its true nature (108, 117, 143, 149, 158), the herd morality's origin in *ressentiment* (132, 182, 185), and the connection between philosophy and morality (64, 174).

2   *The Free Spirit/higher man* (63, 65, 66, 69, 71–6, 79, 87–8, 91–6, 98–101, 103, 105, 107, 109–10, 112, 116, 119, 122, 126, 128–9, 130, 133–5, 140, 146, 150, 152–4, 160, 169–71, 173, 180, 184). A sizable proportion of aphorisms detail Nietzsche's view of the philosophical free spirit and the higher type of man (to whom the former is related). A number of these make reference to Nietzsche's concept of the 'mask', and the part it plays in self-knowledge, the relation of self to society, and the difficult relationship that the philosopher necessarily has to the average person (63, 66, 73a, 91–2, 99, 100, 122, 130, 169). Some aphorisms highlight the difficulties and subtle traps faced by the new philosopher in his search for knowledge (65, 73, 95, 101, 103, 146, 160), whilst others merely outline the qualities and attitudes which should be possessed by such a man (75, 79, 87, 94, 96, 98, 107, 112, 128, 134, 140, 150,[36] 165, 171), and in what way he is different from both previous philosophers and the common man (71–2, 74, 76, 88, 105, 126, 133). Certain sections also reveal how the new philosopher's need to re-evaluate morality will also lead him to be at odds with conventional values, and to come to understand traditional concepts of 'good' and 'bad' (or 'evil') in a different way (69, 93, 95, 109–10, 116, 119, 129, 135, 152–4, 156, 159, 170, 173, 180–1,[37] 184).

3   *Woman* (84–6, 102, 113–15, 120, 123, 127, 131, 139, 144–5, 147–8). Sixteen of the aphorisms are a fore-echo of the comments concerning woman and the sexes in the closing sections of Part Seven (231–9). As noted there, Nietzsche's attitude to sexual equality is somewhat controversial to the modern ear, and he considers female emancipation to be a generally harmful thing (section 147 includes a quotation from an Italian novel which translates roughly as, "good and bad women both need beating"). The topics include: the true understanding of female motivation and psychology (86, 113–15, 127, 148); the key differences between the sexes and the dynamics of their relationship (85, 102, 120, 131, 139, 145, 147); and the social problems faced by the 'emancipation' of women and the change in gender roles (84, 123, 144).

4   *Religion* (65a, 67, 82, 93, 104, 105, 112, 121, 124, 129, 135, 152, 162, 164, 168). The aphorisms on religious topics concern the attitudes of religious believers and the part these play in the formation of religious ideals (65a, 121, 124); a critique of those attitudes (67, 82, 93, 104, 159, 162, 168); and the difference between these religious attitudes and those of the free spirits (105, 112, 129, 135, 152, 164) – among whom he includes Jesus himself (see 164).

5   *Miscellaneous comments* (83, 90, 106, 111, 118, 125, 136–7, 142, 151, 161, 163, 166–7, 172, 175–6, 178–9, 183). The remaining aphorisms are too diverse to group together under one heading, and it is here that it is most clear that all

the aphorisms in this chapter originated from various notebooks, where they were composed over a number of years. Some appear to be isolated thoughts on tangential topics – such as the nature of music (106), poetry (161) and instinct (83). A few comments deal with love (142, 163, 172, 175), and there is a larger loose grouping which can be made of comments that deal with psychological insights: the nature of certain types of people (90, 137, 167, 178), and common psychological idiosyncrasies, flaws and secret motivations (111, 118, 125, 136, 151, 166, 176, 179, 183).

Part Five: On the Natural History of Morals

Section 186

Nietzsche contrasts the "science of morals" (philosophical study of ethics) with "moral sensibility" (sensitivity to, and appreciation of, ethical questions). On the one hand, he argues, Europeans of the time have a very refined response to morality, yet, on the other, they appear to be very clumsy when it comes to studying it. What is missing, he suggests, is a suitably scientific attitude, and what is required is an "assembly of material". In other words, before we start wading in and justifying our own view of 'goodness', we need to appreciate the full range of ideas of 'the Good' which have existed with other cultures, peoples and times – only then can we begin to truly understand the nature of morality.

Philosophers to date have taken morality as 'given', and thus have only attempted to find rational arguments to support it. In doing this, they have only succeeded in reflecting the moral prejudices bred into them by "their environment, their class, their church, the spirit of their times, their climate and zone of the earth" (a point Nietzsche has made a number of times already – e.g. sections 3, 5–6, 46 and 48–50). But, Nietzsche argues, the real problems of moral philosophy do not lie in trying to show why our own morality is right, but rather in comparing "*many* moralities".

Finally, Nietzsche uses Schopenhauer as an example of how a refined and cultured mind can fail to understand the true nature of morality (by considering one of philosophy's purposes to be a search for the "rational ground" of morality – i.e. to base it in rational proofs and arguments). He also points out how, in fact, Schopenhauer's pessimism is quite shallow in that it sees the central rule of morality as *neminem laede* (Latin: 'harm no one'):

> a world-denier and God-denier, [. . .] who affirms morality and plays the flute, [. . .] what? is that actually – a pessimist?[38]

Nietzsche pokes fun at Schopenhauer here, suggesting that the philosopher's pessimism does not in fact run very deep; can one be a pessimist *and* profess a firm moral outlook? Perhaps, then, Schopenhauer is not really a pessimist – or, to illustrate Nietzsche's point another way, just as Plato had a copy of Aristophanes' poems 'under his pillow', did Schopenhauer have a flute under his? (That is, an attitude to life which is different to the one suggested by his philosophy – see section 28 above.)

Section 187

Rather than evaluating a philosopher's views on morality, we should instead ask what purpose those views serve in the philosopher's own life. There are many different reasons why a person holds certain moral views: e.g. to justify themselves to others, to give themselves peace of mind, to provide a subtle form of revenge upon others – this latter motive Nietzsche terms *ressentiment*, a borrowing of a French term, and it is a central notion in his account of the 'slave morality', and therefore of those philosophers whose views spring from or are influenced by it (we will return to this concept in the Critical Themes chapter). In Kant's case, his views promote obedience to the moral law, which is only another way of saying, 'You too should value this attitude'. However, in almost all cases, Nietzsche argues, a morality is a "sign-language of the emotions" – in other words, it springs from the emotional and irrational part of the person who follows it (rather than the rational part).

Key Concept: *ressentiment*

Section 188

Nietzsche begins this section by rejecting the idea that what is "natural" is that which comes most easily to us. On the contrary, he says, it is more natural to seek to impose rules and discipline upon ourselves. In this sense, the artist who is 'inspired' is in fact far from 'letting it all hang out' ("*laisser aller*", from the French, 'to let go'); he is, in fact, concentrating even harder to obey those self-imposed "thousandfold laws" which direct the creative process.

Nietzsche also points out that it is a mistake to think that morality is 'rational'. All moral systems, he argues, have their basis in a desire to impose a restraint upon nature, and in fact upon reason itself. So, we cannot argue that a particular moral stance is 'irrational' unless we have a morality of our own which says that 'irrational beliefs are bad'. But then, what basis would *that* moral attitude have? It must rely, Nietzsche argues, on yet other irrational impulses.

This view of morality essentially underlines Nietzsche's approach in the whole of *Beyond Good and Evil*. Previous philosophers and thinkers have supposed that it is possible to separate the 'rational' (the mental, intellectual, that which we have reason and proof for) from the 'irrational' (desires, emotions, instincts, etc.). However, what he is trying to show is that the irrational actually provides a basis for the rational, and that – furthermore – it is impossible to have an outlook which is not at some level driven by irrational forces. The attempt to find a rational basis for morality – just like the 'prejudices' that philosophers unconsciously employ in their approach to truth – is thoroughly misguided and self-deceiving.

Nietzsche compares moral rules to those we might find in literature and art. "How much trouble the poets and orators of every nation have given themselves!" he says. Why did they adopt such "arbitrary laws" (compare the "thousandfold laws" mentioned above)? Nietzsche's answer – which is central to his view of morality – is that such discipline is a necessary "condition of life and growth". This is true, he says, even where the goals of such processes can later be seen to be "violent, arbitrary, severe, gruesome and antirational" (for instance, the attempt of scholastic philosophers to make everything agree with Aristotle's philosophy). Such attempts, Nietzsche argues, whilst in one sense 'stupid', have also had positive benefits in helping to form the modern European mind's "strength, ruthless curiosity and subtle flexibility". This deliberate submission to arbitrary discipline is true of all "peoples, races, ages, classes", and is natural to mankind itself.

Section 189

The purpose of holidays (*holy*-days or fasts) is to condition the drives that are useful at other times. So, Nietzsche comically observes, the English made Sunday so boring that all the working classes (who don't know what to do with their leisure time – see section 158 above) longed to return to work! These 'fast periods' (when people refrain from certain things) may also occur for longer periods, or even whole generations, and we may interpret certain social trends, philosophical systems (e.g. stoicism) and religious movements (e.g. Puritanism) as examples of times when an enforced discipline is used to "*purify* and *intensify*" certain drives. From this point of view, we can begin to understand how the period of Christian dominance in Europe resulted in a *purification* and *intensification* of the sexual drive (which it generally opposed by considering it 'sinful'), the product of which was a higher expression of the sex instinct ("*amour-passion*", 'passionate love'). Nietzsche seems here to be referring to the flowering of so-called 'courtly love' in poetry and literature from the twelfth century onward. Typically, this involved the idealisation of the female and the portrayal of romantic love as the highest form of spiritual expression (in opposition to Church teachings). Famous examples include the poetry of the French troubadours and the devotion of the Italian poet Dante Alighieri to his beloved Beatrice. (See also sections 260 and 293.)

Section 190

Here, as elsewhere in his writings,[39] Nietzsche distinguishes between the views of Plato, and the views of his teacher Socrates *as expressed by Plato*. Generally, Nietzsche sees Plato as noble and aristocratic, whereas Socrates "smells of the *mob*" (i.e. the views of the common man). Accordingly, Nietzsche sees Plato's attempt to equate 'bad' actions with stupidity (lack of knowledge) as evidence of Socrates' influence upon him. Nietzsche's implication is that 'good' and 'bad' are not to do with knowledge (or lack of it), but rather to do with breeding (or social origin). As an aristocrat – Nietzsche implies – Plato would have known this, and so we can see a struggle in his philosophy as he tries to provide a more respectable framework for Socratic thought. The discussion of 'masks' (as in the next section), also suggests that Platonism is not necessarily the view of Plato himself, but only a doctrine that he taught in order to fulfil a particular purpose (e.g. consider the uses of religion discussed above in section 161, and also the reference to Aristophanes in section 28).

Section 191

Continuing the discussion of Socrates, Nietzsche considers the relationship between instinct and reason. On the face of it, Socrates is the champion of reason: he made a career of questioning the "noble Athenians" as to the basis of their views; men who, as Nietzsche points out, "like all noble men", "were never able to supply adequate information about the reasons for their actions". But Nietzsche sees Socrates' cleverness as dishonest, for could he not have asked *himself* the same troublesome questions as he asked others? He would have realised that what he was asking of others – i.e. to supply a rational basis for their moral views – was something that he could not really do himself.

Plato, in adopting and developing Socrates' views, is less 'crafty' than his teacher, and genuinely believes that such a thing *can* be done. In Platonism, "reason and instinct move of themselves towards *one* goal, towards the good", and all later philosophers have followed this view (except for Descartes, who did not equate truth with 'the Good'). In this, he sees instinct as having triumphed over reason.

This is a subtle and potentially confusing point, so it is worth trying to spell it out in more detail. Instinct (irrational motivation such as desire, emotion, etc.) is often considered opposite to reason (which looks for proof and 'reasons'). For example, if we like a particular food, there may be no reason why that is the case

– we just like it; but if we make a factual judgement (e.g. 'there are many different varieties of apples'), then we must have reasons to support it. As Nietzsche pointed out at the very beginning (see section 1), to consider reason as completely uninfluenced by the instincts (that there is an objective 'will to truth') is mistaken. Therefore, when Plato argues that instinct and reason really have the same goal (i.e. goodness), he is really saying that *we desire truth*, and that, knowing the truth, *it will make us good*. Nietzsche has so far consistently argued that such a view is self-deceiving: the truth may not be 'good for us' – it may even be harmful (see, e.g., section 59). The view that 'truth = good' is therefore a false one, which has been caused by a *desire* (instinct) for that to be the case. Therefore, instinct has triumphed over reason by fooling it (or rather, the philosopher's instinct has fooled his reason).

Section 192

This section expands on the previous idea that the instincts play an important role in falsifying the world and undermining reason. This, he points out, is the basis of all sciences, which first set about making all sorts of assumptions and "premature hypotheses", and only later become more cautious and subtle. In what is now a much-quoted phrase, Nietzsche observes that, "one is much more of an artist than one realises". He then gives various examples, all of which are intended to show how, almost, we view things through a 'filter' of familiarity which turns every new experience into something that we recognise and feel more comfortable with. In most situations, our invented reality (our desire to see things a certain way) is so ingrained in us that it is much more powerful than the actual evidence of our senses.

Section 193

Just as the content of our waking life influences what we dream about, so the opposite is true: what we dream about influences how we live our lives. For instance, a man who could experience the freedom and exhilaration of flying in dreams would carry some of that attitude into his real life. Nietzsche's point here is connected to his comments in the previous section, and it concerns the importance of the way in which the irrational aspects of our personalities influence our outlook on life.

Section 194

Men differ not only according to what they consider good or valuable, but also in the manner in which they wish to possess those things. For instance, there are degrees whereby a man may 'possess' a woman whom he loves: sexually, by possession of her body; in terms of freedom, through submission to his will; and intellectually, through demanding that she have total knowledge and acceptance of his own self ("know him to the very heart"). In a similar way, we may look at all sorts of relationships as determined by the way in which one party seeks to 'possess' the other: a ruler and his people, a mother and her child, the philanthropist and the person helped, etc. In all cases, 'having' is different, and the 'possession' is changed and remade in an image of the possessor's desire. Once more, Nietzsche implies, we see how the way in which we see the world is shaped by instinct (in this case, the desire to possess or have power over something). The last phrase of this section, "From which it follows . . .", suggests a direct link between this process and the culture and ideas of the Jewish people (who are discussed in the next section), who – it is implied – are a culture whose qualities of submission and obedience have been passed on and maintained in this way (i.e. from parent to child). In other words, these qualities have become instincts.

Section 195

Nietzsche considers Jewish religion and culture to be an example of what he elsewhere calls the 'slave morality'. They are the beginning of the "slave revolt in morals" and represent an inversion of the aristocratic and noble values of the pagan ruling classes (e.g. the Romans). Here, for the first time, Nietzsche argues, the term "world" is actually used in a negative sense (because, he implies, the slave finds only unhappiness in his station in this world, and longs for the spiritual consolation of another). Therefore, they call themselves 'the chosen people' (of God) as a means of spiritual consolation for their 'worldly' state (i.e. slavery and oppression).

Section 196

Just as science must discover the influence of things that are not immediately apparent ("dark bodies"), so the "moral psychologist" (such as Nietzsche) must look for the hidden influences upon the formation of a morality (this, essentially, is just a restatement of Nietzsche's general approach).

Section 197

Nietzsche here considers the "man of prey", who does not practise a Christian morality, but rather adopts the law of the "jungle", where the strongest and most ruthless survive. Such a man, Nietzsche argues, is not necessarily tormented by his own guilt, or mentally sick and corrupt – as Christian moralists would have us believe. These are just the moralist's attempts to discredit such a lifestyle, and to scare off others from adopting it, but also to make more "temperate" and "mediocre" men feel justified in their more moderate lifestyles (where their morality is a form of "timidity").

It should be noted here that Nietzsche is *not* proposing the life of such men as an ideal (as those who have distorted Nietzsche's philosophy would have us believe). To him, they are still "tropical monsters", and are mainly of interest in showing that other modes of morality are possible – are even, in some senses, more healthy and honest (because more animalistic and less self-deceiving).

Key Concept: *morality as timidity*

Section 198

Nietzsche continues his analysis of "Morality as Timidity", in other words, the role of morality in controlling the passions and thus subduing passionate – and potentially dangerous and powerful – individuals. In this sense, the moral systems of the Stoics, or of Spinoza and Aristotle, for instance, are merely attempts to provide philosophical justifications for treating everyone as if they were the same. However, Nietzsche argues, such systems "generalise where generalisation is impermissible", and in doing so seek to make individuals of a wide range of different temperaments equally 'timid'.

Section 199

There have always been greater numbers of people who exist in "herds" than those who possess an individual identity. The habit of obedience is more easily passed on and therefore much more common than the ability to command – a fact which has held up the evolution of humanity. Such a habit has in fact become so ingrained that it is almost instinctive, and as a result those who possess it will look around for something to obey – whether it is a person, an organisation or a system of thought – almost as if fulfilling a need. If we imagine that this situation becomes so bad that there would hardly be any "commanders or independent men at all", then we are faced with just such a predicament as exists in present Europe: those who do command are forced to adopt a sort of "moral hypocrisy", whereby they pretend – even to themselves – that they are merely obeying something greater (e.g. God, the law, "the common good", etc.). But even this sort of commander is under threat from being replaced by a group of "clever herd-men" – which is basically the situation when we consider the rulership of a country by a parliament. This process reflects the general desire of the herd to make everyone the same, and for this type of individual to represent "the only permissible kind of man". However, even in this situation, when a genuine commander appears (such as Napoleon was), the 'herd' will accept him out of relief at finally having someone suitable to obey.

Section 200

Men of "diversified descent" (i.e. who bring together genetic and cultural aspects of both the 'herd' and the ruling classes – e.g. St Augustine) are generally weak individuals. This is basically because their instincts are at war with one another, and they primarily desire peace from internal conflict. More rarely, such men also inherit a desire for "conducting a war against oneself" and "self-control" (such as Julius Caesar and Leonardo da Vinci), which results in a process of *self-overcoming*, and a different, much stronger type of man – though the cause of origin of both types is the same.

Section 201

So long as the values that govern the "herd" are meant to keep in check certain emotions and drives that are seen as disruptive to the community, then there can be no genuine "love of one's neighbour" (as Christianity advocates). In pre-Christian pagan societies (such as ancient Rome), the values which Christianity teaches – such as pity, meekness, consideration, etc. – were not absent, but were simply not seen as having moral value *in themselves* (they were "extra-moral", in the sense of being outside of morality – and not to be confused with the 'extra-moral' stage of morality discussed in section 32 above). On the contrary, such societies esteemed values that are now generally considered 'bad', such as "enterprisingness, foolhardiness, revengefulness, craft, rapacity, ambition" – though of course, they called them "under different names, naturally, from those chosen here". Although these values are honoured while a society is under threat from external enemies (and people possessing these virtues – i.e. soldiers – are therefore useful), when that society begins to become established and more secure, the same people – and virtues – now become potential dangers (like soldiers home on leave). As peace becomes established, and "the diversionary outlets for them is lacking" (i.e. war), these 'virtues' now become 'vices'. So, rather than *love*, it is *fear* of one's neighbour that herd morality is built upon. Gradually, the meek values of the herd become esteemed highest of all, to a point where "every form of severity, even severity in justice" (such as capital punishment), is seen as problematic. This attitude reaches its extreme when society takes the side of the criminal himself in proposing the lessening of punishments, even of seeing him as in some way a victim (of poverty, upbringing, etc.). The ultimate goal of this morality – which is generally thought of as "progress" – is to abolish all possible sources of fear.

Section 202

In this section, Nietzsche emphasises one of the main points of this whole chapter: "*Morality is in Europe today herd-animal morality*". The consequence of this is that the notions of 'good' and 'evil' have become fixed, and there is, increasingly, little variance in the moral outlook throughout Europe, but also in those places where European thought is influential (such as in the conquered colonies of certain European nations). Furthermore, the basis of this morality – which is supported by Christianity – is a desire for complete equality and an "opposition to every special claim, every special right and privilege". Viewed from this perspective, even anarchy – which is commonly thought to be in opposition to democracy – is in fact a logical extension of the herd mentality, where everyone is given an absolute equality by the removal of all means of social control and formal government (and therefore controllers). The herd's fear of pain and punishment finally leads to pity and compassion being seen as the "pinnacle of man, the sole hope of the future, the consolation of the present and the great redemption from all the guilt of the past".

Key Concepts: *anarchy*
          herd morality

Section 203

Nietzsche sees the current political, moral and social systems that exist across Europe as essentially a weakening influence upon human development. Where then, he asks, are we to look for hope and direction? The answer is, of course, the 'new philosopher', who will help to reverse the effects of the current herd morality, and reinstate positive, life-affirming values which will allow for the true progression of mankind (and not, as is currently the ideal, the "perfect herd animal"). The new philosophers will teach humanity to rely on its own will, bring an end to the illusion of what is currently seen as historical progress, and prepare it for the hard tasks ahead.

Part Six: We Scholars

Section 204

In modern society, science has become more respected than philosophy (although the reverse used to be the case), to the point where it is "taking it upon itself to lay down laws for philosophy" and prescribing what it can and cannot say. There are a number of reasons for this – such as the view that philosophy is not *useful* – but generally, Nietzsche argues, the reaction stems from the same spirit which drives democracy and the 'herd' mentality. Thus, the scientist rejects philosophy because it represents old, aristocratic values (e.g. belief in the soul), and frequently a disillusionment with *one* philosopher leads the scientist to become disillusioned with *all*.

There is now also a type of philosopher who is influenced by this growth in the status of science: the *positivist*, who restricts the whole subject of philosophy to "theory of knowledge" (and thus, Nietzsche implies, only to those subjects which do not challenge the dominance of the scientific view, and in fact are meant to aid its development). Such attitudes are later to be found in – for instance – *logical positivism*, and the philosophy of A. J. Ayer (among others), who believed that the only meaningful statements were those that could be verified by sense experience. This would be a good illustration of Nietzsche's sense of modern philosophy as a mere "remnant" of what it formerly was – and, more importantly, could be. One of Nietzsche's tasks in this section is therefore to show how science *isn't* independent of philosophy (as it thinks it is), and that it contains all sorts of philosophical assumptions – thus reasserting philosophy's true position as a more fundamental discipline than science.

Key Concepts: *logical positivism*
                    positivism

Section 205

It is very difficult for anyone to become a true philosopher these days. The scientific outlook has become so dominant that the philosopher feels that he needs to specialise in certain areas of philosophy in order to be respectable (just as scientists must specialise in a limited field so that their findings are detailed and painstaking enough to be considered 'academic'). However, in doing this, philosophers fail to achieve the sort of overview necessary to achieve a genuine philosophical outlook.

Nietzsche's point here is an important one: he is criticising modern philosophy for being too narrow – for not stepping back and looking at the bigger questions (about the nature of existence, about whether to answer "Yes" or "No" to life – i.e. to be optimistic or pessimistic). Thus, the philosopher must take big risks, and must resist the temptation to do only what is useful or respectable.

Section 206

If a true genius is like a mother who *gives birth* to ideas, then the contemporary scholar is more like "an old maid" – i.e. they are themselves 'barren', merely collecting and arranging facts, and dealing with other people's ideas. Thus, the scholar is ultimately one of the "herd animals", and possesses all those qualities which are valued by the common people – e.g. industriousness, moderation, a desire to serve, and so on. Out of his own "mediocrity", such a man is resentful of those "natures to whose heights he is unable to rise" (the 'higher' type of man), and will do anything to bring them down to his own level. Similarly, he will also try to "relax every bent bow" – in other words, seek to remove the natural and social obstacles that stand in the way of his ideals of true equality and compassion. But these ideals are opposite to Nietzsche's, who sees such obstacles as *opportunities* to develop greater resilience of spirit and overcome one's own limitations.

Key Concept: *the scholar*

Section 207

In this section, Nietzsche argues that the sort of objectivity that is so highly valued in science is not an end in itself. The ideal scholar, he argues, "is only an instrument, let us say a *mirror*" that "belongs in the hand of one who is mightier" (i.e. the true philosopher). Objectivity, which seeks to create a view which is completely independent of all human interest, must in fact ultimately *serve* human interest (for what, he implies, is the point of knowledge which serves no purpose?). So, rather than take the view of the pessimist (who sees a world that has not been designed for humans, and so looks at it negatively), Nietzsche suggests that we should go *beyond pessimism* (this echoes sections 39 and 59, where a positive value is attached to the degree of objective reality that an individual can cope with).

The remainder of this section describes the character and qualities of the ideal 'scholar' or objective man. He is "a man without content, a 'selfless' man", which makes him an ideal instrument for objective investigation, but – as a result – such detachment makes it difficult for his type to react 'normally' to situations. Such a man should "be respected and taken good care of", Nietzsche points out, but he is not in himself an ideal, merely an instrument in service of a greater cause.

Key Concept: *objectivity*

Section 208

Nietzsche argues that the sceptical, objective and scientific attitude outlined in this chapter is so pervasive these days that people are unsettled by the very thought that someone *might not* share these values. The main fear is pessimism (the negative view of life), but there is also fear of a fervent belief in the *positive* value of life (in whatever form).

Such scepticism can be very sophisticated and alluring, he argues, and there is almost a sense in which anything *but* scepticism is considered 'bad taste' or as unsophisticated. But the sceptical attitude is actually a "sickness", resulting from the mixing of "races or classes". This mixing of values and instincts, he suggests, leads to a doubting of the self, and the contradictory and competing drives within the individual "will not let one another grow and become strong". Scepticism is a sort of "paralysis of will" where, instead of having a firm belief in the rightness of its own values, and seeking to dominate over others, the culture of modern Europe is riddled with doubt and scepticism towards itself and its former beliefs.

Nietzsche predicts (quite accurately) that future European politics will involve countries where the will is strongest (such as in Germany, England and – most of all – Russia) in a struggle to dominate the *whole world*.

Key Concept: *scepticism*

Section 209

Having described scepticism as a "sickness" in the previous section, Nietzsche here outlines a possible way in which this attitude may develop into something stronger and more healthy. He takes as his example Frederick the Great of Prussia, whom he sees as heralding "a new species of scepticism", and which consists of "audacious manliness, which is related most closely to genius for war and conquest". This attitude, Nietzsche argues, has become a central part of the German spirit, and indicates a *proper* use of scepticism, which at times must call for "intrepidity of eye, [. . .] bravery and sternness of dissecting hand, [and] tenacious will for perilous voyages of discovery". Thus, Nietzsche's admiration for the *military* prowess of Frederick becomes (in part at least) a metaphor for his ideal of the *philosophical* conqueror. (Nietzsche will detail many of the ideal qualities needed by the new philosopher in the following sections.)

Section 210

Carrying on from the previous discussion of scepticism, Nietzsche points out that although the type of future philosopher that he envisages will occasionally employ this type of scepticism, *that is not all that they will do*. Rather, he says, they will be closer to what we might call "critics". He then sets about distinguishing between the sceptic and the critic: unlike the sceptic, the critic is certain of his values, just as a critic of music, art or literature will have clear ideas as to what represent 'good' and 'bad' examples. However, whilst the new philosopher will share this quality, he will also be different from the critic, because he will not be afraid to investigate and question the very values that he employs. Thus, the new philosophers will be *sceptical*, and yet not *sceptics*; *critical*, and yet not *critics*. What, then, are they? He answers this in the next section.

Key Concept: *the critic*

Section 211

Nietzsche distinguishes the "philosophical labourers", "men of science" and all other "servants" of philosophy from the true philosopher himself. The main difference, he says, is that whilst the philosopher must at some time perform the same tasks as such men, he is the only one that actually *creates values*. Previous philosophers, he argues – such as Kant and Hegel – have merely accepted "former *assessments* of value" (from their education, culture, etc.), and saw their task as to reduce such "truths" to "formulas", making them "clear, distinct, intelligible and manageable". But for the new philosophers, the search for truth (their "will to truth", recalling section 1) will become "*will to power*". Here, in a nutshell, is Nietzsche's definition of the new philosopher.

Section 212

Philosophers and their ideas are almost always at odds with the accepted truths of their time; they are the "bad conscience of their age", criticising the 'virtues' promoted by the morality of the time. However, because times and cultures differ, the thing which makes the philosopher great will itself be different in each case: in the sixteenth century, where the prevailing attitude was one of pride and selfishness, it was necessary to promote humility and selflessness; in ancient Greece, where the aristocrats had become hypocritical, pleasure loving and self-deceiving, Socrates' job was to ruthlessly point this out by dissecting their characters and revealing their flaws.

In contemporary Europe, the herd mentality dominates and there is a general weakness of will, as well as a distrust of anything or anyone "rare, strange, privileged". The modern philosopher therefore needs to be hard and determined, teaching strength of will and independence, and turning his mind to as many different subjects and disciplines as he can (rather than being lured into some specialism or narrow field of study).

Section 213

In this final section of the chapter, Nietzsche argues that philosophers are born, not made. All those who imagine what a philosopher's task is, or how he should work – but are not themselves, by nature, fit for the job – get it wrong. Not only does this refer to the common people, but also to the intellectuals of the day – the "nimble commonplace minds or worthy clumsy mechanicals and empiricists" (e.g. scientists, philosophical positivists, etc.). Such minds, who are not "bred" for philosophy, commonly imagine that it is hard work, that philosophical truths must be "slow, hesitant, almost as toil", whereas in fact true philosophy can be "easy, divine", joyous and almost a "dance".

It is interesting to note here that, in this final section, Nietzsche has almost come full circle. In the first chapter, the prejudices of philosophers were linked to their 'breeding' and environment; now, when we come to the new philosopher, we find that he too is a product of similar forces:

> Many generations have worked to prepare for the philosopher; each of his virtues must have been individually acquired, tended, inherited, incorporated.[40]

This, ultimately, raises two important questions: firstly, whether we are predestined to adopt a particular attitude in life according to our biological inheritance (which would make Nietzsche a *determinist*); secondly, whether these influences are the only difference between Nietzsche's ideal and the ordinary philosopher (which would make him a *eugenicist*).

It is worth noting that here, and later in section 264, Nietzsche employs a concept of evolution that is closer to *Lamarckism* than to Darwinism. Jean-Baptiste Lamarck was a French naturalist who suggested, in contradiction of Darwin, that evolution could be moulded by the behaviour and choices of its creatures, implying that nature was more than just a blind mechanical force (*mechanism*); it was a living one (*vitalism*). However, Darwin would not concede that this was possible; in his view, evolution was 'blind', and had no inherent purpose. Therefore, in arguing for the inheritance of acquired traits, Nietzsche would seem to favour Lamarckism. I will come back to these questions in the Critical Themes chapter.

Key Concepts: *eugenics*
                    Lamarckism
                    mechanism
                    vitalism

Part Seven: Our Virtues

Section 214

Given his criticism so far of the current values held by the majority of modern Europe, Nietzsche considers what things – if any – the new breed of

Jean-Baptiste Lamarck

philosopher will consider 'virtues'. Such virtues could not conflict with the sort of philosophical investigations which the new philosopher must undertake, so if they are to exist at all, then there is a real danger that they may be "lost" as they themselves are questioned. Also, in looking for such virtues, we will find the values of previous generations ("our grandfathers") which we have inherited. However, even though we must admit that we may at the moment share such values, this will not necessarily be for long (for the new philosopher will go *beyond* them in his search for new ones).

Section 215

Just as two suns may influence the course of a planet, or cast different lights upon it, so Nietzsche argues that the actions of a modern man can be seen in differing lights (according to the different moralities which the actions are influenced by). Here Nietzsche is once more implying that the influences upon our morality may not be wholly conscious, and may spring from a mixture of *unconscious* and competing influences (compare this, for instance, with Nietzsche's discussion of the man of "diversified descent" in section 200).[41]

Section 216

Carrying on from the notion of there being "differing moralities" which influence our actions, Nietzsche contrasts the conscious attitude of 'love thy neighbour' with the *unconscious* attitudes which accompany it. Changes in these attitudes, he argues, can also represent moral progress, as our conception of how we express our moral attitudes changes (i.e. we no longer partake in "puritan litanies" and "moral preaching"). So, he implies, whilst modern man seems to continue to hold to Christian doctrine, his unconscious attitudes ("the dance in our spirit") are altering.

Section 217

Here Nietzsche gives a short illustration of how such differing moralities can influence and explain action. He pictures the sort of individual who wants to be seen to be a moral example to others (an example of the "moral preaching" and posturing that he sees modern man as rejecting in the previous section). Since the *appearance* of being moral is more important to such men than actually acting morally, a witness to any moral "blunders" that such a person makes will become the target of his revenge. So, beneath the surface morality lies a different morality, driven by different motives.

Section 218

Rather than studying the middle classes, psychologists would better profit from studying the common people. It is here, Nietzsche argues, that the greatest complexity exists in the way that the "rule" (the average person) instinctively reacts to the "exception" (the higher type of man). But since such psychologists are themselves examples of the "rule" (the herd), such an exercise would also mean that they must actually study themselves.

Section 219

Carrying on from the previous section, Nietzsche outlines some of the subtle ways in which the "spiritually limited" common person takes revenge on the more refined, exceptional type of person. For the common man, the belief that all men are equal before God is a doctrine that helps console them for their lack of the qualities that they envy in others, and allows them to condemn the actions of those who consider themselves to be 'better' – thus, it is their form of revenge upon the more gifted. Atheism, therefore (since it endangers this doctrine), is vigorously rejected by such people.

But it may be possible, Nietzsche argues, to convince the common man that an order of rank among human beings – and in the world itself – is a just and necessary thing. To do this, he says, one would explain it to them not by arguing that the morality that they profess is incompatible with genuine "spirituality" (which would insult them), but rather by pointing out that the higher, exceptional man represents the ultimate development of these qualities, having arrived at them not only through years of "discipline and practice", but also as a result of breeding ("the course of whole chains of generations").

Key Concept: *order of rank*

Section 220

The "average man" is not drawn to "those things which interest and stimulate every higher nature" (such as the search for truth), and so calls such pursuits "disinterested" (i.e. objective). But the search for truth *cannot* be disinterested; it is, rather, "a *very* interesting and interested act" – but to realise that we must also realise that it is a very refined and elevated sense of self-interest which is involved here (such as is only natural to the refined and elevated soul!).

Nietzsche then goes on to imagine two objections to this argument: love and sacrifice. Aren't these examples of "disinterest"? But, Nietzsche counters, how can an act of love *not* be based on self-interest? Similarly, as regards sacrifice, there is always something that the sacrificer *wants* in return for his sacrifice.

The final image in this section is of truth as a woman, pretending to be bored in order to avoid the impertinent questions of her interrogators. You may recall that Nietzsche has compared truth to a woman before (in the Preface), and it is an image that he is fond of – for instance, in *Zarathustra*, we find:

> Courageous, untroubled, mocking, violent – that is what wisdom wants us to be: she is a woman and always loves only a warrior.[42]

But why does he use it? The reason for this is probably that it represents almost an opposite to the notion that the quest for truth is a straightforward – though difficult – enterprise; it is a search where the attitude of the lover or warrior is better than that of the plodding scholar. Perhaps, Nietzsche is suggesting, Truth may be 'modest' and not want us to see her without her makeup! She may deceive us, or play games, and there may even come a point where it is 'good manners' to stop asking questions! In other words (if we overlook the possibly sexist metaphors), the search for truth is not disinterested or objective, and there may be limits to the answers we can seek.

Incidentally, it should be noted here that by the phrase "average man" Nietzsche does not simply mean, 'the man in the street', but also 'the educated', 'scholars' and 'philosophers'. What he is referring to here is the type of mindset which springs from the outlook of the 'herd' (which, in the modern world, has begun to permeate all levels of society).

Section 221

Carrying on the discussion of self-sacrifice and unselfishness, Nietzsche argues that such attitudes are only valuable when they serve a purpose (i.e. a 'higher', *selfish* purpose). But to propose unselfishness as a moral virtue for *all* types of people is wrong, and in the case of those "destined for command", and the "higher, rarer, privileged" individual, would in fact be "a waste of a virtue". In other words, he is saying that there are different types of virtue for different types of people, and for the higher types it would be harmful and unhealthy for them to adopt an "unegoistic morality". Once again, Nietzsche's main point here concerns the 'slave revolt in morals', where the democratic spirit (stemming from the 'mob') tries to make everyone equal (whereas, in reality, this can't – and shouldn't – happen).

Section 222

In modern Europe, pity and compassion are preached as the chief virtues. However, if we listen carefully, we can see that such 'virtues' are in fact born out of self-contempt and dissatisfaction. This religious emphasis on the idea that we are all 'fellow-sufferers' is an attempt to make inadequacy more bearable. Such people replace self-pity with compassion because they cannot admit to themselves that, actually, they loathe and pity themselves because of what they are. Elsewhere, Nietzsche argues that it is necessary to overcome one's self and one's own pessimism in order to arrive at truly positive and life-affirming values (in light of which, Nietzsche views such values as pity and compassion as signs of negativity, pessimism and moral ill-health).

Section 223

The modern European is self-conscious of his place in history, and adopts certain historical attitudes from the past and other cultures in an attempt to find something that "fits" (think of the modern obsession with 'retro' styles). However, nothing does fit for long, and there is a sense in which our originality as a historical age lies in this trying on of different 'masks' – maybe, in fact, through this process, we are gradually learning that we can perhaps *invent* who we are. As with the idea of 'self-overcoming', Nietzsche is also implying that this process can take place at a social level (i.e. a society as a whole can discover its prejudices and limitations and thereby 'overcome' itself).

Section 224

The "historical sense" described in the previous section (i.e. our capacity to understand and 'take on' the values and attitudes of previous ages), is a fairly recent thing, arising first in the nineteenth century. It is the democratic spirit, Nietzsche argues, which has led to this, with its "mingling of classes and races". So, whereas more "noble" cultures (such as seventeenth-century France) simply dismiss or fail to understand more 'barbarous' ones, we "modern souls" – with our mixture of instincts and ideals from various cultures and classes – can understand things that they could not. We can understand 'semi-barbarous' literature – such as that of Homer and Shakespeare (which embodies this mixture not only of 'high' and 'low' values, but those of different cultures) – because, ironically, of this *lack* of noble taste. So, whilst such modern attitudes do possess some virtues (e.g. we are "unpretentious, selfless, modest" and so on), they are in general in opposition to noble values, and we find such aristocratic attitudes both difficult to understand and distasteful to us. Strangely, then, because we have a taste for everything, we have no real 'taste'. Lastly, Nietzsche points out, because of this lack of restraint (taste, or "measure"), we yearn for the "unmeasured" – the boundless or infinite. Perhaps, ultimately, in this dangerous yearning to go beyond limits, we may be elevated beyond our "semi-barbarism".

This is quite a difficult section to fully understand. Mostly, in *BGE*, when speaking of 'we', Nietzsche is referring to the free spirits or new philosophers. Here, however, he is referring to the man of modern ideas, whom in other sections he is critical of. The point to be understood is that whilst the new philosopher *is* a type of modern man (he cannot help his culture, upbringing, etc.), there is an important sense in which he must use the virtues of modern thinking (i.e. its "taste and tongue for everything") in order to understand and *overcome* this very lack of being 'civilised'. Modern man's yearning for the "unmeasured" (which is itself a lack of taste) – his love of "danger" – must therefore be combined with a refinement and nobility in order to produce a new type of individual.

Section 225

Nietzsche rejects all doctrines that base their values on pleasure and pain. The 'we' and 'our' referred to here once again become the new philosophers, and the enemy is once more the man of modern ideals. The main point on which Nietzsche disagrees with the modern man is concerning the desire to abolish suffering and the emphasis on pity as a chief virtue. The new philosopher feels pity too, he argues, but not because of the fact that people suffer, or feel pain, or are deprived in some way, but rather because, in trying to abolish suffering, modern man is making himself into a pitiable creature, and removing the very cause of his own evolution and progression:

> The discipline of suffering, of *great* suffering – do you not know that it is *this* discipline alone which has created every elevation of mankind hitherto? That tension of the soul in misfortune which cultivates its strength, its terror at the sight of great destruction, its inventiveness and bravery in undergoing, enduring, interpreting, exploiting misfortune, and whatever of depth, mystery, mask, spirit, cunning and greatness has been bestowed upon it – has it not been bestowed through suffering, through the discipline of great suffering?[43]

Thus, in removing the causes of suffering, we are also removing the means whereby it is possible to develop those great qualities (e.g. courage, ingenuity, endurance) which only suffering can provoke. Man is both "*creature* [a thing which has been made] and *creator*", so it is his own job to work upon himself (like a sculptor or craftsman) to forge a new self – the means of which is suffering. A philosophy which denies this, and which stops short of higher ideals by concentrating on promoting pleasure and reducing pain, is ultimately shallow and naive. (This section, with its talk of "tension of the soul", recalls the earlier discussion of the "tension of the spirit" in the Preface; both show that Nietzsche believed that such dynamic opposition was vital for both societies and individuals to progress.)

Key Concept: *suffering*

Section 226

The new philosophers appear to modern man as immoral because such free spirits do not share the prevalent morality of the day. The world which such "immoralists" are concerned with is very different from the one which the man of modern ideals sees. In fact, the latter (who are mere "clumsy spectators") are too naive to even know that such things as concern the new philosophers even exist. Because of this misinterpretation, the man of modern ideals considers the "immoralists" to be without any sense of duty – whereas, in fact, they have a very keen sense of duty and dedication to their investigations, but this is something that the other, by his nature, cannot recognise or understand.

Section 227

Carrying on from the previous section, Nietzsche identifies honesty as one of the key virtues of the new philosopher. Yet this honesty is not of the common kind (as in being upright and moral), but rather of the kind suited to the type of philosophical investigation that the free spirit will undertake. Also, we should be on the watch that this key instrument in the investigation does not become blunted, or that we give in to the temptation of the comfort of a less strenuous life. The free spirit must "remain hard", and not be afraid of employing those qualities which common morality often rejects (for, he implies, it is not the attitude itself which is significant, but the use it is put to). Therefore, it is justifiable to feel "disgust at the clumsy and casual", and to "go to the aid of our 'god' [our ideal] with all our 'devils' ['bad' qualities]" (which is a point already made – see section 34). But most of all, the free spirit must be on guard against identifying himself with a particular attitude or idea (e.g. honesty), and thus cease to question his own nature (becoming "saints and bores" of their new morality).

Section 228

All moral philosophy up until now has been presented in a boring and tedious manner, mostly to suggest that there is nothing of great interest involved, and that the answers to the questions considered will not lead anyone to seek drastic change – in society or in themselves. For example, the English *utilitarians* would like nothing better than for their moral conclusions to uphold a certain conception of the English way of life (and it is almost as if it is "immoral" to question the basis of this morality – which, Nietzsche ironically points out, is a curious attitude for a "moralist"!). But not one of these mediocre philosophers (who are merely "ponderous herd animals") actually realises the truth: that to seek one ideal for everyone – for "the cause of general welfare" – is actually harmful to the development of "higher men", and that there is an *"order of rank"* not only between individuals, but also between *moralities* (therefore, perhaps it is best that such philosophers continue in their own way to justify their *own* lifestyles – and, Nietzsche implies, leave 'higher men' to *their* own morality).

Key Concept: *utilitarianism*

Section 229

In modern, civilised societies, which are proud of overcoming the base animal instincts in man, there is still a great deal of fear that such urges might yet regain control. But no one seems to recognise the fact that, not only have these urges not disappeared, they actually form the basis of all *civilised* morality:

> Almost everything we call 'higher culture' is based on the spiritualization and intensification of *cruelty* – this is my proposition; the 'wild beast' has not been laid to rest at all, it lives, it flourishes, it has merely become – deified.

This is quite a startling proposition, especially if we consider that Nietzsche considers Christianity to be as equally based upon cruelty as – for instance – the ethics of ancient Rome. He then lists various examples of how this cruelty lives on, and how certain Christian virtues, such as self-sacrifice and puritanism, share the same "enjoyment of suffering" as a delight in bullfights and public executions.

The point here is that cruelty is actually an essential form of disciplining the instincts. To turn against one's instincts, whatever they are, is to inflict a form of cruelty upon oneself – whether for religious, moral, intellectual or even artistic purposes. Cruelty, Nietzsche argues, is the basis of all knowledge.

Key Concept: *cruelty*

Section 230

In this important section, Nietzsche continues an analysis of the role of cruelty in seeking truth (see also his view of the role of suffering in culture in sections 44 and 225 above). Firstly, he revisits a phrase that he introduced in the previous section, "the fundamental will of the spirit", and what follows is basically an explanation of the will to power in relation to the mind. Nietzsche does this in three stages:[44]

1 One of the basic mental drives – and expressions of the will to power – is the desire to master new knowledge and experience (which we might call the *will to knowledge*), almost as if we were trying to make what is new submit to what we already know (the categories of our knowledge and experience). In doing this, the mind must necessarily simplify the complex, and find familiar features in the strange and foreign. (This is obviously a theme that Nietzsche has discussed already – for instance, section 4).

2 However, there is also an apparently opposing drive, which seeks to limit or even falsify knowledge (to let ourselves be deceived). This tendency is also expressed in a desire to deceive others by creating a 'mask', so that our real selves are hidden. This *will to ignorance*, as it may be called, would appear to be in opposition to the first drive (that which seeks knowledge), but this is in fact not the case, because it springs directly from the need to simplify or falsify the world in order to master it (through knowledge); both are aspects of the same fundamental drive which seeks to arrange our knowledge of the world in such a way that is *useful* to us.

3 Finally, Nietzsche shows that the role of the true philosopher is to question and analyse the effects of these two tendencies; to strip away the "ancient false finery" which surrounds the search for truth, and reveal the "*homo natura*" (natural man) underneath. Thus, by revealing the 'prejudices of philosophers', and pointing out how their philosophical systems are related to *natural* drives (such as the fundamental instinct to have power over others), Nietzsche is trying to combat the harmful effects of the will to ignorance. But such a will is very strong, and is so closely allied to our basic drive to knowledge (and mastery), that to go against it requires almost an act of cruelty against oneself. Here, then, is the main difficulty in philosophy: if our search for knowledge is driven by a desire for power and mastery, and there are times when such a desire can be served equally well by falsity and self-deception as by truth, why then should we seek truth at all? Nietzsche finishes this section by leaving this trailing question unanswered, presumably to be taken up in the following section. But it may also be argued that the question *does* remain unanswered because it is an open question. In other words, Nietzsche implies, the philoso-

pher's cruelty against his own "spirit" (his instincts) is actually an *expression* of this question; it is much harder to ask ourselves why we seek truth than it is to take truth as pre-existing. But as to why, fundamentally, we ask this question, it remains unanswered – and unanswerable . . .?[45]

Key Concepts: *will to ignorance*
                    will to knowledge

Section 231

Acquiring knowledge feeds and nourishes us, so that we grow and transform. What is it that grows, or that is fed? What drives this process? There is, Nietzsche argues, something "at the bottom of us, 'right down and deep'", which determines and selects which knowledge is meaningful, and what answers might be useful to us. Our beliefs and convictions are at least partly expressions of this most fundamental nature. Nietzsche does not seem to be talking about a soul, here, but rather (since he will, in the next section, go on to talk about the 'nature' of woman), about some physically determined set of instincts. Philosophy is therefore a constant questioning of this "right down deep", an analysis of the "problem which we *are*". This and the previous section therefore represent Nietzsche's ultimate position on the nature of truth and its relation to philosophy.

Section 232

Nietzsche regrets the new developments in Europe that see woman seek to change her traditional role. This can only have bad consequences, and draw attention to her less admirable qualities – which have until now been kept in check by male dominance and direction. On the other hand, woman has many talents and characteristics that are valuable – such as her charm, her ability to bring consolation, and to make light of things. However, the so-called "enlightenment" which has resulted in a change of gender roles has also led woman to begin to play a part in those activities which have up until now been the concern of man (e.g. science, politics and the general search for truth). But woman, by nature, is not fundamentally concerned – or equipped to deal – with truth (which in general represents a painful *stripping away* of appearance), and, in taking part in such pursuits, she must have some ulterior motive (i.e. a desire for power over man). In fact, woman's greatest skill lies in her ability to manipulate reality, for "the lie", and the surface control of "appearance and beauty"; these important skills allow her to make light of man's natural seriousness, and generally allow him to forget his cares (which, ultimately, is why he is so attracted to her). For this reason, he says, woman is also not the best judge of what woman should be like! Ultimately, though, Nietzsche wants woman to maintain her traditional role, to "cease compromising herself through enlightenment".

Section 233

The prominent women who are held up as exemplars of what woman can become (in the modern, emancipated sense), are no more than signs of a "corruption of the instincts", and actually represent strong "*counter arguments*" against the change in gender roles.

Section 234

As an example of woman's unfitness for certain purposes, Nietzsche cites cookery, where (he implies) if a man were in charge then the health of the human race would be much better than it is now. The reason for this is that woman does not have a scientific attitude to food and nutrition.

Section 235

The quotation here embodies the essence of what Nietzsche considers to be the strength of the traditional female attitude – to be able to turn one's back on "seriousness", "gravity" and "profundity" (mentioned in section 232 as typically male characteristics), but also the general cares of the world. Nietzsche is therefore implying here that an aspect of this ability to 'deceive' is essential to life.

Sections 236 and 237

Whilst man can at times idealise woman, it is perhaps less noticed that woman idealises man, and that (Nietzsche implies) much of her behaviour concerns and is directed towards man. The eight short aphorisms in section 237 highlight – quite humorously – some of the central features of femininity, and echo many of the points already made. What follows is a loose identification of some of the themes treated (my summary is not a direct translation of each one).

Woman is concerned with appearance, and most of her concerns centre on what people – especially men – think of her. Truth is less important than surface reality, and her skill at manipulating this allows her to get what she wants (which is based on appearance also). For this reason, woman is fundamentally different in nature to man, and represents to him an almost irrational creature, as if of another world, that he is both enchanted by and afraid of.

Section 238

To find no distinction between the sexes, and to dream of 'sexual equality', is, Nietzsche argues, a sign of shallow thinking – and more generally, that the thinker is not fit to consider the harder, more profound questions that face true philosophers. The best example of the correct attitude towards women is to be found in ancient Greece and Asia, where woman is treated

> as a possession, as property with lock and key, as something predestined for service and attaining her fulfilment in service.[46]

There is a sense, of course, in which Nietzsche is being provocative here (a tone which is not new – it pervades much of *BGE*). What makes *these* comments harder for the modern mind to accept is that we mostly live in societies where female equality is – if not a fact – then at least an accepted ideal. For this reason, as with his views on slavery (as the basis of culture), some readers will no doubt find such ideas difficult to take seriously.

It is worth noting, however, that what Nietzsche is expressing here is simply an extension of his views on class: just as certain 'types' of individual are unfit by nature for philosophy, leadership, etc., so, he argues, the female instincts as they have been nurtured and bred over the centuries – whilst they *may* partake in other, traditionally male pursuits (albeit less effectively, on the whole) – are better suited to more traditional roles. Ultimately, then, the root of Nietzsche's 'sexism' is that, like the effect of democracy on the classes, female 'equality' confuses and pollutes the natural instincts, and effectively lessens woman's natural power.

Section 239

The greater respect accorded to women in the modern age has merely produced in them the desire for more (more rights, more freedoms). This, in turn, has led to a decrease in woman's *fear* of man, and a corresponding abandonment of her "womanly instincts". One of the reasons for this is that the instance of the traditional ideal of manliness has also lessened (i.e. that which originally inspired fear and desire in woman), and the end result is that the democratic spirit is leading to the deterioration of both sexes.

Ironically, in gaining these increased freedoms and rights, "woman degenerates", and thus the liberationists who seek female emancipation are in truth acting *against* woman's best interests.

> Since the French Revolution the influence of woman in Europe has grown *less* in the same proportion as her rights and claims have grown greater.[47]

This movement is actually quite stupid, Nietzsche argues, in that it makes woman move away from "the ground on which she is most sure of victory" and causes her to neglect her "proper weapons" – things of which a "real woman" would be ashamed. Thus, "a fundamentally different ideal is wrapped up in woman", and woman is capable of an equally powerful but *different* type of strength (such as powerful women throughout the ages have always wielded). The "slavery" and lack of freedom which woman has traditionally been subject to is not a limitation on her, but rather a *condition* of the development of her true feminine qualities (just as slavery itself has been the basis of "every higher culture" to date). As he has already argued, one reason for this is the decline of "manliness" in modern society, and it is such men (weak 'herd animals') who seek to encourage this change of gender roles (so that, he implies, everyone in society is reduced to the same common denominator – the herd).

The effect of all these changes on woman herself is disastrous: hysteria and nervous disorders in women are gradually increasing, and these in turn endanger her ability to produce healthy children. This is all part of a gradual process of "enfeeblement" of the will (natural instincts) of the individual within society. Historically, when women have been strong, it has always been through force of will, and not education. Woman is much closer to nature than man, and is more animalistic – which man is attracted to, and both pities and fears. However, through this process of 'education', woman is being made "boring". Thus, the blurring of gender roles is merely a more general sign that the whole of Europe is being 'carried off' by the monster of 'modern ideas'.

Part Eight: Peoples and Fatherlands

Section 240

Nietzsche sees the character of the German people reflected in the music of Wagner. There is, he says, such a mixture of different influences that we get no real sense of there being a unified character to the music. The different emotions, tempos, styles, etc. all suggest that – like the German people as a nation – Wagner has not succeeded in digesting all of these different ingredients – in fact, is almost proud of the fact, and is "most at ease" amidst the "refinements of decay" (i.e. the outdated things of the past that were once held in high esteem). However, this love of the past is also mixed with a desire for innovation and newness. Therefore, just like the music, the German people show the same love of the past mixed with a desire for progression; they are "of the day before yesterday and the day after tomorrow – *they have as yet no today.*"

Richard Wagner

Section 241

Just as Wagner's music represents a sort of patriotic celebration of all things German, so patriotism is a similar sort of inability to 'digest' the things of the past and move forward – to become, in Nietzsche's phrase, "good Europeans". Underlying this is Nietzsche's vision of a future where national identities give way to a broader perspective, driven by science and guided by philosophy. Patriotism is a hanging on to the past, and to national divisions which hold back true progression.

The two patriots whose conversation Nietzsche reports here represent the old and new attitudes within Germany at the time: the first patriot is critical of political developments that see Germany becoming more powerful and unified, but at the same time sacrificing many of the characteristics that made it – in *his* eyes –

great (i.e. it now seeks power for power's sake, but once it had values and nobility); such power and unity are meaningless and empty, because there is no great vision behind it, only a desire for power and dominance over other countries. The second patriot disagrees with this: the achievement itself is great, he says, regardless of the motive – to which the former replies, "strong and mad! *Not* great!"

In one sense, Nietzsche is here more sympathetic with the first patriot; he sees the changes that are taking place (driven by shallow nationalism and a desire for political dominance) as a move in the wrong direction. On the other hand, since he is ultimately a 'good European', he is in truth in opposition to *both* patriots. Just as in Wagner's music, a clinging to the past and a desire for the future must both be sacrificed for the *present* – that is, for the formation of an attitude which represents a genuine step forward. In Nietzsche's view, as I have already pointed out, this entails being a 'good European', with no limiting national ties. Therefore, one positive consequence of the new developments is that it will force others to develop stronger characteristics, and react by becoming *less* nationalistic (i.e. good Europeans).

Key Concept: *the good European*

Section 242

The democratic forces that are shaping Europe are also having an effect upon the physical (genetic) makeup of the individual. By mixing together the various classes, nationalities, cultures, etc. the process is thus producing people who are not tied to certain ways of life or thought, and can adapt to different environments and situations more easily (compare the comments on 'semi-barbarism' in section 224). The occasional rise of nationalist or – even – anarchist movements can only slow down (and not stop) this process, which will ultimately give rise to two different types of man: on the one hand, the "useful, industrious, highly serviceable and able herd-animal man" governed by 'modern ideas' (whom Nietzsche sees as an example of the *slave* mentality who require leadership); on the other hand, it will also produce "men of the most dangerous and enticing quality" – of the *master* mentality, in Nietzsche's sense – who will be all the stronger for having to come to dominance under the influence of the democratic spirit. As Nietzsche points out, such spiritual and intellectual "tyrants" are by no means necessarily a bad thing.

Section 243

Nietzsche uses the fact that our sun is approaching the constellation of Hercules[48] as a metaphor for his hope that the new type of man discussed in the previous section will soon emerge. There is also a suggestion here that such a 'Hercules' will need enormous strength to face the 'tasks' ahead of him (that is, of redefining Europe and leading it to a new age).

Section 244

Traditionally, Germans have been thought to be "profound" or deep thinkers. But this quality has fallen out of fashion, and there is a desire in modern Germans to 'get rid' of it. The German character is difficult to define, and – as Nietzsche has argued up to this section – this is mainly because it is a mixture of lots of different qualities. For this reason, many have tried to define it without success, and because of this mixture of contradictory personality traits, where "the noblest and the commonest here stand side by side", anything one says about the Germans is "seldom wholly wrong about them". German profundity is a sort of slowness in 'digesting' these various qualities, and the German character is still in a state of "becoming" or development – it is not yet complete (it has as yet no "today" – section 240). However, it is quite useful for Germany to hide behind these traditional qualities of profundity, slowness, openness, etc. whilst this new character is developing. (In this sense, Nietzsche considers that a nation may possess a character 'mask' in the same way that individuals may.)

Section 245

Here, Nietzsche continues his analysis of the relationship between music and the national character of Germany. Mozart, he argues, is of a very different spirit to Beethoven: the former is light-spirited and graceful, and represents the end of a "centuries-old European taste", whilst the latter is merely a transition between different styles, and represents a mixture of the new and the old. Appreciation and understanding of Mozart's music will outlast that of Beethoven's, because the political and cultural factors which influenced Beethoven have now changed completely. Even the Romantic movement that followed is now dead, and only represented an 'intermission' between the old Europe and the new democratic one. In the Romantic period, only Felix Mendelssohn's music stands out for its "lighter, purer, happier" air, whilst at the other extreme, Robert Schumann's "petty" taste, which appealed only on a narrow, local level, was justly and quickly forgotten.

Sections 246–7

In these two sections, Nietzsche moves on to the subject of German language and writing. German writers and readers both lack the ability to understand the roles of tempo, rhythm and sound in the meaning of the written sentence. So, because the Germans have no "ear" for these qualities, they would consider certain writing styles similar which are, in reality, very different.

As a sign that the German is "deaf" in this sense, even the writing style of German musicians is bad, and the modern tendency to read silently is a further sign that the German reads only with his eyes, and that "he has put his ears away in the drawer". The skill of reading aloud was at its height with the ancient Greeks and Romans, for whom all reading was public, but this skill is now neglected, and the closest thing that Germany has to eloquence in speaking is the religious sermon. Here, at least, deep religious feeling has produced a book (Luther's translation of the Bible) which conveys at least some understanding of the spoken qualities of words. It is this fact alone that makes Luther's Bible Germany's best book.

Sections 248–9

Nietzsche identifies two different types of genius: the active, creative sort, and the passive, nurturing variety. The first produces new things, whilst the second takes outside ideals and develops and perfects them. Just as with individual geniuses, so with influential nations and cultures, which are either of the first or second kind. The Greeks and the French were of the passive kind, whilst the Romans, Jews – and possibly the Germans? (Nietzsche adds with a question mark) – are of the active sort. Perhaps, he implies, just as the Romans and Jews produced ideas and qualities which other nations went on to perfect, so the Germans will play a similar role in the development of modern Europe. As with men and women, both types seek this relationship, but also as with the two sexes, there is misunderstanding and quarrel.

Every nation, he argues, has its own "tartuffery" (hypocrisy) in regard to its own characteristics or virtues: it thinks and says that they are of one sort, but in reality, they are of another, unknowable sort. Here, as he earlier did in relation to the motives and drives of the individual (e.g. section 231, above), Nietzsche is arguing that 'good' and 'virtue' have ultimately hidden meanings, and that it is a matter of deep instinct as to what these motives are. In other words, the ultimate reason why individuals and nations value certain things as 'good' cannot be known; it is just a consequence of what we ultimately are 'deep down'.

Section 250

Europe owes a great deal, good and bad, to the influence of the Jewish people, but chiefly it is their attitude to morality, which sees 'good' and 'evil' as opposing moral absolutes, and morality as a divinely ordained set of commands. So, on the one hand, Nietzsche recognises the harmful, limiting effect that this attitude has had on

European morality and philosophy, whilst on the other he also sees how such an influence has created – through discipline and tension – the sort of conditions necessary for a new philosopher with a new attitude to morality to emerge.

Section 251

When a country becomes nationalistic, then it is likely to also suffer from prejudicial attitudes towards certain countries and peoples – in Germany's case, towards the French, Polish and Jewish. Once again, Nietzsche uses the metaphor of digestion to suggest that Germany, despite having a similar number of Jews to countries such as Italy, France and England, has not been able to absorb – 'digest' – them as these countries have – to such an extent that, even where German politicians criticise anti-Semitic attitudes, it is more a criticism of the way in which those attitudes are expressed (the "distasteful" feelings involved) than a criticism of anti-Semitism itself. Underlying this attitude is a fear that the German character will be erased by the stronger Jewish culture, which is itself a further sign that Germany has not yet developed a strong idea of what it is and what it stands for.

The Jewish people, on the other hand, are much more fully formed and certain of who they are than almost any current European nation. Their culture changes very slowly, and their chief virtues are that they can survive under the worst possible conditions. It is these qualities, Nietzsche argues, together with the Jews' "genius of money and patience", and their possession of "a little mind and spirituality", which the ruling classes of Germany are currently without – though, unlike the Jews, they do possess "the hereditary art of commanding and obeying". So, Nietzsche suggests, rather than allowing anti-Semitism and being overprotective of the German character, it is better to "eject the anti-Semitic ranters from the country" and "enter into relations" with the Jews with a view to "breeding a new ruling caste for Europe".

It is important to note here that this section contains not only a clear indication that Nietzsche was not an anti-Semite, but also his public apology for ever having had anti-Semitic sympathies:

> May it be forgiven me that I too, during a daring brief sojourn in a highly infected area, did not remain wholly free of the disease and began, like the rest of the world, to entertain ideas about things that were none of my business: first symptom of the political infection.[49]

This is a reference to the anti-Semitism of Wagner and his followers, with whom Nietzsche was briefly associated, and a number of anti-Semitic remarks made by Nietzsche himself in the 1860s.[50]

Section 252

Nietzsche considers the English – especially the English empiricists (Bacon, Locke, Hume)[51] – as having no talent for true philosophy. In their desire to explain reality in a mechanical way, they are lacking that "real *depth* of spiritual insight" which would allow them to go beyond their dry philosophical systems to something more meaningful and alive. The English are thus a coarse, vulgar people, who need the "antidote" of Christianity to spiritualise their nature, which is even "gloomier, more sensual, stronger of will and more brutal than the German". Finally, in an echo of the earlier sections on music, Nietzsche points out that the English are fundamentally unmusical – a further sign of their lack of sophistication.

Section 253

On the other hand, the type of characteristics possessed by the English remain useful for discovering certain types of truth, and certain "respectable but mediocre Englishmen", such as Charles Darwin, John Stuart Mill and Herbert Spencer, are currently providing important contributions to European thought. In fact, such men are necessary, because they allow the men of genius (the "exalted spirits") to concentrate on the task of creating a new way of *being* (rather than the limited, mediocre men who are only concerned with new knowledge). But it should not be forgotten that the English are the people responsible for these "modern ideas" (empiricism, and the scientific and democratic spirit) which have become so dominant in Europe, and have in fact influenced the decline of France – once, in Nietzsche's eyes, the highest expression of everything noble and cultured – into copying these attitudes, and thus becoming a shadow of its former self.

Section 254

The France of the previous section, the "seat of Europe's most spiritual and refined culture", still exists, Nietzsche argues, but in a few, hidden places. The men who still embody it resist modern ideas, and also the influence of pessimism through German philosophy and music (such as through Schopenhauer and Wagner) – which have nonetheless become very influential there. Despite this, French culture still possesses three things which make it superior to the rest of Europe: firstly, their dedication to creativity and 'art for art's sake'; secondly, their fascination with, and knowledge of, the psychology of human beings; and thirdly, their ability to blend aspects of the cultures of northern and southern Europe, tempering the occasional gloominess and "anaemia" (lack of vitality) of the north with the life and spirit of the south. It is this very balance which is embodied in the music of Bizet, and is the theme of Nietzsche's own philosophy (which he elsewhere characterises as the 'joyful science').

Section 255

In this section, Nietzsche continues the theme of northern and southern European temperaments in relation to music. As he has already noted, German music can be very ponderous and lacking in light-heartedness, whereas the music of the south is an antidote to this, and provides a release from the pessimism and gloominess of the north. The challenge to German music – and by association, German and European culture as a whole – is to develop a hybrid of these attitudes; at once, to be capable of light, joyful spirit and profound, meaningful insights. The new music that Nietzsche envisages, like his vision for his own philosophy and attitude to life, is to transcend national characteristics, and become truly pan-European.

Section 256

Despite the occurrences of patriotism that spring up from time to time to divide nation from nation, the general trend in Europe is towards unity. All great Europeans – Napoleon, Goethe, Schopenhauer, even Wagner – have supported this ideal. Nietzsche then concentrates on the latter in an attempt to show that, despite his apparent patriotism, Wagner was – in spite of himself – the beginnings of a 'good European'. Here, Nietzsche is being deliberately antagonistic to those who see Wagner's music as expressing the essence of what it is to be German, and at the same time undermining the patriotic attitude by showing that Wagner's music (as he points out in section 240) is actually a synthesis of many different cultural influences. Ultimately, Wagner stopped "before the Christian Cross" (in accepting Christianity late in life, and not seeking to go beyond Christianity), like other great men before him, and in this sense it is left up to Nietzsche himself to explain the significance of the lives of these great men in the development of a unified Europe, and to further point the way towards a new philosophy of life which goes beyond the traditional Christian values, and creates new ones.

Part Nine: What is Noble?

Section 257

Nietzsche's concerns in this chapter focus mainly on the nature of aristocratic society and 'noble' values, and this first section underlines their importance for the development of humanity as a whole. Firstly, he argues, without the notion of aristocracy, of the idea that one class of persons is superior to another, there would be no sense of self-improvement and development – and no culture (see his comments on 'order of rank' in sections 219 and 228). It is these very notions of rank, rulership, social order and slavery that allow us to strive towards what he calls "self-overcoming" – that is, by thinking that we are better than others we also learn to look at our own qualities and characteristics with a critical eye, and seek to 'overcome' or better ourselves. The key concept here is the notion that refinement of character leads to what he terms a "pathos of distance" – a keen sense of one's own difference – whether looking 'down' upon one's own 'lower' self, or the aristocrat or noble type looking down on the 'lower' classes.

But how does such an aristocratic society originate? Let us not fool ourselves, he warns: the first aristocrats were simply a stronger people than those they conquered – not only in a physical sense, but also in a "psychical" one. In other words, whilst they may have been to all intents a barbaric culture ("beasts"), they were also more complete and alive human beings – or rather, "more complete beasts".

Key Concept: *pathos of distance*

Section 258

When a society or individual becomes corrupt or diseased, it is an indication that the emotional or instinctive foundation has been undermined. For instance, if we look at the French aristocracy before the French Revolution, we can see that they had lost their total belief in their right to rule. Once a ruling class starts to question itself in this way, and to give away or lessen its privileges, then it is the start of its decline (and, in France, this process had begun long before the actual revolution and overthrow of the aristocracy – which was merely, as he says in section 46, "the last great slave revolt").

A healthy aristocracy therefore does not look to justify or explain itself, but rather considers itself to be the very reason that the society it governs actually exists; the purpose of society is to ensure that the 'higher' form of life which the aristocracy represents can exist and flourish.

Section 259

Here Nietzsche begins to contrast traditional aristocratic values with Christian ones. The principles of equality and mutual respect (of 'love thy neighbour' and 'do as you would be done by') cannot, he argues, form the basis of a society. They may be useful codes of conduct where strength is equal, or values are shared within a group – where, in fact, there is genuine equality (such as between members of the ruling class). However, if such principles are applied universally, then they become a "*denial* of life". The reason for this, he argues, is that, if we look at life in a natural setting, we can see that it is essentially undemocratic, where the stronger thrive, and the weak are oppressed and exploited. Therefore, if such processes are essential to life, then to deny them is in fact to be *anti-life*. Here, once again, is Nietzsche's concept of 'will to power': when the spirit of the ruling class seeks dominance and power,

> to grow, expand, draw to itself, gain ascendancy – not out of any morality or immorality, but because it *lives*, and because life *is* will to power.[52]

Such exploitation, Nietzsche argues, is the "*primordial fact* of all history", and the basis of all healthy society. Yet most of Europe has had difficulty in accepting this truth, and as a consequence the ideal of a just and equal society persists. One final thing to note here is Nietzsche's observation that the very terms we use to describe the true life-process ("exploitation", "severity", "suppression") are coloured by democratic and Christian values, and it is very difficult to think of them except in a negative way. This important point is only really hinted at here, and he will return to it later on in this chapter.

Section 260

In this important section, Nietzsche begins to set out, in detail, what he identifies as the two main types of morality: that of the 'master', and that of the 'slave'. The master morality is that of the ruling classes, and their conception of 'good' springs from those qualities that they value in themselves. So, the "proud states of soul", honour, truthfulness, strength, courage, and so on, are all seen as positive, 'good' qualities, whilst the opposite qualities, such as cowardice, timidity, concern only with the utility (usefulness) of a thing, as well as other qualities associated with the lower classes (the ruled and enslaved), are despised and considered 'bad' (though not 'evil' – this concept springs from the slave's value system, which Nietzsche returns to later in this section). For the aristocrat, these qualities determine the 'order of rank' in a society.

In understanding this division, it is helpful to try to relate how the different qualities relate to social position. For instance, Nietzsche argues that aristocrats traditionally value truth, and consider that "the common people are liars". However, it is not simply the case that the common people are less moral, but rather that there may be a reason for not always telling the truth – for instance, to hide some fact from those in authority for fear of punishment. Similarly, timidity can be seen as a further act of self-preservation, for it might not pay to appear proud or arrogant towards those with power over you. But if fear can be said to explain the attitudes and values of those who are ruled, then equally, lack of fear can explain the attitude of the rulers. This in turn explains other aristocratic attitudes, and so we can begin to understand how certain central qualities (e.g. fearlessness and fearfulness) form two opposite networks of values.

A central difference between the two moralities, Nietzsche observes, is that the noble type creates his own values, which are based on "self-glorification", whereas the values of the slave come from outside (they are, in a way, determined for him). For instance, for the noble type, compassion or pity is not considered a chief virtue in itself, but is rather a consequence of having an overabundance of power. In helping the unfortunate, the noble individual is motivated by an urge to spread their wealth, and to communicate their power through generosity. Pity in the form of sympathy is alien to the noble character, and there is almost a sort of pride that such a person takes in having a "hard heart". This is because, whilst the aristocrat does not feel pleasure at another's suffering, neither does he wish for a world where such suffering does not exist. The noble type honours the man who has "power over himself", and to do so, he must admit the role of "severity and harshness" in having power over himself and others (compare the earlier comments on cruelty and suffering, sections 44, 225, 229 and 230). The noble type also honours tradition and old age, and it is the man of 'modern ideas' who shows disrespect in this regard.

If we unpack Nietzsche's ideas a little further here, we can see the connections between these assertions: the noble man venerates what he has, his own wealth and achievements, but by extension, also those things which gave birth to him (i.e. his family, the values they share, tradition and the past, and so on), because they are, ultimately, *an extension of himself*; on the other hand, the man of modern ideas (which Nietzsche considers an expression of the slave morality), is attempting to turn his back on the past, to create a new world of 'equality', and is primarily concerned with change and the future. This latter type of man is therefore at odds with old age and tradition, in that they represent everything that is wrong with the world (in his eyes), and that which he is trying to escape from and change. These views are perhaps surprising to those readers coming to them for the first time, and who perhaps are used to seeing ancient pagan (noble) values through the lens of Christian morality and notions of progression (i.e. as 'barbarous' and immoral). Did the Romans value their elders more than we do? If we see modern society as marginalising and ignoring the views of the aged, abandoning them to care homes, and generally treating them as spent forces, then perhaps so.

A further contrast with modern ideas is that the noble man has duties to those of equal status (other aristocrats), but not to those below him. Even in regard to enemies and matters of revenge, these are only things which concern those of equal rank (whilst his behaviour towards his inferiors is not governed by the same codes).

In contrast, slave morality springs from the common people and those who are subject to the rulership of the aristocracy (and not just literally the 'slaves'). Nietzsche argues that their experiences and their situation in life leads them to be pessimistic about the nature of the world and existence, and sceptical of the virtue and happiness of those in power. (See, for instance, Socrates' doubt as to whether Archelaus, the Tyrant of Macedonia, can actually be considered 'happy' because he was not a 'good' person, in Plato's *Gorgias*;[53] and also Nietzsche's earlier discussion of "Morality as Timidity" and the "man of prey" in sections 197–8 above.) The qualities that are valued by the slave morality are those that help to alleviate their own suffering and generally make their existence easier:

> here it is that pity, the kind and helping hand, the warm heart, patience, industriousness, humility, friendliness come into honour – for here these are the most useful qualities and virtually the only means of enduring the burden of existence. Slave morality is essentially the morality of utility.[54]

What does Nietzsche mean by this last remark? It is that the slave's morality is dictated by that which makes his life easier, and that what is *useful* (what has "utility") in doing this, is therefore considered 'good'. The distinction between 'good' and 'evil' is born from the slave's attitude to power: since the powerful man inspires fear, then power cannot be 'good'; but since such power cannot be considered 'bad' (in the common sense that a certain thing is literally 'bad' for one, causes extreme dislike, is 'rotten', etc.), it must be 'evil'. The term 'evil' for the slave therefore takes on a meaning that goes beyond the idea that something is 'good' or 'bad' in relation to oneself (as is the case in the master morality), and becomes something almost otherworldly. Furthermore, the slave morality's attitude to even its own version of goodness is tinged with an expression of disrespect, for to be truly good, a man must be totally harmless – almost stupid. In other words, Nietzsche argues, 'good' must be so far from being fear-inducing that it becomes difficult even for those who hold it as an ideal to treat it with full respect.

Finally, Nietzsche distinguishes between the two moralities' attitude to freedom: the slave morality values freedom for the very reason that, in the world, slaves are not free, and desire to escape from their position of slavery and submission; but for the noble type, who has complete physical and social liberty, there is a reverence for devotion and submission to something higher. Such a submission is meaningful to the aristocrat because he is free to do it (whilst the slave is not). Consciously and willingly giving away one's freedom (through devotion, passionate submission, etc.), but whilst also valuing oneself highly, is the highest expression of one's ideal. In this sense, Nietzsche argues, love as a passionate devotion to another person or thing can only have originated from the master morality.

(For more on reverence as the characteristic of the noble type, see sections 263 and 287.)

Section 261

Men of noble type find it difficult to understand vanity (i.e. having a false opinion of oneself), because they find it difficult to imagine why someone should want to believe in a false picture of their own character and qualities. As a result, they tend to disbelieve that it exists in most cases. Of course, noble men may be modest, or accept the compliments of friends because they value both those friends and their opinion, but they still do not allow themselves to be deceived as to their own worth.

As mentioned already (e.g. section 46), this is a key difference between master and slave: the former create their own values (for themselves and others), whereas the latter must receive their opinion of themselves from others (be it good or bad, accurate or unfair). Now, because of the mixing of slave and master types through the rise of democracy, Nietzsche predicts that the noble tendency to value oneself will spread, but alongside it so will the slave's tendency towards vanity (false estimation). A vain man will equally value all good and bad opinions, however true or false, rather than (as with the noble type) only those opinions of himself which are true or useful to him. However, the latter is older, more widespread, and more ingrained, so the temptation to vanity will be stronger than the need to define one's character accurately, and so the general trend among most people will be to give in to the older, deeper habit. Thus, vanity is an "atavism" – that is, a throwback to the mental habits of the slave type.

Section 262

In this section, Nietzsche outlines the evolutionary history of aristocratic societies, and how they eventually come to decline, in three distinct stages. Firstly, he says, an aristocratic community becomes strong through a long and constant struggle against "*unfavourable* conditions". The reason for this is that favourable conditions – "plentiful nourishment and an excess of care and protection" – would only produce a weak society, rich in variation of types of person ("marvels and monstrosities"), but ultimately unfit for the hard task of rulership. The society learns which qualities have allowed it to survive and flourish, and it calls these qualities "virtues", seeking to teach and nurture them in its members with the greatest strictness and severity.

After this first stage of development is over, and the society as a whole begins to experience easier conditions (peace with its neighbours, greater and more available supply of food and resources, and so on), the great emphasis on discipline and strict behaviour relaxes. This allows for the appearance of individuals of all different types – both 'higher' and 'lower' – and the general breakdown of the old moral code. Thus, as individuality and personal freedom increases, each person finds themselves more at a loss as to how to live. There is a great mixture of forces and influences, "decay, corruption and the highest desires horribly tangled together", and the society begins once again to experience danger, but this time from its own members, who no longer have a common code to unite them, or teach them their social duty or rank.

Finally, the third stage is a response to this potential anarchy. Since the growing individualism is threatening to tear the society apart, the only solution is to become "mediocre", and to deny those qualities that threaten society. Such a new code speaks of "moderation and dignity and duty and love of one's neighbour", but in reality, it is simply a means to keep society together, to keep everyone safe by seeking to make everyone equally *harmless*. In Nietzsche's eyes, such a system is designed solely to breed the 'herd' type of man (as opposed to the noble and aristocratic type), who is not a danger to society. It is this system which Nietzsche sees as coming into place all over Europe with the spread of democracy and 'modern ideas'.

Section 263

The ability to recognise whether something is worthy of reverence (is of "high rank") is itself a sign that the person with that ability is himself of noble type. This is true even when the thing concerned has not been publicly recognised as being worthy of veneration. Thus, common people often react with hostility to something they instinctively recognise as in some way 'different', needing to be taught that such things are special and how to adopt the proper attitude towards them (e.g. the Bible). In this sense, since the masses have been trained over generations to react in this way, they are often more cultured in this respect than the middle classes (who have had less 'training').

Section 264

Here Nietzsche asserts that a person's character and qualities are always traceable to their ancestors – whether noble or common. He alludes to the words of the Latin poet Horace, "Try to drive out nature with a pitchfork, it always returns."[55] In this sense, a man cannot hide from what he is in terms of his genetic inheritance (which, for Nietzsche, includes certain habits, attitudes and behaviour), and all education can only really deceive in this respect (it changes nothing, only disguises the individual's true nature).

Section 265

The noble type of person is egoistic, and accepts the fact that others will serve him and submit to him as completely natural and just; but when among equals, he respects others as he respects himself. Nietzsche here uses the metaphor of stars, where each 'respects' the orbit of the other and is thus able to coexist in genuine 'equality'. But the aristocratic type's nature causes it only to admit equality or superiority – it is not inferior to anything (it does not look 'up').

Sections 266–7

These two short sections provide further examples of the noble attitude, and its difference from that of the slave mentality in relation to its concern for self-preservation. The first quotes the German poet Goethe with approval, stating that the noble type is not motivated by fear and concern for one's self (unlike the common man). The second section contrasts "late" (modern) civilisations with old, aristocratic ones (e.g. ancient Greece and Rome), where people in the former are 'smaller' than those in the latter. In other words, they are taught not to stand out or express their individuality too much in case they endanger themselves. (Incidentally, the Chinese proverb quoted by Nietzsche here is similar in meaning to an old Japanese proverb: "The nail that stands up gets hammered down.")

Section 268

Nietzsche here discusses what makes the common (in people, ideas, etc.), and starts off by distinguishing between concepts and sensations. For instance, he says, whilst a people may speak the same language, or even use the same words for things, it is their experiences – and more specifically the way in which they experience things (their sensations) – which help them to mean the same thing (or, *have things in common*). Where a group of people grow up in the same environment, and experience the same needs, dangers, etc., they will also understand the same physical sensations by the same words. In fact, he says, fear of this not being the case (of being misunderstood or not 'seeing things in the same way') is the basis of all caution between members of the opposite sex!

This tendency towards having common experiences is so strong among groups of people that it is in fact difficult for there to exist people who see things differently to the majority. This, ultimately, is the problem of producing the different type of man whom Nietzsche sees as an ideal: if the natural processes of living produce a large number of people who have experiences in common, then how is the rare or refined person to exist? "Tremendous counter-forces have to be called upon", he says, so that the exceptional man can develop. (Compare the comments on social "tension" in the Preface, the notion of arbitrary discipline in section 188, and the effect of democratic forces in mixing classes and races in section 242, which can be seen as key factors in cultural growth and the development of the exceptional man.)

Section 269

The psychologist who studies the 'higher' type of man must often feel pity at the inner state of such individuals. This is because, throughout history, the higher type (artists, poets, philosophers, etc.) have, due to their nature, faced difficulties of all sorts, and this frequently leads to their destruction. As noted in the previous section, life is much easier for the common type of man, and the psychologist will seek out the company of such people almost as an antidote to his insight into the exceptional man's suffering. Yet the psychologist must hide his true feelings when amongst the 'mob'; he sees the truth behind the pictures of the "great men" that they admire, and he realises that the public face of such men often conceals an inner flaw or cause of suffering which may influence them towards extreme behaviour that the common man cannot understand. A woman can often have an intuitive grasp of such suffering, but even when this leads her to try to rescue him through love, this is not enough, and her attentions are often misread by the common people (who, perhaps, might consider her a 'gold-digger'?).

The final part of this section concentrates on the person of Jesus as an example of a higher type of man whose nature led to his own destruction. Having introduced the topic of love, and pointed out how, in fact, it is "more prone to destroy than save", Nietzsche himself becomes the psychologist, interpreting the life of the flawed, tormented, higher man. Jesus, he suggests, was possibly an example of someone who sacrificed himself through knowledge of love – that is, through knowledge of the inadequacy of humanity's ability to love. This knowledge led him to create a God of pure love who could love humanity *despite* its failings.

Nietzsche's point here, developing on that of the previous section, is that the exceptional type of man is rarely a whole and sound individual. Because of the difficulties and strains involved in being exceptional – in being misunderstood, in being isolated from people, and so on – such a man is always at risk of buckling from the great inner tensions that he feels, which, unlike the feelings of the common people, have little social outlet. Such a man, like Jesus, is often going to be disappointed by the gap that exists between his own understanding of the world, and that of most other people.

Section 270

Those who have suffered deeply – and the extent to which someone can suffer is often an indication of how 'noble' their character is – frequently feel superior in terms of their knowledge of life. Since few can have experienced what they have, they feel set apart from others: "Profound suffering ennobles; it separates." So, because such suffering can rarely be understood by others, the person who has suffered in this way often feels a need to hide behind a mask so as to keep the fact of their suffering hidden. Such men "*want* to be misunderstood", and mask their suffering through certain attitudes: they may be Epicurean (i.e. love the 'good life'), and display courage and an apparent disdain for suffering; they may be constantly cheerful; they may be men who use the scientific attitude for its good-tempered detachment and apparent concern with superficial problems (as opposed to philosophical or existential ones). Such people, as Nietzsche has pointed out in the previous section, are "broken, proud, incurable hearts". The use of a mask, therefore, can be a sign of the refined nature of the higher type of man who wants to put off inquisitive 'psychologists'.

Sections 271–2

No matter how much goodwill one person feels towards another, the one thing that will always separate people is their differing standards of "cleanliness". By this word, Nietzsche does not mean a literal sense of hygiene, but rather a detachment from common feelings (those of the mob), and a desire to rise 'above' them. The saintly type of man, whose different experiences and outlook on life have set him apart, feels pity for the concerns of the common man. However, Nietzsche implies, there is a yet higher type of individual who rises above pity itself (this would be Nietzsche's ideal, and his main criticism of Christianity is that it does not do so).

The next, short section gives part of the reason why the noble type does not feel pity: he has his own duties and responsibilities, and – unlike the saint – does not wish for others to abide by his own rules, or consider that he has a duty to others. In other words, the saint feels pity because others are not like him, whereas the noble type accepts that they are different from him – necessarily so – and that he must concern himself only with the duties he has to himself.

Section 273

Continuing the idea of personal duty, the higher type of man considers others as either a means of achieving his goals, or else as obstacles. He can only be truly good to others when he has achieved his goal (achieving his true purpose and 'overcoming' himself and his personal demons), and until then he knows that he cannot help others (which, by implication, is the mistake the saint makes: he tries to help others without having achieved his goal of self knowledge).

Section 274

This section concerns the problem of at what point the higher type of man comes into being. In many cases, Nietzsche says, there are men of great potential who simply miss the opportunity to realise themselves. Perhaps then, he suggests, the only difference between men of genius and these men who wait too long is that the former recognise the right time to act decisively in relation to some important issue in their lives.

Sections 275–7

These three short sections point out further differences between the noble and common type. Firstly, the common man will focus on the 'low' aspects of a higher man's character (e.g. his worst points, his character flaws, idiosyncrasies, etc.), thus revealing his own common, non-noble nature.

Secondly, carrying on one of the main themes of this chapter, the common man is better equipped to deal with life than the noble man; the latter faces more dangers, and when they suffer injury or loss, the former is more robust, and will face the loss more easily. An analogy here (not Nietzsche's) might involve two types of machine: a simple mechanical device may take a lot of damage and still work, or else be easily repaired; but a complicated piece of technical equipment may sustain only a little damage, but, because of its complexity, be difficult to get working again.

Thirdly, using the analogy of house building, Nietzsche suggests one of the main difficulties for the un-common man, who must build his character himself, and may finish the task only to find that a vital principle has been ignored. The metaphor of building here suggests a key aspect of the higher man: he must overcome himself, and seek to establish values which go beyond the conventional ones shared by those around him (go 'beyond good and evil'). Finding out that there was "something which one absolutely *had* to know before one – began to build", is therefore only one of the pitfalls listed in this chapter which face the higher type of man.

Sections 278–9

Section 278 is difficult to clearly interpret, but the character of the Wanderer appears in a number of other places in Nietzsche's writings (Zarathustra himself is described as such).[56] In this case, the figure would seem to be Nietzsche himself, imagining that he is being questioned by an "inquisitive man". The Wanderer appears indifferent to all human emotions, showing no reaction to anything, and in this sense may be considered a metaphor for Nietzsche's own philosophical ideal (someone who can draw back and look at things without involvement). What would such a man desire? "A second mask!" he replies. In other words, the image of the dispassionate philosopher is only a mask, an exaggerated attitude which allows him to do his work – but which also causes curiosity from others. A genuine relief would be another mask that would allow him not to have to answer such questions! Once more, the point here involves the difficulties faced by the true philosopher/higher man – a point made in section 279, where "men of profound sorrow" (such as higher men so often are), reveal themselves in their eagerness to grasp true happiness when it arrives (as it does for them so rarely).

Section 280

A man goes backwards in order to better ready himself to jump forwards; but what is this "big jump", and in what sense is Nietzsche going "backwards"? The big leap envisioned is obviously the world of new values that Nietzsche sees the new philosopher as founding; the backwards step is the necessary preparation of analysing past philosophies and cultures, with a view to better understanding what the future task is.

Section 281

This section, enclosed in quotation marks, seems to be Nietzsche talking about himself. He has, he says, concerned himself very little with self-knowledge, preferring instead to turn his philosophical attentions outwards. In fact, he is sceptical of the very possibility that one can 'know oneself' without actually deceiving oneself – as do those philosophers who believe in the possibility of 'immediate certainty' (see sections 16 and 17 above). Perhaps, he muses, there is something in his nature which makes him sceptical. However, this is not a problem he can solve himself, and he leaves it to others, remaining a riddle to himself.

Section 282

In this section, Nietzsche uses the metaphor of dining to illustrate what he feels is the current predicament of the noble type of man. Such a man does not share the same tastes as the masses, and yet, because of the way society currently is – and there are few people who share his outlook on life – he is at times forced to "eat out of the same dish" (share the same experiences as most other people) or else "perish of hunger and thirst" (become lonely and isolated, starved of the experiences he needs). This, Nietzsche says, often leads to "dyspepsia" (indigestion), and he may at times be driven almost to madness through the stress that this causes him (he "smashes the plates, throws the table over, screams, raves, insults everybody"). (On the gap in feeling and experience between the exceptional and common man, see also section 269 above.)

Section 283

This difficult passage once again concerns the idea that a philosopher or deep thinker very often must hide his true ideas beneath a mask. In this case, the mask is to "praise only where one does *not* agree", and so deliberately be misunderstood by others. Unfortunately, this is less possible nowadays, as praise is likely simply to convince non-noble – and therefore less subtle – types that you agree with them (and that you therefore have something in common). Perhaps a better way of understanding this attitude is to consider the way in which philosophers of the past – e.g. Descartes and Francis Bacon – have used the dominant ideology of the time (in this case, Christianity) as a support for their ideas.[57] So, for instance, Descartes is at pains to point out not only how his philosophy is not at odds with Christian teaching, but also how it may help to bolster faith. In this way, he avoids the attentions of the 'unenlightened', whilst appealing to those who see his real, philosophical purpose.[58]

Section 284

The strategy proposed in the previous section is but one of a number of methods which the philosopher may employ in order to increase and preserve his detachment. For even one's opinions, "one's for and against", are merely "horses" which one may ride for a while. The point here is that the process of examining one's attitudes, of using them as ways of approaching certain problems or questions, is an essential part of philosophical enquiry. Solitude is necessary for such purposes, not only in a literal sense of being alone, but also in the sense of being detached. This is the significance of Nietzsche's talk of masks: they allow such detachment even whilst in the company and conversation of others. Such detachment is necessary because all company in some way makes the philosopher "unclean" and "common" (i.e. it compromises his detachment and his search for what is rare and noble).

Section 285

The thoughts of a great philosopher or thinker ("spirit") can take a long time to be understood, just as current events may take a while to be understood in the context of history, or the light from stars can take a long time to reach the Earth. In fact, until that light arrives, the stars do not appear to exist; so, in relation to great thinkers, they are only considered great sometime later, when their ideas have been more fully digested.

Section 286

The quotation here is from the last scene in Goethe's *Faust*, which ends with Faust's soul rising upwards to heaven.[59] The words are spoken by an onlooker in the spectacle, and the significance of the quotation is that the divine is located 'up'. The noble man, who – as noted in section 265 – is already "at a height", does not look 'up' (in adoration of something higher), but 'down', or on a level.

Section 287

What marks out someone as of noble type? It is not, Nietzsche says, his actions (which can be interpreted in different ways), or his "works" (if, for instance, he is an artist or a scholar), because the noble soul does not need to express itself in achievement. Rather, the defining quality of a noble man is that he has "reverence for himself". In other words, he has a clear sense of what he is worth, of what he is; he can be said to have faith in himself, and does not need to prove himself in action or work.

Section 288

People of enthusiasm ("spirit") are apt to appear as "more stupid" than they truly are. This is another example of a mask behind which the higher man may hide himself and his true motives and opinions. Such enthusiasm may also be expressed in their virtues, or moral attitudes. Therefore, Nietzsche implies, the moral enthusiasms they express may hide other moral opinions from the majority.

Sections 289–90

In the first of these sections Nietzsche compares the attitude of a hermit with that of a philosopher. In a sense, a philosopher is a hermit who has "stopped digging" – in other words, stopped actively exploring and questioning. The philosopher publishes books, and in doing so, seeks to express his "final and real opinions"; but for the hermit, the act of so doing would represent a giving up of the investigation, because deeper realisations – Nietzsche implies – await the man who questions the desire to publish and to arrive at complete and final thoughts. Beneath every philosophy, another, deeper philosophy exists. Here, then, Nietzsche is pointing out that the process of philosophical inquiry is never-ending, and that even to think oneself a philosopher is just another 'mask'. (Compare the comments on Plato and the copy of Aristophanes' works 'under his pillow' in section 28.)

Section 290 carries on this idea of philosophy as presenting another 'hiding place', another mask. In one sense, the philosopher is hurt at being misunderstood, but this is preferable to being *understood*. The reason for this is that he then feels sympathy for the person who truly understands him, and partly wishes that he could save him from the same lonely and difficult fate.

Section 291

In a point harking back to a theme that has occurred a number of times already (e.g. sections 24, 192), Nietzsche attributes the apparent simplicity of man's psychological makeup, his morality, etc., to his need to falsify knowledge in order better to make use of it. This might almost be considered an 'artistic' process, thus making creativity (in this wider sense) a much wider and more important activity than is popularly supposed.

Section 292

The philosopher is prone to a wide range of sometimes disturbing experiences and thoughts. Thus, occasionally, he feels the need to escape this constant inquiry into himself, but is ultimately driven back to study of himself by his own curiosity.

Section 293

Once again, Nietzsche contrasts the way in which the master and slave morality view the notion of pity. He lists many of the qualities that he sees as natural to the noble type (e.g. someone who can defend an ideal, who the suffering and oppressed look to as a leader, and so on), and says that, when such a man as *this* has pity, then it is worth something. However, the "pity of those who suffer", who "preach pity" as an ideal – this is a "cult of suffering" which would like to think it was something elevated and spiritual, but is in fact essentially unmanly and weak, and should be rooted out. The reference to "gai saber" here alludes to the troubadour poets of Europe to whom, in Nietzsche's eyes, it owes many of its most noble attitudes – and which here represent an antidote to the "cult of suffering" and pity (see also sections 189 and 260).

Key Concept: *gai saber*

Section 294

In opposition to the English philosopher Thomas Hobbes's assertion that laughter is "a bad infirmity of human nature", Nietzsche considers the ability to see something humorous in even the most serious issues as a sign of the true philosopher.

Section 295

In this penultimate section, Nietzsche extols the "genius of the heart", the irrational impulse that he considers the guiding force of his philosophical enquiry, which he associates with the Greek god Dionysus. In his first published work, *The Birth of Tragedy Out of the Spirit of Music*, Nietzsche had presented Dionysus and Apollo as the two opposite and yet complementary forces at work within any creative process (and within human nature itself). Apollo represents the rational, logical, limiting force, whereas Dionysus is the irrational, emotional and transcending force. In Nietzsche's view, the Dionysian spirit has been neglected – Nietzsche himself is its "last disciple and initiate" – and he sees his task as providing a source for the reintroduction of the god's healing, creative energies into human thought. The god's tendency to disrupt rigid patterns, to 'tempt' us away from the well-trodden path in search of fresh, new experiences (and perspectives), is itself symbolic of the spirit of Nietzsche's philosophy, and of the man himself.

Section 296

In an echo of section 289, Nietzsche again points out the limitations of written language. Already, he says, his thoughts are beginning to move on from what he has written, and some of the words that he leaves behind already sound "so immortal, so pathetically righteous, so boring!" Thus, "we immortalise that which cannot live and fly much longer", and the spirit which existed in the original thoughts fades away. So, in this final section, Nietzsche leaves us with a sense of the living philosophical attitude which has driven him in writing the book – but is itself no longer present in his words.

From High Mountains: Epode

Traditionally, in ancient Greek poetry, an epode is a short lyric poem which forms the final section of a three-part ode. Nietzsche's final thoughts are therefore presented in poetic form, and represent a call to other philosophical spirits of like temperament to join him in the "high mountains" where he resides (philosophically speaking).

But when such friends show up, they turn out not to be the ones that he had hoped for; they are friends from his previous life, and since he has been transformed by his hermetic existence and his experiences, they no longer recognise him, or he them.

The poem ends with Nietzsche expecting the arrival of "*new* friends", ones who are fit to join him. Zarathustra, the "guest of guests", has arrived, and together they celebrate the "wedding day" of "light and darkness". Zarathustra is Nietzsche's literary and symbolic embodiment of his philosophical ideals, and his arrival signifies that, in one sense at least, his philosophical search is at an end. What is required now is the transformation of the world, and the arrival of the "new friends" who will help with the task. The significance of the marriage of "light and darkness" is as a symbol of Nietzsche's task in *Beyond Good and Evil*: the traditional opposites ('good' and 'evil') have been transcended; the qualities associated with either opposite have been freed, and Nietzsche has indicated how the future morality must combine elements of both to produce new ideals. A philosopher may be 'wicked', 'cunning' and 'cruel' in the pursuit of truth, and thus undo the harm done by the 'slave revolt in morals' which first introduced the false opposition (i.e. 'good' and 'evil'). In doing this, Nietzsche can be compared with the English poet William Blake, whose own *Marriage of Heaven and Hell* presented a remarkably similar attitude to the prevalent morality.

Chapter 3

Critical Themes

Introduction

Because of the difficulties which most students face on first reading Nietzsche, it is understandable that almost all of their initial efforts must be dedicated to fostering a clear understanding of his ideas. But this is frequently as far as students get: the effort of comprehension has been so great that critical analysis is either completely lacking, or else rudimentary and off-target.

This chapter has two central aims: to deepen your understanding of Nietzsche's ideas by reference to his other works; and to put those ideas into a wider philosophical context for the purpose of critical discussion. As regards the first aim, it should be noted that this book is not a comprehensive treatment of Nietzsche's philosophy, but rather an introduction to it via *Beyond Good and Evil*.[1] As such, the main aim is an understanding of the text itself.

For my second aim, in relating Nietzsche's ideas to key areas in past and contemporary philosophy, I concentrate on three main themes:

- *Epistemology*, or *theory of knowledge*: How can we define 'truth' and 'knowledge'? Can we obtain certainty? What is the nature of reality?
- *Moral philosophy*: What is morality? Can we have objective knowledge of right and wrong? How should we define 'the Good'?
- *Philosophy of religion*: Can we prove (or disprove) God's existence? What is the true nature of religious belief? What is the true value and meaning of existence?

There are, of course, other areas of philosophy which we can apply Nietzsche's ideas to – for instance, political philosophy, aesthetics and philosophy of science. However, since such topics are not dealt with in any depth in *BGE*, I felt it was safest to concentrate on the three areas about which he had the most to say. Furthermore, if you are interested in Nietzsche's opinions on these and other subjects, then you will be better equipped to follow those trails once you have a clear grasp of the ideas in *BGE*. In discussing Nietzsche's ideas, I usually begin by briefly summarising his views on the topic in question. Therefore, this chapter may also serve as a general introduction to *BGE*, and may be read before – or alongside – Chapter 2.

One final thing that you should note is that the criticisms and counter-arguments presented in this chapter do not necessarily represent the final word on the topic under consideration. My fundamental concern in the following pages is to generate opportunity for you to consider these ideas for yourself. Nietzsche is a very provocative thinker, and his ideas are a very powerful stimulus. One of my purposes in presenting counter-arguments to Nietzsche is therefore to ensure that you are not overwhelmed by these ideas. (For ease of use, the parts of the text which involve direct criticisms of Nietzsche's ideas – and possible counter-criticisms – appear in shaded boxes.) Furthermore, where I can, I have also attempted to show how Nietzsche might have responded to the criticisms considered, or else how his ideas might be adapted or interpreted in order to counter such criticisms. In this way, I hope that you will respond to the challenge of reading Nietzsche as an opportunity to arrive at a deeper understanding of these difficult questions, and to use it as a spur to develop your own opinions.

Reality, Truth and Philosophical Prejudice

Philosophical Prejudices

In Part One of *BGE*, Nietzsche introduces the idea of philosophical prejudice. There, he proposes that many present and past philosophers have unknowingly been victims of their own unconscious forces, or 'drives'. These drives may be emotional, instinctive, the result of cultural influences, or even of the philosopher's own physical temperament. Whatever their source, they represent an unknown influence upon the philosopher's own conscious philosophical outlook, and so, because he remains unaware of them, they act as philosophical prejudices (i.e. unexamined assumptions and beliefs). We may perhaps trace the beginnings of this idea to the German philosopher Arthur Schopenhauer (whom Nietzsche was initially very influenced by), where it is not *reason* that drives us, but *will* (that is, our desires and instincts). However, Nietzsche has taken this idea and refined and expanded it into a powerful tool of philosophical analysis.

Nietzsche's approach consists in part of attacks upon individual philosophers – what is termed an *ad hominem* argument (Latin: 'against the man'). So, in criticising Spinoza, for instance, Nietzsche sees the rigid, mathematical form of Spinoza's philosophical system as a sort of 'armour' against any would-be critics. In organising his system in this way, "how much personal timidity and vulnerability this masquerade of a sick recluse betrays!"[2]

For Nietzsche, Spinoza's philosophy can be chiefly understood as psychological compensation for the philosopher's own personal failings and weaknesses – but is this fair?

The *ad hominem* attack is usually regarded as an invalid form of argument. For instance, look at the following discussion:

Stacey: I'm a vegetarian – are you?
Tracy: No; I think it's fine to eat meat. Why are you vegetarian?
Stacey: I think animals have a right to life, and should not be used for food when there are acceptable alternatives.
Tracy: What a load of rubbish! You wear leather boots!

Now, Tracy may have a point here: if Stacey really cares about animal rights then surely she would not use their skin for clothing. But her comment does not directly address Stacey's argument; Tracy has said nothing about why she thinks Stacey's argument is wrong, only why she thinks Stacey is a hypocrite. In this sense, then, Tracy's argument is *ad hominem*: it criticises the person, and not the person's reasoning.

There are many forms of *ad hominem* argument, and some of them are quite subtle and difficult to spot. Yet Nietzsche's use of this form of argument is, in a sense, different from that of most others; he is certainly aware of the pitfalls of such an approach, and so we should not assume that we can rescue all of the philosophers whom he attacks simply by pointing out that his argument is *ad hominem*. On the contrary, the *ad hominem* attack is a deliberate choice by Nietzsche; he wants to show that there is a clear connection between the personality, temperament, experience, etc. of the philosopher, and that philosopher's own particular philosophy. But, before we judge the truth of Nietzsche's *ad hominem* critiques of these philosophers, we must assess whether it is in fact true that all philosophies spring from such influences. Furthermore, of course, we can ask how Nietzsche's own philosophy is different in this respect: surely his philosophy is also influenced by his own temperament, education, etc.? We'll look at both these questions later in this section.

This said, Nietzsche's criticisms of philosophers and their ideas are not solely *ad hominem*. In Part One, Nietzsche identifies a number of philosophical concepts which he finds problematic, and his criticisms of these tend to take a more traditional philosophical form. Let's look at these again.

1 The will to truth

Nietzsche argues that the majority of philosophers hold the attitude that truth is an objective thing, and that it is possible to arrive at it through rational enquiry. He points out that such philosophers have ignored the role of *self-interest* (among other things) in the search for truth, and that their notion of objectivity is therefore a false one.

Nietzsche's approach to this area of philosophy (*epistemology*, or theory of knowledge) is often termed *naturalistic*. There are different types of *naturalism*, and the term is often used as a general way of describing philosophical approaches that favour scientific or 'natural' explanations over *metaphysical* ones. So, for instance, let's contrast Nietzsche's approach to knowledge with that of Descartes, for whom certain ideas were capable of providing us with absolutely certain knowledge (such as his *Cogito* argument: 'I think, therefore I am'). Furthermore, such ideas are immediately apparent to us; they are 'clear and distinct', and it is the possession of these qualities which allows us to identify absolutely certain knowledge. Nietzsche, and other naturalists such as Hume, criticised this idea: as Nietzsche himself points out, to argue that the *Cogito* argument is true we must first assume any number of things (e.g. that there is a single 'I', that this 'I' is the cause of thought, and so on); Hume had also criticised Descartes's notion of there being a 'necessary connection' between cause and effect, preferring to argue that such 'connections' cannot be observed, and that the connection is a mental association caused by seeing such things habitually occurring together (e.g. seeing an apple fall leads us eventually to the idea of gravity, but – for Hume at least – we are not discovering a natural connection which exists between objects and gravity, but rather forming a mental association concerning events – which may, in the future, turn out to be wrong; there may be a place in the universe where apples fall up, and where is your certainty then?!).[3]

Descartes's assumptions are not based on experience, but go beyond it; they are not based on the 'physical' but the '*meta*physical' – i.e. those ideas which go beyond what it is possible to observe via experience (*meta* is from the Greek, meaning 'after' – see *metaphysics* in the Glossary). In contrast, Nietzsche's own approach is to explain these assumptions in natural terms: we think of there being a single self or 'I' because it is useful to us (e.g. perhaps having psychological individuality has helped our species survive); absolutely certain ideas do not exist, but it may have been helpful, in our past search for knowledge, to rely on certain ideas over others. In both these cases, as Nietzsche repeatedly emphasises, it is not always the truth of an idea that is most important, but rather what purpose it serves. Truth, then, for Nietzsche, is always related to some purpose or goal. With the higher type of man, this goal can be a very refined and sophisticated one, and he may even reach a point where he appears to seek truth for its own sake (e.g. see section 39, where the ability to see the world without illusion is seen as a sign of strength of character and sophistication). But even here, truth is always related back to the individual – and to the will to power.

However, there are a number of problems for philosophers who adopt a naturalistic attitude to epistemology.

Firstly, it would seem to require giving up the possibility of absolute certainty. Remember, Descartes's certainty is based on there being something which is absolutely certain and beyond doubt. But, as we have seen, many of Descartes's assumptions are questionable from a naturalist's perspective, so a naturalist would need to find a way of guaranteeing knowledge that did not involve similar metaphysical assumptions. Yet herein lies the problem: it is these metaphysical assumptions which form the basis of absolute certainty. For instance, suppose that I leave the house one morning and I'm almost at work, when I suddenly wonder whether or not I've locked the back door. I think I remember doing it, but how can I be sure? Suppose that I say that I have a clear memory of doing it – will that do? But the memory I have may be of another occasion (e.g. yesterday) when I *did* remember to lock the door. Perhaps there is some quality about the memory which makes it true and distinguishes it from false memories? Even if I believe that there is, such an assumption is a *metaphysical* one. It is not logically impossible that I could get that feeling about false memories, or even *fail* to get it with *true* memories.

The point here is that, for absolute certainty to exist, we have to make an assumption that some process involved is reliable. So, there are various ways in which we might check our knowledge – by a tried and tested method, by comparing it with the knowledge of friends, by some quality or feeling attached to an experience – but each of these ways will require some sort of guarantee in order to be considered absolutely certain; the method may prove faulty, your friends may also be wrong, the feeling may be misleading. However, such guarantees are, by their very nature, beyond experience, because whatever is experienced may change or be contradicted by further experience in the future (and that which is absolutely certain cannot be contradicted at any time). In denying the existence of any sort of metaphysical guarantee, a naturalist is therefore open to all those sceptical doubts and problems that Descartes sought to defend himself in the first place.

Continued

A second problem for naturalists is the question of reality. If there is no metaphysical guarantee of truth, then how do we know that it is even *possible* for human beings to understand the world? The idea that the world is tailor-made for humans to make objective sense of is highly questionable, and it might even be the case that human beings are too ill equipped (in terms of our senses, our power of reason, and so on) to come near to understanding it.

Because of these two issues, naturalists tend towards *pragmatism*, or the view that what is 'true' may be changeable, or maybe even only true for humans, and that we must strive to obtain a view of the world that 'works' (and not for a perfect description of some unchanging 'reality'). In this sense, pragmatism seeks to bring philosophy closer to science, where theories can change depending on how successful they are at explaining things, and how useful they are.

But where does this leave Nietzsche? On the one hand, he embraces both these consequences: firstly, he rejects the search for absolute certainty, concluding that it is just an aspect of the will to power of a certain type of philosopher who seeks to impose his philosophical system upon others; secondly, he recognises that the view that human beings have of reality will always be coloured by their own drives and instincts, as well as the limitations of their brains and senses, and we must seek to create a reality which is in line with our deepest will to power.

The problem with Nietzsche's view – at least for the more traditional philosopher – is that it would appear to lead us to an extreme *relativism*. If there is no reality or truth by which to judge my opinions and beliefs, then what is there to stop me from taking any deeply felt belief and treating it as truth? However, this gives us an insight into what will to power really is: truth, for Nietzsche, is not a case of having a set of beliefs which correspond to some external objective reality, but rather of having a set of values which one considers to be superior to those possessed by others. (I will come back to this topic shortly when I come to look at Nietzsche's *perspectivism*.)

2 Faith in antithetical values

Nietzsche argues that part of the way in which we falsify reality is to divide it into opposites. One instance he gives is the idea of cause and effect, and this would be an *epistemological* example of this (i.e. relating to the act of knowing the world). However, Nietzsche also argues that we create opposite values in a *moral* sense, by dividing actions and motivations into 'good' and 'bad' (or 'good' and 'evil'). So, we might consider murder to be a bad act, for instance, and view giving to charity as a good act. But what if someone were to ask you, 'Why is one act considered good and the other bad?' You might begin by answering that giving to charity helps others, whilst murder harms others. Now, suppose the questioner responded, 'But why is helping others considered good, and harming others considered bad?' You might be tempted to answer, 'Because we should treat others as we would like to be treated ourselves' – or, as a Christian might say, 'Do as you would be done by'. 'But,' your questioner replies, 'aren't you really concerned here with self-interest? You choose not to hurt others only because you want not to be hurt yourself.' Now, your questioner has a point: your actions *can* be interpreted as being based in self-interest. So, you have a choice: either you can admit that all acts that we think of as 'good' are ultimately based in self-interest, or you can try to define 'good' in such a way that it has nothing at all to do with selfishness. If you take the latter option, Nietzsche argues, then you create a metaphysical notion of good which has nothing to do with reality – it is a *falsification* of life.

I will return to Nietzsche's *ethical naturalism* in the later section on morality, but for now it is enough to realise that faith in antithetical values can apply to such pairs of opposites as 'good' and 'evil', 'truth' and 'error', and even aspects of the physical world, such as 'cause' and 'effect'. But is Nietzsche's attack on this 'prejudice' justified? We may argue, as Aristotle did, that things either *are* or *are not*; the cup is either on the table, or it is not. This is known in logic as the *law of excluded middle*; in other words, something is either true or not, and the answer cannot reside somewhere in between. Therefore, it may be concluded, such oppositions are justified.

There are a number of possible responses to this. Firstly, Nietzsche would point out, it is wrong to consider this rule of thinking as a 'law', for it is not proven by experience or logic, but rather *forms the basis* of our logical deductions. So, it is, in this sense, yet another example of an arbitrary limit that human beings place upon themselves in order to better understand (or 'falsify') the world.

Secondly, the test of what status we accord Aristotle's 'law' is whether we can envisage a world where it was not the case. This is an important step in the argument, for if we can, then the 'law' becomes merely a convention that can either be adopted or set aside. So, for instance, if we imagine a logic where there were degrees of truth – as opposed to things being simply either 'true' or 'false' – then we might be able to accept Nietzsche's point. Some logicians have in fact argued that so-called *multi-valued* or *fuzzy logic* is possible and meaningful, but there is debate about how useful such things are, and how radical their implications are. For instance, if you ask, 'Is it sunny outside?', I may feel that I can't simply reply with 'Yes' or 'No' – there may be some cloud cover, but not enough to warrant a negative response. If 'Yes' is 1 and 'No' is 0, then perhaps my

Continued

answer would be 0.6. This is different from probability: I'm not saying it's *fairly probable* that it's sunny; I'm saying that it is slightly more sunny than cloudy.

Of course, we could rewrite the statement so that it had a definite 'Yes' or 'No' answer (e.g. 'Is the sky cloudless?'); this would remove the need for fuzzy logic, wouldn't it? But Nietzsche's point isn't that we can't use traditional logic to picture the world *if we wanted to*, but rather that such a picture is a wilful falsification of the world to our own benefit – *and that other pictures are possible*. The task of the new philosopher is therefore to analyse such tendencies, and to ask whether they do in fact still serve a useful purpose. Do we still, at some level, *need* to split aspects of reality into opposites? Why? Nietzsche is therefore not necessarily suggesting that we should get rid of this tendency (and that we can do without it), but rather that we should be consciously aware of what role it serves in our search for knowledge – and to realise that it is a role that we can change, if we wanted to.

A final point to do with faith in antithetical values is that, if we admit that there may be degrees of truth, then we cannot say that one opposite is completely unrelated to the other. If there is a sliding scale of values between 'good' and 'bad', then 'good' must be related to 'bad', even if very distantly. By adopting naturalism, therefore, Nietzsche is saying *both* values have a common cause (i.e. the natural world).

3 Distinction between appearance and reality

One of the first things a philosophy student is usually presented with is the problem of illusion. Whether it is the classical example of the stick that appears bent when half-submerged in water, a mirage, or one of many other examples of how our senses may deceive us, the implication is that things are not what they seem; how things *appear* to be is not how they actually *are*.

So, in regard to the way in which we see the world, a *realist* would say that our senses allow us to see the world more or less as it really is. However, if we were to assume that the world is *exactly* as our perceptions tell us it is, then we could be accused of being somewhat *naive* or overly trusting – the stick in water is not *actually* bent, the stars you see at night are not *actually* in the positions you see them (some are not there *at all*). So, once this is pointed out to you, you are more likely to reject *naive realism* (as philosophers call it) in favour of something a little more sophisticated.

A better alternative is the idea that our perceptions present us not with a *direct* view of reality, but rather an *indirect* one via *representations* of it. So, *representative realism* is the idea that – for example – when I look at a red apple, my perceptions of it are relative to certain conditions: the 'red' colour is dependent on my human eyes (a dog or cat would see it differently), and it is only this particular colour

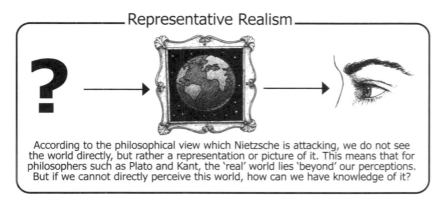

Representative Realism

According to the philosophical view which Nietzsche is attacking, we do not see the world directly, but rather a representation or picture of it. This means that for philosophers such as Plato and Kant, the 'real' world lies 'beyond' our perceptions. But if we cannot directly perceive this world, how can we have knowledge of it?

because of the light conditions at the time. Most philosophers – and most non-naive people – therefore hold to some form of representative realism.

The extreme of this point of view is reached when reality is considered separate and distinct from our perceptions of it. For example, Kant argued that we can only ever experience *perceptions* of things (what he termed *phenomena*), and not the things themselves (what he termed *noumena*). The noumena were permanently unknowable, though we might infer things about them through observing the phenomena for which they are responsible (just as we might understand the nature of a physical object by analysing its colour, texture, shape, temperature, etc.).

A loosely similar position to Kant's (regarding appearance and reality) is held by Plato, who held that the senses provide us with inferior knowledge about reality, and that we must use our reason and understanding to arrive at a more correct picture of the world. He also thought that, underpinning this reality, there exists a separate realm of pure ideas – or what he called *ideal forms*. When we think of a physical thing – for example, a red apple – that thing is related to particular pure ideas ('redness', 'roundness', etc.). So, in order to fully understand the nature of earthly things, we must try to achieve a direct apprehension of these forms.

Nietzsche's criticism of this type of approach is based, once again, on an analysis of *why* the philosopher chooses it. As he points out, we should not be asking – as Kant did – *how* such ideas are possible, but rather, "why is belief in such judgements *necessary*?"[4] The answer from Nietzsche is that, of course, they are not, or at least not for any logical reasons. Rather, they are the result of the individual philosopher's own instinctive drives and will to power.

In another work, Nietzsche clearly outlines his view of what this means:

> In so far as the word 'knowledge' has any meaning, the world is knowable; but it is interpretable otherwise, it has no meaning behind it, but countless meanings. – 'Perspectivism.'

It is our needs that interpret the world; our drives and their For and Against. Every drive is a kind of lust to rule; each one has its perspective that it would like to compel all the other drives to accept as a norm.[5]

Plato and Kant's mistake, then, was to assume not only that the world had a single "meaning behind it", but also that such meaning had absolutely no connection with their own *perspective* on things (which, in turn, was ultimately dictated by their instinctive drives). Such an approach is yet another example of a 'faith in antithetical values', whereby the world of pure ideas is held to be superior and completely distinct from the deceptive and untrustworthy world of the senses.

Perspectivism is the idea that there can be no 'true' perspective on the world, and that what really happens when we arrive at the 'truth' is that a certain desire to see the world in a particular way wins out over other competing desires. This is not only true as regards different individuals who are controlled by different drives, but also within the same individual, where competing drives are struggling for dominance. The perspective that wins out is therefore, in some way, a justification of the nature of the dominant drive, and also a further means whereby that drive can further increase its future power and dominance, and ensure the survival of its 'type'.

The clearest example of this is Nietzsche's interpretation of Christianity. For Nietzsche, Christianity represents part of the 'slave revolt in morals', whereby the old, traditional morality of the aristocrats (the ruling classes) – who valued strength, power and dominance – has been turned on its head. For Christians, worldly power is 'evil', and meekness, humility, lack of pride, etc. are all seen as 'good'. This perspective thereby uses this viewpoint as a means of justifying and legitimising its own power, so that the 'meek' – those who were once without any power (the 'slaves') – could now finally achieve it *via the backdoor*, as it were (i.e. slyly).

The problem with perspectivism is that – as I mentioned earlier when discussing Nietzsche's views on truth – it would seem to leave us with extreme *relativism*. For Nietzsche, there is no one true perspective, but merely a competing array of different perspectives; things are only 'true' or 'false' *relative to* individual perspectives, none of which is ultimately more 'real' than the next. What decides the success of one perspective over others is the extent to which it becomes dominant over others. But even here this may not be a guarantee that the dominant perspective is the best – many of the perspectives that Nietzsche criticises are or have been dominant. Such an *anti-realist* view of things arguably leaves us in a situation where what is and is not 'real' (or 'true') is a matter of complete subjectivity. Reality and truth would both seem to disappear in Nietzsche's view.

Is the situation necessarily this bad? Nietzsche does not dismiss the search for knowledge – on the contrary, he is constantly concerned with getting a deeper understanding of the world. Just because he rejects traditional realism and the idea of objective knowledge does not necessarily mean that all is lost. A possible solution is, rather than seeking to find one perfect perspective, to evaluate *all* perspectives, and to allow each of them to inform our view of the world.[6] This type of idea has been very influential in the late twentieth century, where the views of minorities have influenced and changed the majority view. So, for instance, the movement for racial equality, gay rights, women's liberation and the 'green' movement have all played a part in altering our society and reforming our laws. In philosophy, adoption of sceptical arguments frequently leads to a rejection of former attempts to defend knowledge, and to a new and deeper understanding of the issues involved. This is not to say that any of these alternative perspectives are *true*, merely that a sympathetic understanding of them will necessarily broaden and deepen the common outlook.

So, in summary, whilst a certain view of reality and truth *does* disappear with Nietzsche, it is replaced by a deeper – though more vulnerable – understanding.

4 Atomism

One of the questions with which the early Greek philosophers were fundamentally concerned was that of the constitution of the world: what it is made up of? So, for instance, Thales believed that the fundamental element in the world was water, and that ultimately everything originates from, and returns to, that first state. In contrast, but for similar reasons, Anaximenes held that air was actually the fundamental element, whilst Heraclitus, who thought that everything was permanently in a state of change, preferred to think that the basis of everything was fire. However, it was not until the philosophers Leucippus and Democritus that we begin to get closer to something like the modern scientific perspective, whereby everything is composed of minute, indivisible particles, or *atoms*, which are in a constant state of motion.

Despite the early appearance of this theory, it was not until the nineteenth century that the idea began once more to be entertained seriously. Up until then, Aristotle's conception of the world as split up into the four elements – earth, air, fire and water – had held sway, and the backing of the Catholic Church had ensured that any serious challenge to this view was discouraged. However, the growth of scientific inquiry during the seventeenth and eighteenth centuries led eventually to an empirical investigation of the nature of matter. During this time, scientists such as Robert Boyle and Isaac Newton helped to reintroduce and popularise the idea, whilst later chemists, such as Antoine Lavoisier, gradually cleared the way for an atomistic understanding of matter by using atoms to explain the behaviour of gases in chemical reactions. By the beginning of the nineteenth century, the experiments of other scientists, such as John Dalton, Amadeo Avogadro and James Clerk Maxwell, helped reinforce the credibility of the idea, and so, by the end of the nineteenth century, atomic theory was quickly becoming established as the leading theoretical explanation of what matter is and how it behaves.[7]

Nietzsche's interest in the subject is twofold: on the one hand, he had a genuine curiosity about the scientific discoveries of the time, and did his best to keep abreast of them; on the other hand, he is aware that scientists are no different from philosophers as regards their tendency to exhibit 'prejudices' in their search for knowledge. In sections 12, 20 and 32, he criticises *atomism* or the *atomistic* way of thinking, whereby, he argues, certain thinkers fall into the trap of supposing that there exists a central 'atom' or thing which – for instance – possesses qualities or properties. From a scientific point of view, he finds that the idea of the atom had already begun to be undermined by such thinkers as "the Pole Boscovich",[8] who argued that atoms could be better understood in terms of fields of force, rather than as tiny particles. In this sense, Nietzsche can be seen to have been quite prophetic in his predictions: atomic theory, whilst still a contentious one at the end of the nineteenth century, was fast becoming the main one. Yet, early in the twentieth century, even as the theory became orthodox, other discoveries were already waiting in the wings to undermine it. So, by the time I did physics in school (in the 1980s), what I was learning was already considerably out of date.

It was a model first put forward by the New Zealand physicist Ernest Rutherford in 1911. But Rutherford's model presented as many problems as it solved, and the many attempts to get it to work (or to disprove it) would eventually lead to strange and baffling new discoveries. Despite this, the popular conception is still difficult to shake.

> The picture most people still have, from school or popular accounts, is of an atom rather like the solar system, with a tiny central nucleus around which electrons whiz in circular orbits. This is the place to abandon that picture, however, and to try to approach the bizarre world of the atom – the world of quantum mechanics – with an open mind.[9]

Rutherford's model of the atom is therefore a prime example of the way in which human beings try to understand the world using concepts which have either proved useful to us in the past, or else which are so embedded in our way of thinking as to be almost unnoticeable. But just as the atomic idea can be replaced, so we can root it out of our thinking concerning other matters. So, for example,

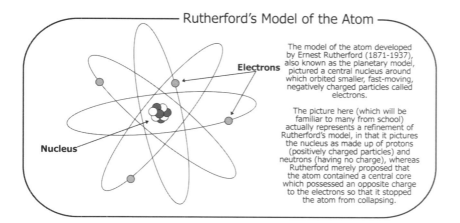

Rutherford's Model of the Atom

Electrons

Nucleus

The model of the atom developed by Ernest Rutherford (1871-1937), also known as the planetary model, pictured a central nucleus around which orbited smaller, fast-moving, negatively charged particles called electrons.

The picture here (which will be familiar to many from school) actually represents a refinement of Rutherford's model, in that it pictures the nucleus as made up of protons (positively charged particles) and neutrons (having no charge), whereas Rutherford merely proposed that the atom contained a central core which possessed an opposite charge to the electrons so that it stopped the atom from collapsing.

Nietzsche criticises Descartes for thinking that there is one, indivisible, immaterial self. Why, he argues, should there be just one, or in fact any finite number of selves? Perhaps, as with the atom, it may be possible to understand the self as a complex unity of different 'selves' – or 'drives', as Nietzsche himself argues – and what we think of as 'I' is a fluid, changeable, loose affiliation of shifting perspectives and influences – not all of which have compatible goals.

So, where does this "atomistic need" spring from? Nietzsche argues that we are tempted into thinking atomistically through the grammatical structure of our language (see sections 16–21 and 34). For instance, take the simple sentence, 'I think'. In grammatical terms, the *subject* ('I') is the thing which either causes or is the centre of a state of being or action, and that action or property which we associate with the subject is called the *predicate* ('thinks'). This pattern is the basis of most of our language – for instance, look at the following statements (I have *italicised* the subject and underlined the predicate in each case):

> *The car* has broken down.
> *She* went to the park.
> *Life* is beautiful.

Now, Nietzsche's point is that we are so used to speaking in this way that, when we come to theorise about the true nature of things (as philosophers do), we also begin to *think* in this way. This is a case of 'putting the cart before the horse' (as they say), because – for instance – in looking for a unified, central self or 'I', we are already *assuming that there is one*.

The twentieth-century English philosopher Gilbert Ryle makes a similar point in a famous passage:

A foreigner visiting Oxford or Cambridge for the first time is shown a number of colleges, libraries, playing fields, museums, scientific departments and administrative offices. He then asks, 'But where is the University? I have seen where the members of the colleges live, where the Registrar works, where the scientists experiment and the rest. But I have not yet seen the University in which reside and work the members or your University.'[10]

This is called by Ryle a "category-mistake" and represents the sort of error we make when we confuse different *types* of thing. So, the foreign visitor sees the various buildings, facilities, staff, students, etc. that make up the university, but still assumes that there is something extra which constitutes the "University" itself. A person would make similar mistakes, Ryle argues, if he went looking for "team spirit" as something separate from the behaviour of the team members; or, when watching battalions, batteries and squadrons of soldiers marching by, searched for something extra called a "division". In the latter case, someone would simply point out that the term "division" is the collective name for a certain number of battalions, batteries and squadrons of soldiers.

However, I think Nietzsche's point here is deeper than Ryle's. Firstly, whilst Nietzsche and Ryle both criticise Descartes's view of the self, Nietzsche sees this as only one expression of the "atomistic need", for it is, he argues, a way of seeing which is tied into fundamental patterns of human behaviour, thought and communication. Secondly, Nietzsche's view of truth is more flexible than Ryle's. For instance, Nietzsche recognises that such 'errors' have played an important role in the development of humanity, and that without them we may not have evolved so successfully – or even survived at all. Atomism, therefore, has been a useful way of categorising the world so as to better master it. What's more, in recognising the limitations of atomistic thinking, Nietzsche is not simply dismissing it in favour of another theory (as Ryle is), but rather asking us to investigate just what purpose it serves – and, where it leads to restrictive dogma (as he argues it has in relation to many areas of philosophy), to question its validity.

One final important point to realise here, but also in relation to the other philosophical prejudices that Nietzsche identifies, is that many of the traditional problems of philosophy – the existence of self or soul, the mind-body problem, the freewill debate, and so on – can be resolved if we abandon the traditional dogmas. In identifying these philosophical prejudices, Nietzsche is not just seeking to undermine the positions of certain past philosophers, but also trying to point philosophy in a new direction. The old philosophical problems are phrased in old philosophical language and concepts, and to seek to solve them in those terms is merely to preserve the values which those philosophers (and philosophies) represent. So, in adopting a new approach, Nietzsche is not only seeking to overcome the old problems, but also to supersede the old values with new ones.

If we were to criticise Nietzsche here, we might begin by asking what evidence he has for his assertion that language has a distorting influence on our understanding of the world. He does not seem to present any conclusive argument that, for instance, the self does not exist, or that 'atomistic thinking' has led us drastically astray in our search for knowledge. In this sense, his position is similar to that of Kant: both philosophers (though for different reasons) assume that humans are limited in their ability to understand the world; Kant puts this down to the necessary categories (time, space, cause and effect, etc.) that we impose upon the world in order to understand it; Nietzsche argues that we *create* such categories, and that, accordingly, others are possible. Both philosophers, however, seem generally to agree that our understanding of reality is relative to the limits of human perception and thinking.

But what proof could there be for such a position? Remember, any knowledge that we have of the world must come through human perception and understanding; if we receive information that suggests that we have a distorted view of the world, then surely that changes our understanding of it (i.e. we overcome the distortion). Kant's position is different: he argues that we cannot, *by definition*, come to a direct perception of reality, and that our understanding will always, to some extent, be lacking. This is different from saying that our knowledge is limited (but capable of growing); it is, rather, saying that, however much our knowledge increases, the real world is *fundamentally unknowable*. Nietzsche, of course, gives up the idea of there being one, objective reality – or at least, he claims that such a reality would be useless to us (*because* it does not take our interests into account). But a similar criticism can be aimed at him as at Kant: if we can discover that our understanding of the world is flawed, then we can overcome that flaw, and thus grow closer to an objective understanding of reality – can't we?

I think, to be fair to Nietzsche, this is largely what he *is* suggesting. Atomistic thinking (as well as other philosophical prejudice) is to be recognised and – where appropriate – discarded. And yet, this does not solve the problem of how we are to be *sure* that such thinking is false, or how we can ultimately know that we are inescapably driven by the human need to simplify and distort things for our own interests. This can be broadened out into a more general criticism of Nietzsche's arguments: there is frequently a lack of clarity and proof concerning his assertions, and we are sometimes left wondering whether Nietzsche's assumptions are any less prejudicial than those of the philosophers he criticises. In one sense, Nietzsche recognises this; he would not claim that his own philosophy is free of non-rational influences – in fact, the idea of the will to power is based on exactly that idea. However, he would claim that he is more aware of these influences, and that his philosophy is therefore *deeper*. The extent to which we can

Continued

believe him is a sign of how willing we are to leave behind more traditional, Western philosophy, in favour of a subtler – but less 'certain' – view. (I will return to this point when I come to consider the will to power in a later section.)

5 Teleological explanation

In 1802, the English philosopher William Paley published *Natural Theology*, a book in which he set out an argument for the existence of God. This argument attempts to argue that the universe shows evidence of having been created or designed, and so we must assume the existence of a designer (i.e. God). This has become known as the *design* or *teleological argument*, and whilst it has become mainly associated with Paley, it actually stretches back at least as far as Cicero, the Roman philosopher and statesman.

The word 'teleological' comes from the Greek word *telos*, which means 'end' or 'goal'. So, to look at something *teleologically* is to consider it in terms of what goal it might serve, and what its ultimate purpose is. For instance, from a religious perspective the world and all its creatures have been designed by God to fulfil a certain role. Everything, from the organs in our bodies to the atoms and particles that make up the physical universe, has a certain function.

In philosophy, this idea goes back at least to Aristotle, who thought that we should think of an object as having four causes. For example, if we think of a work of art (e.g. a marble statue), it can be understood in four different ways: what it is made of is its *material cause* (marble); the shape or form of it, or the idea it represents, is its *formal cause* (e.g. a figure of a man); who or what made it constitutes its *effective cause* (the sculptor); and the purpose it serves is its *final cause* (e.g. to portray and celebrate a certain ideal of male beauty). This 'final cause' is what Aristotle would have called a thing's *telos*.

In section 13, Nietzsche identifies this form of thinking as a major philosophical prejudice. Whether we think in religious terms of the world, of human beings as having a purpose or reason for existence, or whether we simply think in biological terms, of organs and organisms as having a particular fixed function, we are – Nietzsche argues – thinking *teleologically*. Moreover, in doing so, it is *we* who ascribe function and purpose. For instance, we might say that the purpose of the eye is to translate light waves that reflect off objects in the environment into electrical signals, which are then relayed to the brain. Or, more simply, we could point out that the function of the heart is to pump blood. However, in both cases, we are assuming that these functions are somehow *built into* the organs in question. In other words, it is as if they have been *created* with these purposes.

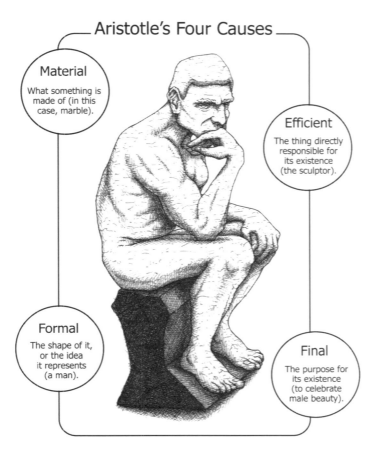

Aristotle's Four Causes

Material
What something is made of (in this case, marble).

Efficient
The thing directly responsible for its existence (the sculptor).

Formal
The shape of it, or the idea it represents (a man).

Final
The purpose for its existence (to celebrate male beauty).

This way of thinking has given rise to some well-known criticisms. Firstly, concerning the existence of a designer (or God), there is nothing that leads us from an analysis of the world to decide the nature of the designer. As Hume has pointed out, it is just as impossible to know the nature of the creator of the world simply by studying what has been 'created' as it is to know anything about the watchmaker from studying his watch.[11] We might, like Sherlock Holmes, make all sorts of clever deductions as to the character, morality and beliefs of such a person, but there is a high likelihood that we will be wrong; so, in relation to the creator of the universe, we have no way of knowing – for instance – whether there is one designer or a whole committee, or even what the morality of such a being would be (nature, after all, is full of cruelty, and displays an alarming lack of concern for human life at times).

Secondly, and more importantly, we do not need to assume that design is the only way in which the complexity of the world can have come about. The nineteenth-century father of the theory of evolution, Charles Darwin, argued that we can adequately account for the complex characteristics possessed by living species if we assume that they are the result of different mixtures of inherited characteristics, and that these then make each creature more or less fit for its environment. So, for example, imagine that there are two islands (A and B), and that a certain species of bird lives on both of them. Now, on one island, there exists a certain type of food – a seed, let us say – which is easier to eat if you have a certain sized and shaped beak, and on the other island, a different type of seed means that a differently sized and shaped beak is preferable. Darwin would predict that, over a long period of time, the beaks of the birds living on the two separate islands would begin to change: the beaks of the birds on island A would evolve in size and shape to feed on the seed that exists on *this* island, whilst the beaks of the birds on island B would evolve to suit the seed that exists on *that* island. However, Darwin argues that there is no design at work here, but merely the law of *natural selection* (or, the 'survival of the fittest', as it has also been called).

It is important to be clear about what is happening here: the birds' beaks on the two islands are not changing shape because the birds want them to, or because some mysterious force is influencing events; rather, the birds' beaks are changing shape because those with the right-shaped beaks are *surviving* and *breeding* (they are the *most fit*, i.e. well-suited, for the environment), whilst those who do not have the right-shaped beaks are not doing so well, have less opportunity to reproduce, and are therefore *dying out*.

Darwin's Two Islands

Darwin's idea of 'natural selection' explains not only how different species thrive (or become extinct), but also how the appearance of design can be explained by a purely mechanical process. So, on two islands, natural variations in the shape and size of finches' beaks, together with different environmental factors (e.g. the presence or absence of different food types on each island) can account for the different varieties of finch which have evolved.

 On island **A**, the main food source for finches is cactus seeds, which require a large, strong beak to break open. So, this leads birds with such beaks to thrive, and birds with unsuitable beaks to struggle and eventually die out.

 On island **B**, the main food source for finches is small seeds, which require smaller, finer-shaped beaks. Therefore, birds with these beaks survive, whilst the ones that thrive on island **A** - with big, strong beaks - do not thrive, and are 'naturally selected' for extinction (from island **B**, that is).

However, Darwin could not fully account for the means whereby such natural variations came about, and it was not until later that his ideas were combined with others in order to produce the modern theory of evolution (or the 'modern evolutionary synthesis' as it is called).

The shape of each bird's beak is part inheritance and part chance. For instance, your nose is the shape it is because you have some of your mother's genes and some of your father's – perhaps you have your father's nose, or your mother's eyes. Yet it is also possible that the genes which determine these things are not the same ones which gave your mother her eyes, or your father his nose. In this case, perhaps you have your *grandfather*'s nose, or your *grandmother*'s eyes (they are what is commonly called a *throwback*). This is because your parents also carry *latent* genes, which do not affect them, but which are passed on to their children; which genes you get is, to a certain extent, a matter of chance.

However, it is not just inheritance that determines the size of your 'beak', as there is also a bigger element of chance involved – that of *genetic mutation*. So, even if there were a way of ensuring that you received your father's 'nose genes', it may still be possible that you end up with a different-shaped nose. This is because when genes are duplicated to be passed on during reproduction, they occasionally *mutate* or change. This can be thought of as a mistake in the copying process: say – for argument's sake – that there is a specific gene that dictates exactly how big your nose is. Now, in the copying process, a bit of information may be left out – or added – to the 'nose gene code' – say a '5' is changed to a '4' – and you end up with a smaller nose than your father (phew!). But it could equally go the other way (never mind: big noses are a sign of refined character – at least that's what I tell myself . . .).

Now, to sum up, Darwin's argument is that we do not need to assume the existence of a designer, or some sort of *telos* or purpose, in order to account for the complexity of the biological world. All we need to assume is that there are limited resources which creatures of different species and aptitude fight over, and that, given the fact that (to an extent random) changes in inherited traits make some species more fit than others, those species will thrive, whilst less well-adapted species will face extinction.[12]

Nietzsche's opposition to teleological thinking is in this respect similar to Darwin's. For both thinkers, the processes of life can be adequately explained without reference to divine planning. But Nietzsche's position differs from Darwin's – and also Schopenhauer's – in that he did not think that the fundamental drive was an instinct for self-preservation. For Nietzsche, all life follows the principle of will to power, and each species seeks dominance over its fellows. Yet it does not do this because there is an instinct to survive (survival is possible without dominance), but rather because there is an instinct which seeks to exert its power over all other competitors. Here, in fact, he differs from Darwin in emphasising the importance of 'instinctive drives' in shaping the development of an organism, as opposed to – as Darwin saw it – merely being the result of the physical characteristics of the organism combined with external factors. So, for Nietzsche, evolution could be seen as a combination of the influence of inner drives, and biological and external factors.[13]

Another interesting contrast with Darwin and Nietzsche can be seen when we consider Nietzsche's concept of the 'higher' type of man. As you may recall (e.g. section 268), Nietzsche has already set out the difference between the 'higher' and 'lower' types of man, arguing that it is much more difficult for the former to thrive than it is for the latter. Therefore, the process of evolution, such as Darwin describes it, does not necessarily serve the production of higher, more complex organisms, but rather that of simpler, more rudimentary ones (which, in terms of complexity, have less to 'go wrong', and so are not so sensitive to environmental factors).[14]

I shall leave criticism of the will to power to a later section, but for now it can be seen that Nietzsche's criticism of teleological principles is part of his general rejection of any underlying metaphysical reality. So, he rejects the idea of God not only as the designer of the universe, but also as the supplier of moral values and meaning (though, perhaps, he does not reject the idea in another sense – I will discuss this in the later section on religion). The only *given* that he admits is the will to power itself, and that is more an urge to dominate, thrive, and achieve full expression of oneself than it is a source of values or meaning (on the contrary, a certain type of will to power is what drives us to *seek* value and meaning in life).

However, once more, we must ask of Nietzsche what basis he has for the assertion that all things are driven by the will to power, and whether, in fact, it is not *itself* an example of teleological explanation. Perhaps, to be fair, Nietzsche would not deny this (he has not, after all, asserted that his philosophy is closer to *reality* than other philosophies – at least not in the sense that he criticises). Perhaps, then, we can interpret the will to power as a *deeper* form of teleological explanation, in that it takes into account and explains a wider range of human behaviour.

6 Immediate certainty

In sections 16 and 17, Nietzsche attacks the idea that particular types of knowledge provide us with immediate certainty as to their truth. The main example he considers is that of Descartes's *Cogito* argument, which attempts to show that whilst we are conscious of thinking and perceiving, we cannot say that we do not exist (more famously summed up as, 'I think, therefore I am').

Nietzsche's main criticisms of the *Cogito* centre on the assumptions that Descartes's argument makes:

- That there is a separate and distinct 'I'.
- That this 'I' is capable of being a cause.

- That the 'I' is capable of causing thought.
- That 'something' must cause thought.
- That it is already clear as to what 'thinking' is.

Nietzsche's main point is that Descartes has already assumed all these things not only to be possible, but true. As he points out, in assuming that there is anything at all that is responsible for thought, "one has already gone too far", because this conclusion "already contains an *interpretation* of the event and does not belong to the event itself".[15] So-called 'immediate certainties' therefore necessarily involve a thought process, or act of interpretation, which disqualifies them from being immediate.

Another target of Nietzsche's which is relevant here is Kant's distinction between *synthetic* and *analytic* judgements.[16] As with many philosophers before him, Kant held that certain judgements could be true *a priori* (true independent of experience) or *a posteriori* (true by virtue of experience). So, that 'all triangles have three sides' is true *a priori*, cannot be doubted (to be a triangle and not have three sides is a logical contradiction), and is therefore *necessarily* true; whilst 'some swans are black' can only be confirmed by experience (it is *empirically* true), and is therefore open to doubt or disproof. However, by introducing the notions of *synthetic* and *analytic* statements, Kant now allowed for *two* ways in which *a priori* and *a posteriori* statements could be true: if they were analytic, then the truth of the statement could be arrived at through an *analysis* of the terms involved; if they were synthetic, then the truth is related to the fact that two otherwise unrelated terms have been brought together. So, 'all triangles have three sides' is true because when we analyse the meanings of the term 'triangle' we find that it necessarily contains the idea of having three sides. On the other hand, if we consider the statement that 'some swans are black', then Kant says that this statement is *synthetic*, because 'black' is not a necessary part of our understanding of the term 'swan' (swans could be any colour, whereas triangles *must* have three sides); so, in this sense, the statement is a *synthesis* of two otherwise unrelated things (swans and the colour black), which extends our knowledge (unlike analytic statements, which only tell us in more detail what we already know).

If we now relate all these distinctions to one another, we find that statements can be understood according to two different categories: regarding how they relate to experience (whether they are *a priori* or *a posteriori*); and regarding how their different *terms* relate to one another (whether they are *analytic* or *synthetic*). Now, if all Kant was doing here is providing another explanation of what distinguishes *a priori* from *a posteriori* statements then it wouldn't exactly be revolutionary. But what he has done is shown that these distinctions are actually separate, and that there are consequently *four* ways in which statements can be true:

- Analytic *a priori*
- Synthetic *a posteriori*
- Analytic *a posteriori*
- Synthetic *a priori*

We can see that the first two of these categories do not really give us anything different from the traditional distinctions: analytic *a priori* statements are necessarily true independent of experience, and do not give us any new information; synthetic *a posteriori* statements are true empirically (by experience) and tell us something new. However, Kant argues, since all analytic truths can be known independent of experience, then they are also *a priori*. So, this means that there is no need to 'discover' analytic truths via experience (*a posteriori*); therefore, there can be no such thing as analytic *a posteriori* truths.

This leaves us with one additional category: synthetic *a priori* truths. Do they exist? Kant argues that they do, for there are statements which both tell us something new about a concept (are synthetic), *but* whose truth is independent of experience. One of Kant's examples is our knowledge of cause and effect. A cause is an event, but the concept of an event does not contain the idea of being necessarily linked to an effect; and, since it cannot be doubted that 'every event has a cause', then the statement must be true *a priori*. Other examples of synthetic truths are mathematical statements. So, whilst '3 + 3 = 6' cannot be doubted (and must be *a priori*), the concept of '6' does not necessarily contain the concept of '3 + 3' – there are many different ways of making up '6' (2 + 4, 12 ÷ 2, and so on). So, mathematical truths must also be synthetic *a priori*.

The existence of such truths would be a very important thing in philosophy. Kant goes on to make great use of them, arguing that synthetic *a priori* judgements are 'contained as principles' in our search for knowledge, and that without them we could not understand the world. As such, then, they form *categories* which we apply to experience, and which also supply limits to our understanding.

If we now look back at section 11 of *BGE*, where Nietzsche ridicules Kant's notion of synthetic *a priori* knowledge, we can see that he is not only questioning Kant's right to make such a claim, but also his motives for doing so. In his *Critique of Pure Reason*, Kant had tried to explain how synthetic *a priori* judgements were possible, but, Nietzsche says, the real question he should have asked himself is not how such judgements are possible, but "why is belief in such judgments *necessary*?"[17] The answer, for Nietzsche, is that Kant's own desire for such statements to exist (his philosophical will to power) is ultimately responsible. Through his use of the idea of synthetic *a priori* knowledge and the notion of categories, Nietzsche argues, Kant is able to argue that the world has a definite form, and that our understanding of it – even our moral understanding – is something which has definite limits, and whose form we cannot question.

For Nietzsche, the ideas of Descartes and Kant are both examples of the philosophical prejudice of immediate certainty. In rejecting Descartes's *Cogito*, he is rejecting the *foundationalist* approach to knowledge (favoured by such as Descartes) which looks for absolute certainty as a basis for our general knowledge of the world; in rejecting Kant's synthetic *a priori*, he disputes the contention that the world – or our experience of it – has a definite logical form. What he is rejecting generally is the idea that there is a metaphysical basis to our knowledge of the world which in some way shapes and guarantees our knowledge. But he is not the first to reject such views; previous *empiricist* philosophers (such as Locke and Hume) would agree that there can be no absolute guarantee for our knowledge, and that we must look – for instance – to the way in which our beliefs relate to and support one another.

But are such philosophers right in completely rejecting the possibility of such certainty? We might argue that in order to doubt something we must at least believe in the thing which is to be doubted. This is really Descartes's *Cogito* argument restated: if I see a chair, then I can doubt its existence (it may be a dream, or some other illusion), but I cannot doubt that I am having the experience. Some philosophers, therefore, prefer to talk of *impressions* or *sense-data* rather than objects. So, the information I have of the chair is made up of mental representations (sense-data), which – regardless of the chair's existence – are in some sense 'real' to me.

Nietzsche's criticism of this picture is to argue that there can be no such thing as *pure* sense-data. So, even to say, 'I have a mental image of a chair', is already an interpretation of sense impressions. In fact, Nietzsche would probably go further than this: nothing is *given* to us *before* interpretation; the act of perception is *already* an interpretation. Certain experiments in psychology would seem to back this up. For instance, look at the illustration below. As you can see, it is possible to see this picture as either a duck or a rabbit. However, since the actual image to the eye is the same, it must be the case that we supply the interpretation ourselves. Other experiments have suggested that the tendency to see the world in a particular way is somehow built into the brain and our sensory systems. So, for instance, babies as young as two and a half months, who are shown 'magic tricks' or other 'impossible' illusions, pay greater attention to what is happening than when presented with normal events. This suggests that, even at this young age, there is some awareness of 'how the world should be'. Obviously, this is not the result of training or education, so we must assume that such assumptions are instinctive.[18] A similar point is made by psychologist Steven Pinker concerning language:

Continued

The Duck-Rabbit Illusion

What do you see in the top image?

Is it a rabbit?   Or a duck?

> A preschooler's tacit knowledge of grammar is more sophisticated than the thickest style manual or the most state-of-the-art computer language system.[19]

What is being attacked here is what the American philosopher Wilfrid Sellars called "the myth of the given".[20] As Nietzsche and philosophers such as Sellars argue, there is no perception of the world which is *given* to us, and which we then interpret; rather, interpretations are part of the way in which we see the world. The 'given' – i.e. a pre-interpreted world of chairs, trees, stars, etc. – is a myth (or, as Nietzsche would say, a philosophical prejudice); furthermore, this is true whether you think that our interpretations of the world are 'hard-wired' into the brain (like a computer), or simply spring from our attempt to understand the world in terms of concepts; either way, there would appear to be no way to get completely 'beyond' such interpretations, for they are the very tools that we use for our understanding.

Not all modern philosophers agree with this. In criticising Sellars, the American philosopher William P. Alston argues that it *is* possible to have *non-conceptual* perceptions.[21] So, I may not have the concept of a mango (for instance), but I can certainly have an experience of looking at a mango, even if I do not know what one is (i.e. I will see a yellow or green patch of colour with a certain roundness). But Alston seems to ignore the fact that there are still concepts involved in this perception: 'roundness' and, of course, the concept of an object itself. So, if we take such concepts as 'given', then we must assume that there is no other possible interpretation. Might a Martian (or some other hypothetical alien species) see the mango in a completely different way – perhaps, not even as a distinct object? They might, for example, think in terms of groups of objects, like a picture, or even put together snapshots from different times of the object's existence – rather like a cubist painting. Whatever the case, if different conceptions are *possible*, then we cannot say that any are present from the start (i.e. are *given*).

7 Causa sui

Nietzsche attacks the idea that a thing may be *causa sui* (Latin for 'the cause of itself'); as if, he scoffs, one might "pull oneself into existence out of the swamp of nothingness by one's own hair".[22] This idea may spring from a number of different sources: for instance, the desire by certain philosophers to provide a defence of free will (the contention that we have freedom of choice in at least some of our actions); or, in the philosophy of religion, to provide an argument for the existence of God (as the first, uncaused cause of the existence of the universe – the *cosmological argument*). In either case, the same idea exists: it is possible for a certain thing to be the cause of an event without itself being an effect of a prior cause. So, individuals are able to freely choose an action that is not itself determined by other factors; and God is able to exist and create the universe without the existence of something which would first create Him.

An alternative view to this is known as *determinism*, and argues that every event has a cause, and that there are no exceptions to this. So, what appear to be an individual's free choices are actually acts which are determined by other events; I choose to buy a certain magazine, not because I make a free choice, but rather – for example – because I have been influenced by certain tricks of advertising. In relation to God, the argument may be used to undermine the whole concept (God cannot exist, because there can be no such thing as an uncaused cause); or, on the other hand, God may Himself be seen as the ultimate cause of all actions.[23]

But before we consider Nietzsche's approach to the problem, let us first examine some traditional solutions. There are three main approaches:

- *Determinism*. This is the view that there is a strict cause-and-effect relationship between events, and that there is no room for free choice or an 'uncaused cause'. This view may also take different forms – for example: someone may be a determinist because they believe that individuals' actions are predetermined by their genes (*biological determinism*); religious believers may also be determinists if they hold that all events are preordained by God (*theological determinism*). Determinism has a strong hold in many scientific perspectives, and is commonly associated with traditional views of causation – as held, for example, by great names in the history of science such as Sir Isaac Newton and Pierre-Simon Laplace.[24] However, following some of the disturbing discoveries of quantum mechanics, this view has been challenged.[25]

- *Libertarianism.* This is the opposite view to the above, arguing that determinism is false, and that free choice is in some way possible. There are different types of libertarianism, and the reason why we are free to choose will differ accordingly (some, for example, might say that it is because we have an immaterial soul or self which is the free cause of action, whilst others might argue that there exists a degree of randomness in the universe which stops all actions being determined). Therefore, many well-known libertarians are also religious believers – such as, for example, Descartes.

- *Compatibilism.* The first two views represent opposite positions, because they both deny that free will and determinism are compatible (i.e. they cannot both be true). These views are therefore both examples of *incompatibilism*. But there is a third position that argues that determinism and libertarianism *are* in some sense compatible, and that they are both in some sense true. For instance, both Thomas Hobbes and David Hume held versions of compatibilism, and argued that, in an everyday sense, we can view certain actions as either forced or free. So, if you are tied up and forced to eat marshmallows at gunpoint, it may be said that your actions are not free; also, there are certain actions which you may have no control over, such as your body's reflexes (e.g. the dilation of the pupils in your eyes, your heartbeat, and so on). However, there are other actions where it is natural to talk of someone having choice, such as whether you decide to cross the road or not.

Nietzsche's own view, not surprisingly, is somewhat difficult to define. On the one hand, as we have seen, he is critical of the idea of *causa sui*, and therefore – on the face of it – at odds with the very idea of free will; but he is also critical of the opposite view (determinism). Where, then, does this leave him?

> Assuming it is possible in this way to get beyond the peasant simplicity of this celebrated concept 'free will' and banish it from one's mind, I would then ask whoever does that to carry his enlightenment a step further and also banish from his mind the contrary of that unnatural concept 'free will'; I mean 'unfree will', which amounts to an abuse of cause and effect.[26]

But in what way is the traditional use of the terms 'cause' and 'effect' unsatisfactory? These terms, he argues, should only be used to help us understand each other in talking about the world, but they should *not* be used as explanations of it. For instance, we may talk about 'looking for the reason' as to why someone acted in a particular way, but it would surely be a mistake actually to go looking for this reason as if it were a separate cause distinct from everything else (i.e. as if it were a *thing*). And yet, Nietzsche points out, that is what we commonly do when we talk of cause and effect; we think of the cause as being the source of that which is produced (as opposed to simply being a way of describing certain events). Furthermore, just as the idea of *causa sui* is something that we have invented in the process of making the world in our own image, so the 'unfree will' (determinism) is reliant upon the same way of thinking. Furthermore, it is a 'mechanistic' picture of causation, in that (like Darwin's theory of evolution) it treats nature as if it were a machine where all decisions are made by 'external' forces. Nietzsche's preferred picture is one where nature is a battleground of competing drives, each of which has its own 'internal' agenda, like a desire which compels it to extend its power and dominance over others.

> 'Unfree will' is mythology: in real life it is only a question of *strong* and *weak* wills.[27]

Here, then, we get to the crux of the matter. For Nietzsche, 'will' is a matter of 'will to power'. In other words, when we feel a sense of freedom in our actions, what we are actually sensing, Nietzsche argues, is the feeling of power or of being alive as we give full expression to a certain 'drive' or instinct. Over time, we come to associate this feeling with being in control, and successfully 'willing' actions. Also, in contrast, the feeling that we associate with the expression of contrary instincts comes to be associated with lack of control. So, in reality, there is no such thing as 'will', only the dominance of certain drives over others.

> 'Freedom of the will' – is the expression for that complex condition of pleasure of the person who wills, who commands and at the same time identifies himself with the executor of the commands – who, as such, enjoys also the triumph over resistances involved but who thinks it was his will itself which overcame these resistances.[28]

Nietzsche suggests that the best analogy of this state of affairs is that of a nation or "commonwealth", where there are lots of competing "wills" or drives which exist together in a "social structure composed of many 'souls'[or drives]".[29] In some cases, different drives join together to serve the same cause; in other cases, drives may oppose the rulers and plot rebellion (just as madness may attempt to overwhelm reason). Accordingly, the 'will' is a convenient myth which we use to describe this complicated state of affairs, and is simply our way of identifying with the "ruling class" (or dominant drive). A unified will might, however, be possible if certain drives were to join together, or one drive were to become so dominant as to rule over all – perhaps, in fact, we might argue that Nietzsche sees this as the ultimate goal of personal development (or 'self-overcoming').

The problem with Nietzsche's view of free will lies in the question of the extent to which this picture can make sense without our traditional understanding of 'cause' and 'effect'. On the one hand, it sounds quite persuasive to argue that the whole problem of free will is a self-made one, and that if we simply abandon or amend our understanding of these terms we can arrive at a more satisfactory picture. In doing this, Nietzsche's position would appear to fall outside of the three traditional responses to the problem outlined earlier; he attacks libertarianism and determinism equally, and his solution to the problem seems basically to amount to a rejection of the basis of the whole argument. Yet when he comes to replace this traditional conception of free will, he does so by what is arguably a deterministic picture. Our nature is determined by our drives, and our drives are in turn determined by factors largely outside of our control – things such as environmental conditions, biology, genetic inheritance, education, etc. Which drive becomes dominant (becomes the "ruling class") would therefore appear to be determined for us.

Despite this, Nietzsche may still have room for freedom. In his concept of the 'free spirit' Nietzsche describes individuals who have evolved beyond their 'programming'. That they do so, initially, is perhaps a matter of chance; either they find themselves with qualities or instincts that make them fit for rulership (and mastery over their own instincts), or else their will arises out of an awareness of inner conflict (and a desire to resolve it – see section 200). This freedom arises through the development of will and discipline in relation to the instincts, and not – as some misinterpretations of Nietzsche have it – a 'letting go' and giving in to the irrational drives. The free spirit is therefore one who has achieved freedom through discipline, which in turn allows him a choice as to whether to express one instinct or another.

In this sense, Nietzsche views the majority of human beings as lacking freedom. They are driven by their instincts, and for this reason pass on their responsibility for their own actions to outside forces (which, Nietzsche argues, is in effect true: they *aren't* in control of themselves). This marks a distinction between aristocratic races (who are bred and raised to acquire self-mastery), free spirits (who acquire it by self-discipline or – initially – by accident) and the so-called 'herd' (who never have it). The latter do not accept responsibility for their actions, whereas the former do, because they know that in doing so they take a step towards self-mastery.[30]

This last point is an important one: Nietzsche's ultimate concept of freedom is the doctrine of the 'eternal return'. In this, he argues that the most positive conception of life would be to wish to live it all over again *exactly as it was*. This attitude is known as *amor fati* (Latin, 'a love of fate'), whereby to accept responsibility for everything that one is provides the basis for true freedom, whereas to desire to change anything about oneself would be to give in to an individual desire and bring about internal conflict (and thereby become 'unfree'). So, in Nietzsche's sense, freedom resides in both acceptance *and* resistance.[31]

8 Reification[32]

The final philosophical prejudice that I shall discuss is that of reification. In section 21, whilst discussing the notions of cause and effect, Nietzsche criticises the more general tendency of philosophers to treat concepts as if they were things. So, in relation to cause and effect, philosophers are apt to assume that there is a specific thing which we may call a 'cause' – perhaps the best example of which would be the idea of 'self'. As we have already seen, Nietzsche criticises such philosophers as Descartes for assuming the existence of a specific 'I' which is the cause of thought (as in, 'I think, therefore I am'). And yet, he argues, there is no logical reason for doing this, and we must be careful to distinguish between ways of speaking which are useful for our everyday understanding (e.g. to talk about oneself and having thoughts), and the precise use of terms in a scientific or philosophical sense. We are, in such cases, frequently misled by grammar: because we use such terms as 'I' and 'self', and we talk in ways that suggest that actions and properties must belong to specific things, we make the mistake of assuming that those things actually exist.

This prejudice has already been mentioned in relation to other topics already discussed (e.g. atomism and *causa sui*), so I will not repeat points already made there. However, it is worth noting that reification is a significant prejudicial tendency in its own right: atomism may assume that there is a central unified core behind certain events or features, and *causa sui* may assume that certain events springing from those 'atoms' are self-caused, but reification represents the general mistake of assuming that these events have a 'real', physical basis. In terms of 'cause' and 'effect', events are not 'things', and if we think so then we have mistaken a useful way of talking about the world for the way the world is itself. This tendency ultimately springs from our experience of the natural world, and the way in which things behave in physical reality also influences the way in which we describe the 'unseen' world.

A topic I have not discussed so far, but which is relevant here, is the question of Nietzsche's *materialism*. As a naturalist, Nietzsche would probably be thought to embrace the idea that all causes are physical in nature (as orthodox science does). So, the idea of *immaterial substance* (or 'spirit'), as proposed by Descartes, would appear to be something that Nietzsche would reject. However, whilst Nietzsche is often considered a materialist, we must be careful here: the mistake of reification is something that he directs not only at those who advocate the existence of the soul, but also the material scientists who only believe in that which can be touched or measured (what is known as *positivism*).

Once more, Nietzsche's attitude seeks to go beyond traditional opposites (which, given its title, it is perhaps not surprising to find is a general theme of the book). But is this view a coherent one? If we interpret Nietzsche in this way (as neither *materialist* nor *dualist*), then – as with the question of free will – we find that he has rejected aspects of two traditional perspectives, but without supplying a clear account of a third alternative.

This problem is most acute in the philosophy of mind, where, on the one hand, certain materialist philosophers (such as Daniel Dennett) reject the notion of an immaterial mind or soul, and try to account for consciousness in purely physical terms; on the other hand, other philosophers (such as John Searle), whilst not wishing to revive Descartes's *dualism* (and all its problems), argue that most materialist accounts of the mind leave out the reality of conscious experience. However, the latter are criticised by the former for not presenting a clear understanding as to how this 'something extra' (i.e. conscious experience) can be understood. Nietzsche's position would seem to be closer to the latter: he does not want to propose a spiritual substance separate from the physical, but neither does he want to be restricted by the world view of the positivists (who are "clumsy naturalists" and cannot "touch 'the soul' without losing it" – see section 12). So, whilst we might consider him a materialist, it is arguably true that he would reject the extreme form of materialism – just as he rejects determinism – because it is merely the opposite side of the same coin.

One attempt to bridge the mind–matter gap can be found in Nietzsche's concept of will to power. In section 36, he suggests that it might help us to overcome the life–matter divide if we imagine that, even at the molecular and atomic level, each thing has its own drives or will to power. These then provide the basis for the more recognisable forms of striving and desire that we see in animals and humans. So, rather than seeing an inanimate universe, Nietzsche is prepared to see continuity between the life force present in higher forms of life and that in atoms and molecules. Whether this commits him to some sort of *vitalism* (which sees the world as pervaded by a purposeful force) it is difficult to say, and, because of Nietzsche's dislike of treating topics systematically, it is not one that we can easily answer (for more on this, see the later section on 'will to power'). But whatever the case, it is possible to see Nietzsche's position as an attempt to overcome the division between mind and matter, and even to rescue at least some concept of the soul. (I shall talk about this last topic in more detail in the section on religion.)

Nietzsche's Anti-Realism

Finally, in this section on Nietzsche's views on truth and reality, I would just like to summarise Nietzsche's overall position regarding these topics. The best way to understand Nietzsche's position is to contrast it with the traditional one. *Realism* is the general view that (a) there is such a thing as a mind-independent reality,[33] and (b) it is possible, to some extent, to gain knowledge of this reality. Both these viewpoints are central to scientific enquiry, for if we did not think that the real world existed, or that it was possible to understand it, then what would be the point of conducting experiments and formulating theories? This view is held, therefore, largely by those philosophers – such as Descartes, Leibniz, Plato and Bertrand Russell, for example – who are not sceptical about the possibility of knowledge.

The answers that various philosophers provide to these two questions can be used to classify their attitudes. For example, Plato is a traditional realist in that he believes that (a) there is such a thing as an independent reality, and that (b) it is possible for us to arrive at a more or less complete and secure understanding of it; Kant agrees with Plato on (a), but argues that (b) we can never experience this reality directly; in contrast, Berkeley disagrees with both Plato and Kant: (a) there is no mind-independent reality, because in order to exist, something must be constantly perceived – for this reason, (b) it is possible to directly apprehend the true nature of things with the mind (because they are, in truth, thoughts in the mind of God).

In contrast to all of the above three positions, an example of an extreme anti-realist position can be found in the Greek sceptic, Gorgias of Leontini, who argued famously,

> (1) that nothing exists; (2) that if anything exists, it cannot be known; and (3) if anything can be known, it cannot be communicated.[34]

Nietzsche's position is not quite this extreme. Firstly, he does not argue that the real world does not exist, merely that the way in which philosophers have treated it has created a 'myth' of an objective – and yet not necessarily attainable – world of perfect, objective knowledge. In *Twilight of the Idols*, in a section entitled, 'How the "Real World" at Last Became a Myth', Nietzsche sets out the six steps through history whereby this concept degenerates (I am paraphrasing here):[35]

1 The real world is attainable by the wise and virtuous (Plato).
2 The real world becomes more elusive, almost mystical, as a reward for virtue (Christianity).
3 The real world exists, but is directly unattainable (Kant).
4 Since the real world is unattainable, it ceases to influence philosophers, who concentrate instead on *appearance* (positivism and science).

5   Since the real world is both unattainable and we have no obligation to it (i.e. in religious or moral matters), then why not abolish it? (The growth of Romanticism, atheism, freedom in morals, etc., where "all free spirits run riot".[36])

6   Since the real world has been abolished, we must also abolish its counterpart, the *apparent* world. This done, we arrive at a new beginning (Nietzsche's philosophy).

This little potted history of the development of the idea is quite useful in understanding Nietzsche's attitude. He is not, as Gorgias appears to be, a complete sceptic; his criticism of the idea of the "real world" is largely that it has become abstract and useless metaphysical 'baggage'. Once, where it was achievable, and played a direct role in the philosopher's life, it had meaning; however, following that, it firstly became abstract, and then the abstract idea came to signify a different order of reality. Like other ideas (such as 'cause' and 'effect', 'self', etc.), it has become *reified* (i.e. the idea has been made into a *thing*). Abolishing it, therefore, allows us to begin anew.

Nietzsche's position is generally considered an example of *anti-realism*. In relation to the two questions we considered earlier – (a) Does the real world exist? and (b) Can we know it? – Nietzsche would generally answer 'No' to both – but with some qualifications:

(a)   The real world does not exist because the distinction between 'reality' and 'appearance' is a false one. What we have instead is our own *perspective*, which we cannot go beyond. (*Perspectivism*)

(b)   We cannot know reality in this sense, because such a world does not exist. So, we must understand reality as, in some way, dependent upon our own natural instincts. (*Naturalism*)

We have already considered these two views in the process of examining the eight philosophical prejudices. Nietzsche's perspectivism is basically the consequence of rejecting this metaphysical idea of the real world and adopting *naturalism*. If we remove the possibility of one, central, objective reality, then we are left with different, competing perspectives (mine, yours, his, hers, etc.). Nietzsche's answer to the second question, (b) 'Can we know the real world?', has already been shaped by his answer to the first question (perspectivism). As we have seen, in (a) he would have answered that the real world is a 'myth', and that we must reject this false duality of 'real' and 'apparent'. But in doing this, and proposing perspectivism, he may justifiably be asked the question, '*Why* can't the "real world" exist?'

The answer lies in Nietzsche's assertion that our motive for seeking truth is not a disinterested desire to get at the 'real' nature of things (i.e. 'truth for truth's sake'), but rather a very *interested* (although semi-conscious) desire to see the world in a particular way. Behind each of the philosophical prejudices considered so far lies an instinctive motive to shape the world – or, our knowledge of it – into a particular form. It is *useful* for us to think of reality in terms of 'cause' and 'effect', atoms, things having a purpose (*telos*), and so on. But, Nietzsche argues, we have now reached a stage of philosophical knowledge where we can begin to be aware of our own prejudices in these matters – and seek to go beyond them.

It should be noted here that Nietzsche is not proposing that we can ever go completely beyond these instincts – there is always, he says, the "right down and deep" which we are always, on the one hand, seeking to understand, and on the other, being motivated by.[37]

The best that one is one does not know – one cannot know.[38]

This is a subtle point: if I consider all my motives to spring ultimately from deep instincts (as Nietzsche does), then to become aware of those instincts is to become capable of not being influenced by those motives. For instance, if I become aware that a deep-rooted jealousy underlies many of my opinions and actions, then I can try to overcome that (if I choose to). However, this desire to overcome my deep-rooted jealousy is in turn motivated by some other desire – perhaps the desire to be in control of my emotions (and thereby, perhaps, feel superior to others). The point is that we can never really escape being motivated by some instinct or other, and that the best that we can strive for in our search for 'objectivity' is to be as aware as possible of these motives – which in turn, perhaps, becomes a sort of 'super motive'.

But, as Nietzsche has already argued, absolute 'objectivity' is not really the goal. Of course, we may strive for a deeper understanding of ourselves and the world in which we live, but that understanding will always be coloured by our deepest instincts. By understanding those instincts themselves, we understand a little better, but such 'objectivity' as we might achieve is only ever relative to our previous understanding. We have gone deeper, but we will never reach absolute truth (because it does not exist). The goal for us must be to analyse our instincts in order to better understand our needs and goals – and possibly to go beyond them.

God, Religion and the Saint

The Question of God's Existence

Nietzsche is generally considered an atheist. However, unlike other critics of religious philosophy (David Hume, for example), there is little direct analysis in his writings of arguments for the existence of God. Instead – and *BGE* is fairly typical in this respect – Nietzsche prefers to concentrate on how belief in God comes about, what role it serves in people's lives, and – for an atheist – what might replace it. That Nietzsche is an atheist is fairly certain, although – as we shall see later – his ideas have appealed to some unlikely followers. Let us consider what reasons Nietzsche has for rejecting religion.

Nietzsche is primarily concerned with understanding religion, or the "religious neurosis" as he terms it. Accordingly, he sees religion as arising from two – or perhaps a combination of two – possible causes:[39]

- *Metaphysical error.* This is the idea that belief in the supernatural is based on a mistake. So, in early primitive societies, people interpreted natural events as the actions of spirits or supernatural forces: volcanic eruptions occurred when the volcano god was angry; accident, disease and ill fortune were seen as the revenge of malevolent spirits whom the victims had neglected to appease with suitable offerings and sacrifices; success in certain ventures was thought to require the co-operation of unseen entities, who might also give their favour in the form of assistance in magical rites and ceremonies. These attitudes, so it is argued, are ignorant misunderstandings of natural phenomena, and the magical practices of these early societies can be seen as a form of primitive science. In this sense, they are a *metaphysical* type of error in that they mistakenly assume the existence of beings and forces beyond the physical world, whilst misunderstanding the nature of the natural world itself. A similar view was famously advocated by the Scottish social anthropologist Sir James Frazer in his work *The Golden Bough*.[40]
- *Projection.* Nietzsche sees much religious belief as a projection of an individual or society's values. This can happen in two ways: in the case of an aristocratic society, where the ruling or dominant class uses the idea of God or gods to embody the values that have made it successful; in the case of a 'slave' or subservient class, where God and heaven represent a justification of their own morality, and a type of revenge (*ressentiment*) upon their 'masters'. In this sense, Nietzsche anticipates the ideas of the Austrian founder of psychoanalysis, Sigmund Freud, who also believed generally that an individual's beliefs concerning certain things are sometimes a compensation or wish fulfilment arising from his own desires. More specifically, in psychoanalysis, projection takes place when someone projects their own undesirable qualities onto another ('He is an awful person – so judgemental!'). Freud also thought that religious beliefs spring from unresolved psychological conflicts (mainly from childhood), and that they represent, on the whole, a failure to deal with the world rationally.

So, God is not rejected primarily because there is insufficient proof (though this is obviously a factor), or because all arguments for God's existence are flawed; it

Sigmund Freud

is not even because the 'God hypothesis' is unconvincing or problematic (though, given Nietzsche's naturalism, it would arguably have been difficult for him to adopt religious belief in any traditional way): rather, it is because the idea that God is a metaphysical error, or a projection of human wish fulfilment, provides a more convincing understanding of how religious belief comes about than any traditional theistic explanation.[41]

Other related issues – such as the existence of the soul – are dealt with once more from the perspective of why people hold such beliefs. So, as we saw in Nietzsche's attacks on atomism and the doctrine of *causa sui*, his main concern is to show that these ideas are prejudices which are related to a deep-seated need to see the world in a particular way. In this sense, Nietzsche is ultimately interested in the *attitude* of religious believers, and the *reasons* which cause them to create, adopt and maintain those beliefs.

In criticising Nietzsche's views here, we might first observe that he may be guilty of what has been called the *genetic fallacy*.[42] This means that, in arguing that religious ideas stem from psychological projection, for instance, Nietzsche does not actually prove that those ideas are false, or that there aren't other genuine

Continued

reasons for them being true. In other words, where an idea comes from (its *genetic history*, so to speak) does not give us any information about the truth of the idea itself. This said, though, Nietzsche would have been aware of this, and he simply considers his own explanations for the existence of religious belief to be more plausible than any other current theory. This aside, let's look at Nietzsche's two possible explanations.

Firstly, the idea that religious belief arises from a type of mistake or *metaphysical error* has been contested by some modern philosophers. The Austrian philosopher Ludwig Wittgenstein argued that it is possible to interpret religious language in a way that avoids assuming a mistake had been made. For instance, in criticising Frazer's view of magic and religion in *The Golden Bough*, Wittgenstein argues that Frazer's understanding of the rain dance performed by certain tribes is a distortion of the actual meaning of the ritual.[43] Frazer argues that the dance is an attempt to influence the weather, fuelled by primitive superstition and belief in magic (a *metaphysical error*). Wittgenstein, on the other hand, argues that the actual purpose is not to implore some deity to send rain, but rather *to celebrate its coming*. Wittgenstein's view is usually termed an *expressive* theory of religion, in that it interprets religious practices as emotional expressions (which, of course, avoids the problem of interpreting religious ritual in a way which would oppose our scientific understanding of the world). The Welsh philosopher D. Z. Phillips has also written a great deal along these lines, utilising Wittgenstein's approach to explain how Christian doctrine can live alongside a scientific perspective without conflict.[44]

The problem with this approach is that it is difficult to see how it can account for all types of magical and religious practice. It is all very well to say (as D. Z. Phillips does) that a person who prays is not actually asking for their prayers to be answered by a supernatural deity, but rather is undertaking a spiritual practice which leads to self-improvement and deeper understanding; however, a person who performs a ritual act at a distance from the intended recipient (e.g. to divine the sex of a child, or to determine the whereabouts of a missing relative), and has no contact with that person, obviously has a different view of their practices. Is such a person 'wrong'? To say so would be to call all such practitioners (who are probably in the vast majority) 'mistaken', and to elect a small minority of more sophisticated believers as being 'correct'. But wouldn't this just be a case of reinterpreting the nature of religion so as to fit in with a modern scientific view?

The second explanation – that religious belief is a projection of man's inner desires and experiences – is, as I have already pointed out, similar to a position held by Sigmund Freud. Such a position assumes that (a) there is no God, and (b) religious terms are *anthropomorphic*. This second point is the idea that, in seeking to understand the world, we give human qualities to it. This is most easily understood in terms of children's cartoons and stories: *Thomas the Tank Engine*, Mickey Mouse, *Jungle Book* – all these and similar stories imbue animals or inanimate objects with human qualities; so, the argument goes, aren't we just doing the same thing with the ideas of God, spirits, demons, etc.? Naturalist thinkers such as Freud and Nietzsche would point out, for instance, that food metaphors abound in the Bible and religious literature generally:

> As newborn babes, desire the sincere milk of the word, that ye may grow thereby: If so be ye have tasted that the Lord is gracious.[45]

> Bread of heaven, Feed me till I want no more.[46]

What's more, many common metaphors also reflect other basic human needs and desires – e.g. sex, maternal comfort, paternal protection, and so on. Anthropomorphic language, therefore, which paints the nature of God in human terms, provides further evidence that religion is in some sense a projection of human wishes.

In his book *The Varieties of Religious Experience*, the American psychologist and philosopher William James criticised this way of thinking:

> Religious language clothes itself in such poor symbols as our life affords, and the whole organism gives overtones of comment whenever the mind is strongly stirred to expression. Language drawn from eating and drinking is probably as common in religious literature as is language drawn from the sexual life. We 'hunger and thirst' after righteousness; we 'find the Lord a sweet savor;' we 'taste and see that he is good.'[47]

So, James's point is basically that, to a certain extent, we cannot avoid anthropomorphic thinking. All our concepts are couched in human terms – as Nietzsche himself would agree – and there is a sense in which we cannot get beyond this. So, even if – for instance – the desire for God is expressed in metaphors which reveal sexual longing, or hunger, this is not to say that the thing which is desired is a complete fabrication. In fact, this is a point which Nietzsche himself makes (section 175):

> Ultimately one loves one's desires and not that which is desired.[48]

We are rational animals, and the tools which we possess to express ourselves are limited by our natures. Furthermore, God is traditionally thought of as impossible for humans to adequately conceive of, and religious language as an

Continued

attempt to bridge the gap between our limited human intellect and an incomprehensible divine reality. So, you may argue, it is completely legitimate that a desire for union with God can be expressed in anthropomorphic terms (as long as we realise, of course, that this is just a metaphor).

Finally, to reiterate a point made earlier, the argument that religious language is anthropomorphic, or that religious ideas are a projection of human desires, does not in fact prove that God *does not* exist. All that this version of the genetic fallacy does is provide a plausible alternative for the explanation of religious belief. A direct refutation of the 'God hypothesis' would require a logical proof that such a concept is in some way impossible or self-contradictory – which is not something that Nietzsche attempts.

Religious Neurosis and the Saint

Nietzsche identifies a particular attitude as the basis of certain types of religion – especially Christianity, Judaism and Buddhism – which he terms a 'neurosis', in that it embodies an irrational need for constant sacrifice and self-denial. Such an attitude, he argues, springs from the 'slave revolt' in morals, where the 'slaves' or powerless members of a society, because they cannot achieve power themselves, make a virtue out of not having it. So, for instance, Christianity advocates self-denial, and promotes the attitude that worldly power is corrupting and evil:

Blessed are the poor in spirit: for theirs is the kingdom of heaven.[49]

Blessed are the meek: for they shall inherit the earth.[50]

Ye have heard that it hath been said, An eye for an eye, and a tooth for a tooth: But I say unto you, That ye resist not evil: but whosoever shall smite thee on thy right cheek, turn to him the other also.[51]

But I say unto you, Love your enemies, bless them that curse you, do good to them that hate you, and pray for them which despitefully use you, and persecute you.[52]

At first sight, such statements appear expressions of selflessness, humility, compassion and peacefulness. Yet Nietzsche sees them in a different way, for he argues that these attitudes are actually a subtle means of achieving power. Since the powerless have no worldly power, they use religion as a means of compensation and revenge, thus achieving *spiritual* power: those values that they associate with their masters (power, pride, love of pleasure), the slaves now consider evil; those values which their circumstances force them to accept (lack of independence, ill treatment, having nothing to be proud of), they make virtues out of.

The culmination of these attitudes is found in the person of the saint or holy man. Through extreme self-denial he has reached a stage where he has developed a very powerful will; however, it is a *negative* will, in that it denies all those things which are the essence of being and feeling alive. In this sense, whilst such self-denial is impressive (and makes those with traditional power both uneasy and in awe of him), such a choice is ultimately a *neurotic* one, and the result of the denial of the life force (or 'will to power'), and hence represents a type of disease.

Interestingly, Nietzsche also views the religious neurosis as something that can exist outside of a religious context. For instance, the scientific need to quantify and objectify life, and to seek absolute certainty, can be seen in a sense to be equally life-denying; as Nietzsche points out, there are those who

> prefer a handful of 'certainty' to a whole cartful of beautiful possibilities; there may even exist puritanical fanatics of conscience who would rather lie down and die on a sure nothing than on an uncertain something.[53]

Paradoxically, the basis of atheism is the religious neurosis itself; as we climb the so-called "ladder of sacrifice", the logic of the neurosis forces us to sacrifice things which are increasingly dear to us, ending with the idea of God Himself (for more on this, see section 55 above). This, ultimately, is the meaning of Nietzsche's famous pronouncement that "God is dead" – though it is usually quoted without full understanding of the context. In *The Gay Science*, Nietzsche tells the parable of a madman walking through the marketplace:

> 'Whither is God?' he cried; 'I will tell you. *We have killed him* – you and I. All of us are his murderers.'[54]

What has died here is not God, but belief in God. Whilst aristocratic societies made their gods in their own image, such divinities were positive projections of the values that made their class dominant, and as such were a positive celebration of those values; yet since the religious neurosis springs from the downtrodden and powerless, its projection is only a celebration of the sacrificial aspect of religion (which, when it becomes the totality of the religion, becomes life-denying). Nietzsche recognises that, even if it has not happened yet (the madman, for instance, laments that he has "come too soon"), it will eventually happen; the religious neurosis will eventually do away with religion – even with meaning itself.

What can we say in response to this picture of the religious urge as a type of mental disease? Firstly, we may question the assertion that this attitude is the basis of all religious belief. The concept of sacrifice plays a part in most types

Continued

of religion, but we do not have to think that it is an essential or even defining characteristic. Furthermore, even if we agree with his assertion that monotheistic religions such as Judaism and Christianity are *essentially* negative, there are other religions and religious attitudes which advocate positive and life-affirming perspectives: many forms of paganism[55] represent a positive attitude to life, and celebrate human existence in the context of a close relationship with nature. But to be fair to Nietzsche, he is aware of this aspect of religion, identifying it with the aristocratic or ruling classes. We might therefore consider his attack upon religious belief to be confined merely to the 'neurotic' attitude which has developed from the 'slave' mentality, and the 'slave revolt in morals'. Nietzsche argues that this attitude pre-dates Christianity, and he identifies its beginnings in Judaism, Platonism and Buddhism.

Secondly, we might also question whether the sort of self-denial which Nietzsche criticises is in fact a negative *life*-denial. The word 'sacrifice' originally means 'to make sacred', and so a religious believer might argue that practices which involve self-denial, or foregoing certain pleasures – such as giving up chocolate for Lent – are actually a means of making room in one's life for God, and of developing the will to serve God. Such practices need not be considered as denying the basis of life, but actually as seeking to get in touch with the source of life itself – i.e. God. Such attitudes as humility and selflessness, which aim at the denial of one's ego, can also be seen to serve a similar goal in that the purpose is to become part of a *greater* self by achieving union with the divine.

Beyond Pessimism: the Übermensch *and the Eternal Return*

Having rejected the religious attitude (or rather, the religious neurosis), Nietzsche is left with a gaping hole where God used to be. He is not the first philosopher to have rejected God – Schopenhauer was also an atheist. Yet unlike Schopenhauer, Nietzsche does not accept that the only attitude that is open to us is pessimism – i.e. the general belief that since there is no God, humans are mortal, life is full of suffering and pain, and the world is generally at odds with human desire, we should take a negative view of life. On the contrary, Nietzsche believed that the best attitude to take to this situation was one where human beings grow and change to meet the challenge of this situation. In this sense, Nietzsche shares the same assumptions as pessimism (which we may call *nihilism*, or a belief in nothing), but comes to a different conclusion.

His answer is called the doctrine of the *eternal return* (or *eternal recurrence*). In *The Gay Science*, he writes:

> What, if some day or night a demon were to steal after you into your loneliest loneliness and say to you: 'This life as you now live it and have lived it, you will have to live once more and innumerable times more; and there will be nothing new in it, but every pain and every joy and every thought and sigh will have to return to you, and all in the same succession and sequence – even this spider and this moonlight between the trees, and even this moment and I myself. The eternal hourglass of existence is turned upside down again and again, and you with it, speck of dust!'[56]

How would you react? Nietzsche asks. Would the thought of an eternity of the same existence appal you? Nietzsche's point here is that, in a sense, this is the worst of all possible scenarios. However good a life you have lived, there will have been moments of unhappiness, pain, boredom, etc. And, what is more, the thought of the exact same life lived over for eternity would be crushing – but why is that? Nietzsche's answer is that it would be a world without any hope, which would test your ability to enjoy only the current moment – whatever that may contain. Such an existence is a test of how positive and strong a person's attitude to life is. A man who could not only live through it, but could in fact "*crave nothing more fervently*",[57] would have the most positive, life-affirming attitude possible; he would have *amor fati* (Latin: 'love of one's fate').

This is where Nietzsche parts with the atheists, pessimists and nihilists: he accepts the responsibility of God's 'death', and sets about establishing an attitude to life which is positive and life-enhancing. It is not a delusional one (there is no consolation of an afterlife or reward in heaven), or one where we hide from the truth (and, perhaps, adopt a hedonistic, forgetful attitude to such unwelcome revelations). Rather, Nietzsche is advocating that we face up to the absence of God with courage, clear vision and strength.

In such a world, our new responsibilities are immense: we must find meaning without either reinventing old prejudices or admitting the 'nothingness' of defeat; we must find a basis for morality which avoids both chaos and self-delusion; most importantly, having rejected God, "we still have to vanquish his shadow, too".[58] In other words, we must not fall back into the patterns of thinking that gave rise to the concept of God in the first place. In a sense, then, we must become the gods of this new age; having announced the death of God, the madman asks:

> Is not the greatness of this deed too great for us? Must we ourselves not become gods simply to appear worthy of it?[59]

In other words, such an individual who could reject the 'God hypothesis', who could look the truths of pessimism in the face and *still* say 'Yes' to life, would cease to be an ordinary human; such an individual would in fact become a *Super-*

human. Nietzsche's term for this was *Übermensch*, [60] and it is meant to designate the sort of person who has gone 'beyond good and evil' and become a 'free spirit' (in Nietzsche's sense of the term).

It is perhaps worth pausing here briefly to put to rest some misconceptions that still surround the popular figure of Nietzsche. Firstly, the *Übermensch* is not intended to be *in*-human; yes, he has transcended the traditional set of values shared and promoted by the 'herd', but in doing this he has merely shown the need to create values for oneself – and, for a man of artistic sensibility such as Nietzsche was, these values should be refined and noble (and not, as some have assumed, beastly and primitive). Secondly, because of Nietzsche's declaration of his opposition to Christianity (and his styling of himself as the *anti-Christian* [61]), some have assumed this to suggest the promotion of 'evil'; yet this would be a misinterpretation. As Nietzsche argues, certain Christian values can be considered life-denying, and so, rather than proposing Satanism (i.e. choosing the opposite side of the Christian 'good' and 'evil' divide), Nietzsche is actually aiming at the negation of the Christian world view itself. [62]

Whilst it is relatively clear from the above sections that Nietzsche is an atheist in terms of the traditional view of God, we may consider for a moment whether in fact his ideas necessarily lead to the death of God and the religious attitude *in all senses*. It may be surprising for you to learn that Nietzsche's ideas have influenced a number of different types of religious believers, and that there are those who believe that they are not incompatible with certain spiritual attitudes. He was, for instance, a great influence upon *Theosophy*, the spiritualist movement that sprang up at the end of the nineteenth century. Theosophy took Nietzsche's prophecy that all current moral and philosophical systems would end in nihilism as a sign that, more than a new religion, the world required spiritual transformation (an idea similar to Nietzsche's contention that "Man is a rope stretched between animal and the Superman" [63] – i.e. that he is an unfinished work, and is in the process of becoming something else). [64] This appeal to religious believers and spiritual thinkers should not, perhaps, be too surprising: existentialism, for instance, has found expression in both religious and atheistic forms. [65]

Firstly, as pointed out earlier, Nietzsche does not entirely reject all religious instincts: he sympathises with and understands the tendencies of aristocratic societies who project their positive values outward in creating their own gods, and he even entertains the possibility that the idea of the soul may be 'rescued' from the materialists and atomists (albeit in a naturalist sense).

Secondly, some have argued that Nietzsche's own attitude is itself a quasi-religious one. As Colin Wilson has argued in his study of the link between creativity and alienation, *The Outsider*, Nietzsche's attitude to philosophy is driven by concerns which are common to religion. Throughout his early life he was surrounded by religious figures, and much of his thought and reading centred upon religious topics. So, even when at the age of 21 he comes to adopt atheism, he is still fundamentally concerned with the idea of 'salvation'.

> And this is the reason why Nietzsche must be considered as a religious man; above everything else, he was aware of the need for what he called 'salvation'. We may disagree with him; we may even agree with a Jesuit theologian that his heresies were 'poisonous and detestable', but we cannot doubt the sincerity of his need for 'salvation'.[66]

Wilson argues, therefore, that although Nietzsche rejected Christianity and its values, as well as other forms of organised religion, he was still at bottom a religious thinker, consumed by a deep desire for meaning and integrity. So, in a way, Wilson argues, Nietzsche rejects Christianity because it was "*not religious enough*". Wilson also argues that at the bottom of Nietzsche's philosophy – underlying such concepts as 'will to power' and his championing of *Dionysian* values – are certain "mystical" experiences from his youth.[67] Such experiences were eventually to find expression in *The Birth of Tragedy* (perhaps Nietzsche's most 'mystical' and romantic work); but, even later, when his thoughts have found a more mature and tough-minded expression, he is still true to these themes. (In the penultimate section of *Beyond Good and Evil*, he still considers himself to be "the last disciple and initiate of the god Dionysus".[68])

Thirdly, in light of the above, we may consider Nietzsche's rejection of the metaphysical need for God as a sort of hard-line spirituality. For instance, in Buddhism there is a saying that, 'If you meet a buddha, kill the buddha.'[69] In a way, this might be considered as being of parallel meaning to Nietzsche's pronouncement that "God is dead": it is the *idea* that is the stumbling block, and if we 'kill' the idea, we realise a much higher truth (that we ourselves are Buddha/God). As Colin Wilson points out, there are significant parallels between the idea of the Buddha and that of the *Übermensch*, and that the "idea of the Superman is a response to the need for salvation in precisely the same way that Buddhism is a response to the 'three signs'" (i.e. that life is imperfect, all things are constantly changing, and that there is no such thing as a soul).[70] In this sense,

> Nietzsche was not an atheist, any more than the Buddha was.[71]

Continued

This contention is also upheld by other commentators. Lesley Chamberlain argues that *The Anti-Christ* is 'a book which would best be named "Against the Christian Church"':

> Nietzsche I feel was often acting out the wisdom of Christ, facing the whole world angrily, as if he had found the moneychangers in the temple.[72]

However, such interpretations of Nietzsche are quite contentious, and there are undoubtedly atheists who would like to keep him for their own, so what I am doing here is merely pointing out that the picture of Nietzsche as a simple atheist should not be accepted at face value.

Others have claimed to recognise an essentially religious attitude underlying Nietzsche's philosophy, but see it as a sign of the philosopher's own self-deceit. For instance, in *Straw Dogs*, John Gray argues that

> Nietzsche was an inveterately religious thinker, whose incessant attacks on Christian beliefs and values attest to the fact that he could never shake them off.[73]

For Gray, whose own position is closer to Schopenhauer's pessimism, Nietzsche does not go *far enough*:

> Looking for meaning in history is like looking for patterns in clouds. Nietzsche knew this; but he could not accept it. He was trapped in the chalk circle of Christian hopes. A believer to the end, he never gave up the absurd faith that something could be made of the human animal.[74]

Here, Nietzsche becomes, like many of the prejudiced philosophers he has identified, a dupe of his own hidden longing for a religious sense of meaning and purpose. However, unlike Wilson, Gray sees this as a delusion; he sees Nietzsche as *claiming* to have rejected God, but in reality as being influenced by the same fundamental religious need to see mankind as more significant than they are.

I think, whether Gray's view is true or not, that it is an interesting one. You may recall that Nietzsche himself pointed out that the religious viewpoint need not itself be religious; the 'religious neurosis' had sacrificed God and could now be found at the basis of positivism and the scientific world view. It would therefore be heavily ironic to find Nietzsche himself as the unwitting victim of a similar prejudice.

However, there are also good reasons for questioning Gray's conclusions. He points out that Nietzsche was aware of the human tendency to find meaning where none inherently exists ("looking for patterns in clouds"), but still accuses him of holding to an "absurd faith" that humans are more significant than any other animal or form of life. This would seem to me to ignore Nietzsche's own emphasis on the *creative* role that the new philosopher must play in the search for meaning and value. Nietzsche has not said that such values already exist – he explicitly denies that. What he has said is that, in going beyond pessimism and nihilism, we must decide and create our own values (which animals can't do). Furthermore, Nietzsche is fully aware that we are driven by irrational forces – and, what is more, forces that we may never fully fathom. To call this move "faith" is therefore misleading; faith implies belief in something which may or may not exist, but which we cannot currently claim knowledge of; Nietzsche's view, on the other hand, would seem rather to involve *choice*. Call it an 'absurd choice' therefore, if you will, but to call it 'faith', and to accuse Nietzsche of being an unwitting dogmatist, would seem to make a *straw man* of him.[75]

Morality, *Ressentiment* and the Will to Power

Ethical Naturalism

In Part Five of *BGE* Nietzsche further explores the link between morality and the natural impulses. As should now be apparent, Nietzsche sees morality as fulfilling a natural purpose (e.g. to strengthen and refine certain appetites), and the effects of various moral codes are not always the ones that moralists think are consciously being aimed at. For instance, a puritanical Christian might consider certain types of sex to be 'sinful', and so will prescribe strict rules of conduct concerning it. Whilst on the face of it this would seem to aim at making people 'better' (and less 'sinful'), it actually also serves other, unforeseen purposes: the sex drive becomes more refined and intensified, and this leads to other, higher forms of sexual expression (such as notions of 'chivalry', ideals of romance and chaste love, etc. – see *BGE*, section 189).

Nietzsche's main complaint about moralists and philosophers is that they fail to notice these moral subtleties, taking their own version of 'good' as simply being true, whereas what is needed is a *comparative* study of morality, in which different moral codes are analysed in relation to such things as environment, history, culture, and other factors which are traditionally ignored. Accordingly, Nietzsche may be considered an *ethical naturalist*: the belief that morality doesn't spring from God, or from some metaphysical reality, but rather from our natural impulses and desires.

The choice between ethical naturalism and some metaphysical notion of good is an important one in the history of philosophy, and it can help to categorise the various ethical theories that have developed in the past. So, for instance, a classical *utilitarian* (such as Jeremy Bentham) would argue that what we term 'good' is ultimately based on pleasure and happiness. So, bearing in mind that we would all like to be happy (and avoid unhappiness), then it makes sense to choose actions which maximise everyone's happiness and cause minimum suffering. Another philosopher might object to this: pleasure is not always good, and there are times when it makes sense to ask, 'This action would make lots of people happy, but is it the *right* thing to do?' This argument comes from the English philosopher G. E. Moore, who tried to show that 'good' cannot be defined in terms of other qualities (such as pleasure or happiness), because we can always ask whether such things are good or bad. This is different, he said, from simply saying that something was good because it gave us pleasure, or simply made us happy – this is fine, as long as we do not say that 'good' is the *same* as 'pleasure' (Moore called this type of mistake the *naturalistic fallacy*).

Moore's position here is similar to that of other philosophers who have argued that 'good' is a term which cannot be defined merely by reference to those things which we consider it to apply to (i.e. pleasure, happiness, self-fulfilment, and so on). But if we cannot analyse goodness in this way, then what is it? Moore is often considered an *intuitionist*, and he believed that when we use the term 'good', we have an *intuitive awareness* of what it means. Similarly, other philosophers have argued that goodness cannot be defined by reference to natural qualities: Plato argued that there exist separate ideas or *ideal forms*, which provide us with the reference points for the use of such terms; Kant believed that all our actions are either good or bad inasmuch as they accord with the moral law or not, and whether they occur out of a sense of duty.

So, in this sense, these three philosophers have all chosen to define good in *non-natural* terms (and for this reason they may be termed *non-naturalists*). We have already seen that Nietzsche may be considered a naturalist in relation to truth and knowledge, but we may also consider him an *ethical naturalist* in that he considered all morality to stem from *natural* motives (the deepest of which is the will to power). So, in his criticisms of Kant and Plato, we find him making similar points: the concept of 'the Good' in these cases is a creation of the philosopher himself, who claims to have 'discovered' it. But what is really happening is that the philosopher has rejected the *naturalistic* interpretation of morality (i.e. that it is pleasure, or self-interest, or – in Nietzsche's case – will to power), and unwittingly defined it in a way which ignores what Nietzsche sees as the *real* cause of the morality (the secret drives of the philosopher himself). It is not reason which is the basis of these 'discoveries', but rather the philosopher's own desire for it to be that way. In this sense, non-naturalist philosophers have a type of 'faith' that such opposite values exist, and that they themselves are completely uninfluenced by natural motives.

However, in proposing this view of philosophy, has Nietzsche committed Moore's *naturalistic fallacy*? Not necessarily so, for whilst Nietzsche *does* try to explain morality in natural terms, the concept of the 'will to power' is flexible enough to explain many different types of behaviour: for instance, at one point Nietzsche describes how the will to power is different from the survival instinct, and that through it an individual might even sacrifice its life in order to give greater expression to its own will to power. Furthermore, in Nietzsche's view, there is no one natural property which can be called 'good' – pleasure and pain can both serve a higher goal of the individual, and there are many different expressions of will to power, resulting in a different emphasis upon different qualities (strength, intelligence, love, etc.) for different purposes, or at different times.

A Natural History of Morality

In Part Two, 'The Free Spirit', Nietzsche sets out his view of morality as having developed through three stages (for a more detailed account of this, see section 32 above):

- *Pre-moral*: This stage stretches from prehistoric times right up to the first major civilisations, 10,000 years ago. Here, actions were simply right or wrong according to their consequences (*consequentialism*).
- *Moral*: This is the age that we are currently in. Here, actions are 'good' or 'bad' according to where they come from, or the intention that lies behind them (*intentionalism*).
- *Extra-moral*: This is the future age envisioned by Nietzsche. Here, moral values will be analysed and evaluated according to an understanding of their place in the natural development of humanity.

For critics of Nietzsche, this division is questionable: what is his basis for this threefold division? He presents little or no evidence in support of designating the first two stages as he does, and it would seem overly simplistic to characterise the whole of prehistoric morals as being *consequentialist*, and modern morality as *intentionalist* – how does he know? What is required in order to make such sweeping judgements is a detailed study of cultures throughout history – something which Nietzsche himself advocates (e.g. section 186), but nonetheless does not himself undertake.

Continued

Secondly, the presentation of the extra-moral stage is problematic: is Nietzsche suggesting that it is inevitable that humanity takes this course? If so, what is his argument for this? Again, there appears to be none – other than his dissatisfaction with the current state of morality, and his claim that we *must* undertake a 'revaluation of all values' in order to move forward.

In this sense, Nietzsche's historical overview is similar to that of the political philosopher Karl Marx, who analysed the economic history of mankind as a progression from *feudalism* (where the nobles ruled over and owned the *vassals* or peasants), to *capitalism* (where a small number of individuals privately own the *capital*, or means of production). The final stage in Marx's analysis was *communism*, where the means of production would be equally shared, and all members of society would be equal. Critics of Marx have pointed out that this third stage is more of an ideal than an analysis: communism, whilst it has come about in certain countries (more or less unsuccessfully), has not led to the utopia that Marx predicted. It would appear, then, that it was not inevitable that communism would come about. Similarly, we may make the same criticism of Nietzsche: there would seem to be no compelling reasons why the extra-moral stage should come about, and we may consider it to be an ideal, or merely an option (where others are possible).

Not to misrepresent Nietzsche, it may not be a criticism of his analysis that the extra-moral stage has not yet come about. Nietzsche has also been credited with having predicted the decline of religious belief, and shown how the growth of democratic ideals, science and industry has led to a growing nihilism. The extra-moral stage may not, therefore, be a prophecy, but rather the philosopher's opinion as to the only way in which modern society can escape nihilism.

Ressentiment

One of Nietzsche's key ideas is that of *ressentiment* (from the French, 'jealousy or resentment'), which is the idea that the modern, Christian-influenced notion of 'good' is an inversion of traditional moral values. In his work, *On the Genealogy of Morals*, Nietzsche explains this using a parable:

> That lambs dislike great birds of prey does not seem strange: only it gives no ground for reproaching these birds of prey for bearing off little lambs. And if the lambs say among themselves: 'these birds of prey are evil; and whoever is least like a bird of prey, but rather its opposite, a lamb – would he not be good?' there is no reason to find fault with this institution of an ideal, except perhaps that the birds of prey might view it a little ironically and say: '*we* don't dislike them at all, these good little lambs; we even love them: nothing is more tasty than a tender lamb.'[76]

The birds of prey are the strong, those who are fit to rule by virtue of their dominance, and their values spring from their own nature. The lambs are the ruled, the weak, and their values are a *reaction* to being ruled, and also to the values of the birds of prey. In other words, the lambs' morality is based on dislike: they hate and fear the birds of prey, so they define themselves as their opposite. However, as Nietzsche says, there is nothing 'wrong' in the fact that the lambs do this – he implies that, just as the birds of prey develop a morality from their qualities of strength, it is natural for the lambs to develop a morality which takes account of their own weakness and powerlessness. In this sense, for both lamb and bird of prey, their morality is directly related to their respective natures. The problem arises when the morality of the lamb becomes dominant, and seeks to change the nature of the bird of prey – or, in fact, tries to show that we are all really 'lambs'.

It should be obvious to you by now that by "lambs" and "birds of prey", Nietzsche is referring to the 'master' and 'slave' moralities. The figure of the lamb, in fact, is aptly chosen, because, for Nietzsche, the source of slave morality is Christianity and Judaism, where the lamb represents the ideal of meekness, goodness and sacrifice. In the history of morality, the slave morality, through the dominance of Christian thought, managed to achieve what Nietzsche calls a 'slave revolt in morals' – that is, an inversion of traditional master values in order to produce a dominant slave morality. This, in effect, is will to power at work: the slave morality makes *everyone* equal, and by doing so makes everyone equally *weak*; thus, those who are most weak (or humble or 'good'), become, ironically, the most powerful. But, Nietzsche argues, this should not happen, because it leads to a weakening of humanity in general. To quote further from the same section in *On the Genealogy of Morals*:

> To demand of strength that it should *not* express itself as strength, that it should *not* be a desire to overcome, a desire to throw down, a desire to become master, a thirst for enemies and resistances and triumphs, is just as absurd as to demand of weakness that it should express itself as strength.[77]

Or, as the poet William Blake put it:

> One Law for the Lion & Ox is Oppression.[78]

And yet, this is what the slave revolt in morals has achieved: out of jealousy, fear and frustrated desire for power, the 'slaves' have craftily undermined the 'masters' and created a new morality which justifies their dominance. This, in essence, is *ressentiment* – but is it true?

Firstly, we may question Nietzsche's division of morality into these two tendencies. Once more, we must ask ourselves what evidence he has for this. Throughout his writings, Nietzsche analyses and comments upon different cultures, individuals, philosophies, etc., and through this process tries to show that, in most cases, there is a lack of moral self-knowledge present. This is because the morality aimed for is almost never the morality which is practised; it is only, in fact, when we come to understand the will to power that we can really begin to understand the true nature of morality. For instance, a person may practise humility, but in reality what they are secretly seeking (perhaps unconsciously) is a subtle sort of superiority over others ('I am more humble than you are!'); on the other hand, a person may perform a cruel act, but in reality they are doing something which, in the greater scheme of things, can be viewed as a healthy sense of detachment (a 'pruning of the tree' to make it stronger). The point here is that the individual who practises the morality concerned frequently does not have a true sense of why they do so. Undeniably, this is an important point when thinking about morality and moral motivation, and in this sense Nietzsche and Freud are right. Furthermore, our understanding of human nature would certainly be poorer if we rejected the idea of unconscious motivation altogether.

But there is also a sense in which these observations have become part of our common way of thinking: we may talk of 'false humility', or of someone being hypocritical; we occasionally also talk of 'being cruel to be kind', or making hard decisions based upon pragmatic concerns (such as turning off life-support machines, or performing abortions). Do we need, as Nietzsche does, to distinguish between two different *moralities* at work here, when it may be possible to account for differences of moral outlook within a *single* morality?

Yet, other alternatives to Nietzsche's perspective are possible: we might account for these moral differences by proposing a *range* of different moralities, each with a different end in view; or, it may be possible that the traditional Christian-type morality actually represents moral progress, and that what we have seen in the 'demise' of the master morality is actually a growth in compassion and understanding, and a moral development away from selfishness and brutishness.

The problem in deciding this question lies perhaps in the extent to which we can fully understand the motives of another person. If we employ the type of approach that Nietzsche does – one which he shares, to an extent, with Freud – then true moral motivations are hidden and difficult to discern. What's more, because of this we cannot easily check whether such statements are true or not. Critics of Freud have pointed out that some of his theories are, in effect, unverifiable: we cannot know whether someone has or has not got this secret motive or desire, for even if you can make a convincing argument and bring the *person concerned* to see it, there is still the possibility that all you have done is *convince him* (self-knowledge is a tricky thing . . .). As far as scientific proof goes, then, Freud has been found lacking. In her essay, 'Can Intuitive Proof Suffice?', Barbara Von Eckardt argues that Freud's main criterion for the truth of a theory seems to be its "explanatory power" (i.e. the extent to which it can account for all the questions under consideration):

> this was so because he regarded a high degree of explanatory power as suffi-cient for the justification of a theory. But, as we have seen, according to the standard scientific methodology this is not enough. A theory is not suffi-ciently justified unless it has been submitted to a variety of good scientific tests. And here Freud's methodology systematically falls short.[79]

Similarly, then, Nietzsche's theory of *ressentiment* is open to the same criticism: can we really know if compassion conceals a hidden desire to be better than another person? Nietzsche also seems to have been swayed by his theory's "explanatory power". So, whilst this may not invalidate Nietzsche's theory, it does make it difficult to prove.

But perhaps the truth of the theory does not necessarily lie in whether or not we can know someone's actual motives. Nietzsche's main contention is that morality is will to power, and that, by turning its back on the natural desire to dominate through strength, power, courage, etc., the slave morality has become *anti-life*. The question of whether *ressentiment* is true is therefore dependent on whether will to power is true; if Nietzsche can show that all morality *is* in fact based on will to power, then his case for Christianity being an example of *res-sentiment* – or for any morality which denies these qualities – becomes all the stronger.

We will now look at Nietzsche's doctrine of the will to power.

Will to Power

In an earlier section on the philosophical prejudice of teleological thinking, I mentioned that there are key differences between Nietzsche's conception of will to power and Darwin's theory of evolution. So, whilst thinkers such as Darwin believed that creatures were driven by a will to survive (and that survival instincts evolved through natural selection), Nietzsche thought that survival was not in fact the main driving force. As we read in section 13:

> Physiologists should think again before postulating the drive to self-preservation as the cardinal drive in an organic being. A living thing desires above all to *vent*

its strength – life as such is will to power – : self-preservation is only one of the indirect and most frequent *consequences* of it.[80]

So, Nietzsche is not denying that self-preservation is a motive in some actions, but is simply proposing that it is not the most *fundamental* one. The most fundamental of all is the desire of something to achieve "ever greater vitality and life-enhancement", and includes "not only human motivation but the behaviour of all that lives".[81]

Another important thing to consider about will to power is that it can take many different forms. For instance, the will to power can be that which causes a plant to grow and spread its seed; that which causes a wild animal to become leader of the pack and defend its position; or that which causes a human being to devise a philosophy on life that expresses his personal ideal. All of these things are expressions of will to power, and, concerning the last, Nietzsche says, "philosophy is the most spiritual will to power" – that is, the most subtle, and therefore the type of power-seeking dominance most likely to go unnoticed. However, Nietzsche does not consider will to power just to regulate all living processes, but also the 'inanimate' world of physical atoms; in this way he makes a bridge between life and matter that is perhaps lacking in the modern scientific perspective.

The difference between Darwin and Nietzsche is nicely summed up by anthropologist H. James Birx:

> Nietzsche saw the explanatory mechanism of natural selection as merely accounting for the quantity of species within organic history, but (for him) it is a vitalistic force that increases the quality of life forms throughout progressive biological evolution. He held that nature is essentially the will to power. Evolving life is not merely the Spencerian/Darwinian struggle for existence but, more importantly, it is the ongoing striving toward ever-greater complexity, diversity, multiplicity and creativity. In short, reminiscent of the interpretations offered by Lamarck, Henri Bergson, and Pierre Teilhard de Chardin (among others), Nietzsche's vitalism had substituted Darwin's adaptive fitness with creative power.[82]

It is clear from the above that Nietzsche agreed with certain principles of Darwinism (i.e. that more complex species evolved from simpler ones, the process of natural selection) – in fact, as has been pointed out, "Nietzsche shares more with Darwin than he does with most of Darwin's opponents".[83] And yet, at best, Nietzsche considered Darwinism to be only a partial explanation of the evolutionary process. Nietzsche's main problem with Darwinism may be summed up in three sets of competing explanations:

- *Mechanism vs. Vitalism.* Nietzsche thought that Darwin's picture of nature left out the life force. So, Nietzsche, whilst he did not want to assume a sort of spiritual essence to things, did argue that there is more behind natural forces than simply mechanical cause and effect. Accordingly, he has more in common with such thinkers as Lamarck.[84]
- *The Fittest vs. The Most Highly Evolved.* As already noted, Nietzsche believed that the highest type of human was not always the one best suited to cope with what the world had to throw at him (section 276). Frequently, the type of being which would best survive would be, in many ways, the most mediocre, less-evolved type. So, less-intelligent, simpler and less-sophisticated beings have often more chance of surviving than their more evolved counterparts, because there is less to go wrong, and they have numbers on their side.
- *Will to Survive vs. Will to Power.* The crucial point for Nietzsche is that natural selection *will not* produce a higher type of individual, but rather *the most mediocre* type. Therefore, whilst it explains certain characteristics of species, and how some survive and others die out, it does not account for the inherent drive that leads nature to seek to produce higher and higher expressions of the life force.

Of course, all of these points are highly contentious, and Darwin's defenders would no doubt take issue with each of them. Let us analyse each of them in turn.

Vitalism

Firstly, concerning vitalism, it must be noted that the majority of modern scientists now prefer a mechanistic account of nature. In other words, if we can explain how nature works purely in terms of physical cause and effect, and without resorting to mysterious substances or principles, then we should. This is known as the *principle of parsimony*, or *Occam's razor*: all else being equal, if one of two explanations is the simpler (makes fewer assumptions), then we should prefer that one. The key phrase here, of course, is 'all else being equal'; the two explanations must be otherwise identical in terms of their power to account for the thing in question. If, for instance, the more complicated explanation *does* explain more than the simpler one, then of course we should prefer *that* one – this is not a case of 'simpler is better *no matter what*'. However, if there is nothing to separate two theories apart from their respective complexity, then simpler *is* better. Accordingly, in its quest to explain the physical world, modern science has by and large tried to account for things purely in terms of material processes.

Continued

Vitalism, on the other hand, argues (a) that living things cannot be explained purely in terms of physical forces, and (b) that each living thing contains some essence or vitality that is distinct from these physical forces. We have to be careful here: such a definition is very close to 'spirit' or 'soul', and it would probably be misleading to picture Nietzsche as holding that sort of view. Perhaps the closest to what Nietzsche means is the idea that living things are not defined by the physical laws which describe their behaviour. After all, a law simply describes what we know about a thing, and it may not necessarily describe all that it is capable of. In this sense, Nietzsche's vitalism pictures a sort of spontaneity and freedom that Darwin's picture lacks; Nietzsche's organisms are not just machine-like bits of matter, 'going through the motions', but rather small entities with 'wills' and 'desires' of their own. This latter point also shows that, for Nietzsche, the world is alive, and even whilst it may stretch language to speak of tiny living things having 'desires', this is closer to what Nietzsche means. Such a picture, he argues, is more accurate than one where physical matter goes through various stages and processes, governed by impersonal physical laws.

The problem with this view, of course, is that it is difficult to prove. Non-vitalists often interpret vitalists as proposing that something exists *in addition* to matter, and then point out that physical tests have not found anything in addition to physical processes. But this is not necessarily the case: vitalism (and Nietzsche) can be interpreted as simply saying that matter is *a different sort of thing* than has previously been supposed. So, in a sense, Nietzsche may simply be pointing out that we misinterpret matter by assuming it to be inanimate, and by assuming that we can know all there is to know about it from a purely external perspective. But if there *is* something different about matter which is *internal*, then it is easy to see how this aspect has been ignored: we cannot know what it is like to be a rock, a tree, an animal, or even in fact another person; all our knowledge comes from our own experiences, which we then project outwards. However, whilst this works with other human beings (we can understand them through supposing that they have similar motives and feelings to ourselves), we think it ridiculous to think of smaller entities having 'desires' or 'motivations'. Of course, in a sense, this is right: apart from larger mammals, it is difficult to imagine a plant or a tree having such internal processes – which is not to say that *they do not have simpler versions* of such feelings.

Once again, it comes down to the principle of parsimony: why not simply accept the simpler explanation? A reason for not doing so may in fact lie in our own experience of the world. A parallel discussion to the vitalism/mechanism debate (already mentioned) exists in the philosophy of mind, where the majority of philosophers are materialists who consider the brain to be a sort of extremely complicated machine. By extension, human beings themselves are also very complicated machines. In opposition to this, other philosophers (whom we can call *non-reductive realists*) have argued that seeking to account for consciousness in this mechanistic way necessarily leaves something out of the explanation – i.e. what it is like to *be* conscious. In other words, if we were nothing but machines, then surely we could build a machine that would be conscious in exactly the same way as we are – wouldn't it? Of course, both sides of the debate take this possibility to prove their point: the materialists think that such a robot could exist, whilst the realists argue that such a robot (whilst it might be able to 'think', in the sense of 'compute') would not be conscious at all.

The conclusion of this argument is that the debate is a living one (excuse the pun). Whilst the principle of parsimony may be a valuable rule of thumb, it does not necessarily mean that it provides a definite answer in this case; even if experiments cannot detect a vital principle, that is not to say that such a thing does not exist.

Fittest and highest

Nietzsche's contention that the goal of evolution is to produce higher types of individual is at odds with Darwin's concept of 'natural selection' (or the 'survival of the fittest'). As we have already seen, Nietzsche argues that the higher type of man is commonly more fragile than the lower type – as the survival of a rare orchid is more precarious than that of a common dandelion. For these reasons, whilst the fittest do in fact survive and prosper, the real goal of evolution – according to Nietzsche – is the production of higher and finer expressions of life.

Is Nietzsche misreading Darwin here? It may be argued that Darwin is not in fact proposing that the strongest and most noble creatures survive, or even that they represent progress, but merely that those creatures which are best suited to the environment survive over those which are not. Darwin does in fact suggest in places that evolutionary changes "tend toward progress and perfection",[85] suggesting almost that evolution "works solely by and for the good of each being",[86] but such views are not central to Darwinism itself, and he may only have put such ideas in to soften the news to the religious traditionalists that we are all descended from apes! Therefore, is Nietzsche simply using a *straw man argument* (i.e. setting up a distorted version of Darwin's theory in order to criticise it)?

I think, on the one hand, Nietzsche's criticism is not harmful to Darwin's central thesis: if cockroaches or bacteria prove to be the best able to survive in all environments, then they are undoubtedly the fittest. However – and this is where Nietzsche's point has more power – neither cockroaches nor bacteria may be said to be the highest development of nature (in terms of complexity,

Continued

sophistication, etc.), and so we may possibly argue that this would weigh in favour of Nietzsche's main point (i.e. that nature has an aim over and above mere survival). Yet, in siding with Nietzsche in this, we may be introducing a teleological process into evolution. One of the strengths of Darwin's theory is that, at its purest, it does away with all teleological principles (i.e. nature has no purpose or *telos*). But if we start to differentiate between 'higher' and 'lower' forms of evolution, then we begin to introduce values into the situation – e.g. we value more complex things over simpler ones, or more intelligent and sophisticated organisms over more basic ones. This, arguably, begs the question: is the will to power a teleological principle?

Survival and power

Darwin proposes that each living being has survival instincts – such as hunger, the need to reproduce, desire to avoid pain, and so on. At first, this looks like a teleological principle (i.e. the goal of each individual species is to survive). However, these instincts can be explained as a simple by-product of the evolutionary process: those beings which avoid the experience of pain (and physical damage) simply live to reproduce; those whose behaviour does not adapt itself to pain stimuli die out; thus, the instinct to avoid pain is passed on as a survival instinct. In this sense, the survival instinct can thus be seen to be a secondary principle to that of natural selection.

Nietzsche, on the other hand, dismisses the idea that the survival instinct is fundamental to living organisms. It doesn't really matter here whether Nietzsche has misread Darwin (in thinking that Darwin holds the survival instinct to be fundamental), because the point is still the same: Darwin has overlooked the existence of the will to power, which is the most fundamental instinct of all.

The problem here is that Nietzsche's contention is difficult to prove. If the will to power is more successful in accounting for evolution and natural forces than Darwinism, then there should be cases where will to power wins out over Darwinism. But since this discussion is one that best takes place in the field of biological science, we have a problem: modern science is based on materialism, which by its nature denies vitalism; similarly, Darwinism is a materialist, non-vitalist, non-teleological theory, and so is the best fit for a modern scientific view of nature and evolution (which has been hugely successful to date). So, even if there were theories that favoured a Nietzschean interpretation of evolution, they are unlikely to be successful, because this would require switching from materialism to some form of vitalist (and possibly teleological) theory – which would require a huge shift in the scientific world view. Consequently, until the hypothetical day when materialism's shortcomings are exposed, Nietzsche's view of the natural world would seem to be waiting in the wings.[87]

Appendix:
Overview of *Beyond Good and Evil*

Part	General topic	Main arguments
Preface	Identification of philosophy to date as dogmatic	Most philosophy is dogmatic, based on the personal prejudices of each philosopher; certain philosophical prejudices represent a stage of intellectual growth, but must now be discarded; the modern philosopher must struggle against Platonism and Christianity (which is "Platonism for the people").
1: On the Prejudices of Philosophers	Identification of philosophical prejudices, problems with traditional philosophical approaches	1: Objective "will to truth" (1st prejudice). 2–3: Faith in "antithetical values" (2nd prejudice), role of instinct in philosophy. 4: False judgements as essential to life. 5: Role of instinct, most philosophers "innocent". 6: Role of drives, possibility of objectivity. 7–8: Epicurus and Plato. 9: Stoicism a distortion of nature, philosophy as spiritual will to power. 10: Appearance and reality (3rd prejudice), nihilism, positivism, modern ideas. 11: Kant and the synthetic *a priori*. 12: Atomism (4th prejudice). 13: Will to power, teleological explanation (5th prejudice). 14: Science and positivism. 15: Refutation of idealism. 16–17: Immediate certainty (6th prejudice), Descartes's *Cogito*. 18–19: Free will controversy, Nietzsche's view (commonwealth of souls). 20: Grammar as basis of metaphysics (e.g. atomism). 21: Free will controversy, *causa sui* (7th prejudice), reification (8th prejudice).

Part	General topic	Main arguments
		22: Link between reification (8th prejudice) and democratic spirit, herd morality, will to power. 23: Explanation of criticisms, new philosopher (free spirit) must adopt "psychological" approach to truth.
2: The Free Spirit	The nature and concerns of the "new philosopher", the free spirit and truth	24: Importance of will to ignorance in knowledge, must be analysed by free spirit. 25: Criticism of Bruno and Spinoza (martyrs for truth), tragic philosophy. 26: True philosopher's need for isolation. 27–8: Link between language, thought and temperament. 29: Isolation of free spirit. 30: Different needs of free spirit and common man. 31: Philosophical maturity rejects reactionism and need for black and white answers. 32: Pre-moral, moral and extra-moral stages of humanity. 33: Need for psychological interpretation of selflessness and objectivity. 34: The reason for error (will to ignorance), philosophers generally naive (e.g. immediate certainty), free spirit must be suspicious (bad) character, truth and falsity, Descartes (atomism). 35: Naivety of Voltaire (truth and goodness the same). 36–7: Will to power, cause and effect better understood as acts of will, rejection of causation unpopular with modern science. 38: Idea of progress as distortion of history. 39: Truth and happiness not the same, man measured by degree of truth (suffering) he can stand, free spirit must cultivate "severity and cunning". 40: The nature of masks. 41: Detachment important quality for free spirit. 42–3: New philosophers are "attempters", not dogmatic, not concerned with popularity. 44: Distinction between philosophical and political free spirits.

Part	General topic	Main arguments
3: The Religious Nature	Religion and the religious viewpoint, the saint and the religious neurosis	45: Religion should be interpreted psychologically, study is vast and suitable scholars too few. 46: Religious belief as reflection of temperament and environment (Pascal, Cromwell, Luther, Greece and Rome), Christianity as slave revolt in morals, difference with master morality. 47: The religious neurosis and the saint. 48: Link between temperament and types of belief (north and south). 49: Gratitude basis of ancient Greek culture, fear basis of later Greeks and Christians, difference between noble and common. 50: Belief and upbringing. 51: Difference in will to power in saint and aristocratic ruler. 52: Difference between Old Testament (rich culture) and New Testament (poor in comparison). 53: Progression of religious neurosis to science, philosophy and politics. 54: Concept of soul. 55: Religious neurosis, ladder of sacrifice. 56: Pessimism, the eternal return. 57: Ideas as intellectual toys for growth. 58: Link between scholars/modern ideas and herd morality, both antagonistic to true religious attitude. 59–60: Will to ignorance and fear of truth prevalent in religious attitudes, love of mankind based on fear of mankind. 61: The uses of religion in the hands of the true philosopher. 62: Growth in pity in religion result of slave revolt in morals.
4: Maxims and Interludes	Various	Philosophical and moral prejudices: 64, 68, 70, 75, 77–8, 80–1, 97, 108, 117, 132, 138, 141, 143, 149, 157–8, 174, 177, 182, 185. Free spirit/higher man: 63, 65, 66, 69, 71–6, 79, 87–8, 91–6, 98–101, 103, 105, 107, 109–10, 112, 116, 119, 122, 126, 128–9, 130, 133–5, 140, 146, 150, 152–4, 160, 169–71, 173, 180, 184. Woman and the sexes: 84–6, 102, 113–15, 120, 123, 127, 131, 139, 144–5, 147–8. Religion and the religious attitude: 65a, 67, 82, 93, 104, 105, 112, 121, 124, 129, 135, 152, 162, 164, 168. Miscellaneous topics: 83, 90, 106, 111, 118, 125, 136–7, 142, 151, 161, 163, 166–7, 172, 175–6, 178–9, 183.

Part	General topic	Main arguments
5: On the Natural History of Morals	Study of morality from a historical perspective, role of instinct and irrational forces	186: Science of morals versus moral sensibility, search for rational basis for morality naive (Schopenhauer). 187: Morality as expression of irrational drives, *ressentiment*. 188: Morality and art both results of discipline of arbitrary laws (condition of growth), morality irrational (will to power). 189: Purpose of religious discipline (intensification of drives). 190–3: Difference between Plato (noble) and Socrates (common), influence of instinct upon reason, unconscious attitudes' influence upon consciousness. 194: Different degrees of possession (personal and national), Jewish culture. 195: The Jews, slave morality, origin of term "world". 196: Hidden influences upon morality ("dark bodies"). 197: The Man of Prey and moderate men, morality as timidity. 198: Morality as timidity in Spinoza and Aristotle. 199: Herd morality and true leaders. 200: Men of diversified descent (Caesar, St Augustine, da Vinci), self-overcoming. 201: Analysis of how herd morality comes to dominate in society. 202: Herd morality dominant in contemporary Europe, expression in democracy – even anarchy, pity as highest value. 203: True progression of mankind not "perfect herd animal" but new philosopher.
6: We Scholars	Criticism of modern attitudes to knowledge, science and philosophy	204: Science (herd) now legislates for philosophy (noble), positivism. 205: Specialisation not good for philosophy. 206: Contemporary scholars "barren" (collectors of facts), anti-elitist, mediocre (herd morality). 207: Objectivity not an end in itself (instrument of new philosopher). 208: Scientific scepticism prevalent, belief out of fashion, scepticism as "paralysis of will". 209: Proper use of scepticism (Frederick the Great). 210: Free spirits critics not sceptics. 211: New philosopher creates values (not "philosophical labourer"), will to power not will to truth. 212: Philosophers need to be "bad conscience" of their age. 213: Philosophers born not made, qualities needed by philosophers.

Part	General topic	Main arguments
7. Our Virtues	The values of the new philosopher, difference with man of modern ideas, criticism of female emancipation	214: New philosopher's virtues will change through investigation. 215–16: Actions influenced by hidden motives, contrast between conscious and unconscious. 217: Psychology of moral posturing. 218: Common man most interesting psychological study, most psychologists stem from herd. 219: Common man's revenge on higher type (*ressentiment*), order of rank. 220: Average man not fit to search for truth (criticism of disinterest), truth as a woman. 221: Selflessness, different moralities necessary for different types. 222: Pity and compassion chief virtues but stem from self-contempt. 223: Modern age self-conscious (no fixed identity), historical masks, self-overcoming at social level. 224: Historical sense recent result of mingling of classes (democracy), modern taste broad, lack of "taste" fuels development. 225: The value of suffering as a discipline. 226: Misunderstanding of new philosophers by modern men (immorality). 227: Qualities needed by new philosophers (honesty, courage, hardness). 228: Contemporary moral philosophy "boring" (utilitarianism) because based on unquestioned accepted values, order of rank between moralities. 229: Fear of instincts and ignorance of their true role, value of cruelty. 230: Will to knowledge versus will to ignorance. 231: Philosophy as analysis of our fundamental nature. 232–5: Female emancipation a bad thing (corruption of instincts), traditional role more powerful, woman not naturally suited to "serious" pursuits, strength lies in manipulation of "appearance" (surface reality). 236–7: Difference between men and women (aphorisms). 238: Sexual equality naive, traditional role best. 239: Female equality lessens woman's true power.

Part	General topic	Main arguments
8. Peoples and Fatherlands	National character, current political forces, the good European	240: German people similar to Wagner's music (mixture of different ages, tastes), no unified spirit. 241: Criticism of patriotism (two patriots – traditional versus modern), rejection of both, qualities of "good European". 242: Democracy mixes classes and races, two individuals produced (herd animal and new master type). 243: New man is emerging (Hercules). 244: German character difficult to define because still emerging (undigested mixture – mask). 245: Music as expression of different aspects of German character (Mozart – traditional, Beethoven – transitional, Mendelssohn – light and pure, Schumann – provincial). 246–7: German writing has no "ear", Luther's Bible one exception. 248–9: Two types of genius: active (Romans, Jews – Germans?) and passive (French, Greeks), fundamental nature of national character is unknowable. 250: Influence of Jews on Europe (good and bad). 251: German anti-Semitism a result of fear and inability to assimilate, anti-Semites should not be tolerated, importance of certain Jewish qualities to future Europe. 252–3: English people and philosophers dry and unimaginative (source of modern ideas) but useful to new philosophers, modern decline of France. 254: Celebration of true French culture (creativity, psychology, synthesis). 255: Characteristics of northern and southern music and culture, new spirit will be pan-European. 256: General trend in Europe towards unity (attitudes of great men – Napoleon, Schopenhauer, Goethe, Wagner), Christian values as obstacle.

Part	General topic	Main arguments
9: What Is Noble?	The qualities of the noble type, master and slave morality, the nature of the quest of the higher man	257: Aristocracy necessary for cultural development (pathos of distance), aristocrats originally "more complete beasts". 258: Aristocracy is reason for society to exist, corruption of this belief leads to sickness. 259: Comparison of aristocratic values (life-affirming) and Christian values (life-denying), all healthy society based on exploitation. 260: Detailed analysis of master and slave moralities. 261: Master and slave morality in relation to self-estimation. 262: Account of decline of aristocratic societies (three stages). 263: Reverence as characteristic of noble type. 264: Inherited qualities (not education) as source of character. 265: Egoism and equality in noble type. 266–7: Noble type not concerned with self (Goethe), modern civilisations based on fear. 268: General tendency for people to seek common experience not conducive to producing exceptional man. 269: Higher type of man often suffers greatly (Jesus). 270: Suffering separates individuals, need for masks. 271–2: Importance of "cleanliness", higher type of man transcends pity (duties only to self). 273: Higher man can only do good to others after achieving self-knowledge (others are obstacles or aids). 274: Importance of recognising key moment for self-development (difference between great men and others). 275–7: Key differences between noble and common type. 278–9: The Wanderer, true philosopher's need for mask. 280: Going backwards (analysis of past) to make "big jump" forward (future). 281: Nietzsche as a riddle to himself (for others to solve). 282: Noble cannot eat at same table as common man (indigestion). 283: Past philosophers' use of masks to support controversial ideas (Descartes, Bacon). 284: Use of masks to preserve philosophical detachment. 285: Philosophical ideas may not be understood until much later. 286: 'Heaven' is "up" (Goethe's *Faust*), but noble man is already at a height.

Part	General topic	Main arguments
		287: Self-reverence as defining characteristic of noble type. 288: Enthusiasm as a mask of the higher type. 289–90: Comparison of hermit and philosopher (hermit keeps questioning, philosopher is just another mask). 291: Man as "artist" of truth. 292: Philosophers disturbed by discoveries but driven on by curiosity. 293: Master and slave notions of pity, "cult of suffering" should be rooted out. 294: Importance of laughter (lack of seriousness) for true philosopher. 295: Nietzsche as "last disciple" of Dionysus, neglect of Dionysian spirit in modern age. 296: Limitations of language, Nietzsche's thoughts have already moved on.
From High Mountains: Epode	Call to the new philo-sophers	Nietzsche's philosophy as a call to like-minded spirits to join him in the "high mountains", but the old friends who turn up no longer understand him – or he them, new friends are expected, Zarathustra arrives, "wedding day" of "light and darkness" (old values are transcended).

Notes

Introduction

1 Friedrich Nietzsche, *Twilight of the Idols/The Anti-Christ*, translated by R. J. Hollingdale (London: Penguin Classics, 1990), 'Foreword', p. 31.
2 *Twilight of the Idols*, 'Maxims and Arrows', maxim 42, p. 37.
3 From his introduction to Nietzsche's *On the Genealogy of Morals and Ecce Homo*, edited and translated by Kaufmann and R. J. Hollingdale (New York: Vintage Books, 1967), p. 4.

1 Background

1 The biographical account here is based on details taken from a number of sources: Walter Kaufmann, *Nietzsche: Philosopher, Psychologist, Antichrist* (Princeton, NJ: Princeton University Press, 1974), pp. 21–71; Crane Brinton, *Nietzsche* (New York: Harper & Row, 1965); R. J. Hollingdale, *Nietzsche* (London: Ark Paperbacks, 1965); and Rüdiger Safranski, *Nietzsche: A Philosophical Biography* (London: Granta Books, 2002).
2 Nietzsche was named after the then King of Prussia, Friedrich Wilhelm IV, probably as an expression of loyalty, but also more significantly because they both shared the same birthday. Nietzsche, however, who grew not to share his father's patriotism, later dropped 'Wilhelm' from his name.
3 The German Confederation was an alliance made up of 39 sovereign states, which existed from 1815 to 1866. It had been created at the Congress of Vienna to re-establish unity between many of the states that had made up the Holy Roman Empire. However, this eventually became the German Empire in 1871 (or what is sometimes known as the 'Second *Reich*').

4 Up until 1815, Nietzsche's birthplace would have been part of the Kingdom of Saxony. However, after supporting the losing side in the Napoleonic wars (i.e. France), 40 per cent of its realm (including the area surrounding Lützen) was annexed by Prussia. Nietzsche's awareness of this history thus seems to have made him more interested in understanding the forces at work than in taking sides. Despite his utilisation by the Nazis for propaganda purposes, it should be noted that Nietzsche was not a nationalist in any narrow sense, and rather liked to think of himself as having a broader view of the unity of European culture (hence sometimes referring to himself as "the good European").

5 Hollingdale, *Nietzsche*, p. 11. However, there is still some debate over this.

6 Hollingdale, *Nietzsche*, p. 12.

7 Brinton, *Nietzsche*, p. 13.

8 Quoted in Kaufmann, *Nietzsche: Philosopher, Psychologist, Antichrist*, p. 23.

9 Kaufmann, *Nietzsche: Philosopher, Psychologist, Antichrist*, p. 22.

10 Quoted in Brinton, *Nietzsche*, p. 17.

11 For instance, *Beyond Good and Evil* (hereafter *BGE*), section 22, p. 52.

12 It is interesting to view these principles still at work in *BGE*. Late in the book, Nietzsche portrays himself as a "disciple" of Dionysus, in that he sees his task as partly to overthrow the rational dominance that has – in his view – blinded philosophers as to the true nature of philosophy.

13 Also sometimes translated as *Thoughts Out of Season*.

14 Much the same as he uses in Part Four of *BGE*.

15 It should be noted here that 'gay' has nothing to do with homosexuality; it is rather used in the older sense of 'joyful' (Nietzsche's title has also been translated *The Joyful Wisdom* and *The Science of Joy*). The inspiration for the title is a term used by the troubadour poets of the fourteenth century to describe the correct combination of knowledge, skill and emotion in writing poetry. Incidentally, the book was published in 1882, followed by a second edition five years later with an additional section (Book 5).

16 However, Lou Salomé was not the only woman Nietzsche showed interest in. He had previously proposed marriage to Mathilde Trampedach in 1876, having only known her for a few hours, but was again unsuccessful.

17 Zoroastrianism is thought to have originated with Zoroaster around the ninth or tenth century BC in Persia (modern-day Iran). It is monotheistic, but some schools emphasise a duality between good and evil. Other characteristics include after-death reward and punishment, and a day of divine judgement at the end of time.

18 Brinton, *Nietzsche*, p. 64. Frankly, it is comments like this which make one wonder why Brinton should spend time and effort in writing a biography of a man in whom he finds almost nothing to like or admire. *Ressentiment*, perhaps?

19 Brinton, *Nietzsche*, p. 71.

20 See Dr Leonard Sax, 'What Was the Cause of Nietzsche's Dementia?' *Journal of Medical Biography*, 11 (2003), pp. 47–54. Sax presents a well-argued case for a benign tumour (meningioma) behind the right eye, which not only would explain the migraines and the enlarged right pupil that Nietzsche suffered with through-out his life, but would also account for the gradual progression of the disease as the tumour developed. Sax's main argument is that the doctors who diagnosed him where unfamiliar with the patient's medical history, and took as recent developments certain symptoms which Nietzsche had actually displayed for most of his life. Sax also shows how, in fact, not only is the diagnosis a shaky one, but also that the only other piece of 'evidence' that suggests Nietzsche had syphilis – a rumour that he was treated by doctors for it in his student days – does not have any support. There is no documentation or record that states that Nietzsche had such treatment, nor even that any doctor at all treated anyone by the name of 'Nietzsche' at the time and place it was meant to have occurred (i.e., during his student days in Leipzig).

21 Nietzsche's opinion on these matters is summed up in section 241 (Part Eight), where both attitudes are expressed in terms of the conversation of two patriots.

22 This should not be confused with the book of this title which Nietzsche's sister published after his death, and which represents a somewhat distorted and heavily edited selection from Nietzsche's unpublished *Nachlass* (notebooks). For a more detailed account of the *Will to Power* project, see, for example, Hollingdale, *Nietzsche*, pp. 166–72.

23 For instance, Safranski, *Nietzsche: A Philosophical Biography*, pp. 285–6.

24 Hollingdale, *BGE*, 'Translator's Note', p. 27.

25 Michael Tanner, *BGE*, 'Introduction' to Penguin translation, p. 7.

2 Explanation and Summary of the Main Arguments

1 Throughout the book I will make reference to 'most philosophers' or Nietzsche's attitude to them. However, it should be borne in mind that Nietzsche's acquain-tance with philosophy obviously ends somewhere in 1889, and subsequent phi-losophers (who have been very influenced by his ideas) may therefore not be open to similar criticisms. So, whilst some of Nietzsche's criticisms may still apply to some modern philosophers, it should not be assumed that he is any longer alone in holding such views.

2 In the story of the Greek myth of Oedipus, the hero was the first person to answer a riddle posed by a terrible monster (the *Sphinx*) that had been terrorizing Athens. In solving the riddle, Oedipus freed the city of the curse and claimed the throne.

3 *BGE*, section 3, p. 35.

4 *BGE*, section 3, p. 35.

5 *BGE*, section 4, p. 36.

6 Incidentally, these examples are not from Nietzsche but are, I would say, in the spirit of Nietzsche – later, we will see the way in which he applies similar arguments to the notion of 'self'.

7 Hence the modern use of the word *Epicurean* – though it is now generally used to signify someone who is devoted to sensuous enjoyment, especially of food and drink.

8 The conflict between Epicurus and Plato – who were contemporaries – parallels the conflict between a non-moral, scientific interpretation of the world (Epicurus held, with Democritus, that the world consisted of atoms), and a moral/religious interpretation of life. The implication is that Plato 'won' because he was a 'better actor' – i.e. that he could present a more attractive case to the audience (the common majority). In his bitterness, Epicurus is merely pointing mockingly to this fact. See Laurence Lampert, *Nietzsche's Task: An Interpretation of 'Beyond Good and Evil'* (New Haven, CT: Yale University Press, 2001), pp. 32–5.

9 The medieval Mystery and Miracle plays developed from the tenth to the sixteenth century in Europe, and were a popular form of entertainment, dramatising biblical stories in church, often with accompanying music.

10 *BGE*, section 9, p. 39.

11 Isaiah 11.6 (note: all biblical quotes are from the King James version). For some reason, this passage is often misquoted as 'the lion shall lie down with the lamb'. The full passage actually reads: "The wolf also shall dwell with the lamb, and the leopard shall lie down with the kid; and the calf and the young lion and the fatling together; and a little child shall lead them."

12 See the section on the sixth philosophical prejudice, 'Immediate Certainty', in Chapter 3.

13 *BGE*, section 11, p. 42.

14 "Sensualism" as used here should not be confused with 'sensuality'. Nietzsche uses the former term to mean a scientific emphasis on material fact (the evidence of the senses), whereas the latter commonly refers to an enjoyment of sense experience or sexual pleasure.

15 See Lampert, *Nietzsche's Task*, pp. 43–5.

16 There is also a hint here of Nietzsche's doctrine of the master and slave moralities: the senses are "plebeian" and "a mob", whereas the attempt to control them and impose a purpose and meaning on experience is considered "noble". I will return to this in more detail later.

17 The debate concerning the degree to which our knowledge of the world is socially determined – or whether it can ever be considered 'objective' – is a still-raging one, and has generally become known as 'the science wars'. For instance, see Ziauddin Sardar, *Thomas Kuhn and the Science Wars* (London: Icon Books, 2000).

18 See René Descartes, *Meditations on First Philosophy*, Meditations 1 to 3.

19 As an aside here, and somewhat in support of Nietzsche, we should remember that he is not the first to question this notion of "immediate certainty". In relation to the notion of cause and effect, for example, the Scottish philosopher David Hume made a similar point when he argued that our sole knowledge of cause and effect comes from experience (i.e. of seeing one thing 'cause' another many times over in "constant conjunction"), and that there is not (as philosophers such as Descartes claimed) an absolutely "necessary connection" involved (or at least, none that we can identify with any certainty). Nietzsche's point here – though maybe not Hume's – is that seeing the world in terms of 'cause and effect' is not something that is dictated by the way the world is, but is rather something which is *useful* to us (and that it might be possible to see things differently). This is a subtle point, and one which I shall return to in more detail later. (For Hume's argument regarding cause and effect, see *An Enquiry Concerning Human Understanding*, sections IV to VII inclusive.)

20 *BGE*, section 19, p. 49.

21 *BGE*, section 19, p. 48.

22 *BGE*, section 19, p. 49.

23 The Ural–Altaic language family is a hypothetical group of languages thought to be the basis of the languages of Asia ('Altaic') and certain parts of Europe ('Uralic'). Altaic languages include Turkic, Mongolic, Tungusic, Manchusic, Japanese and Korean, whilst Uralic languages include Finnish, Hungarian, Estonian and Lappish. German would share a language family with most European languages (such as French, Italian, Spanish, etc.), but also with Latin, Greek, Indian (Sanskrit) and Persian. However, there is dispute among modern linguistic scholars as to the correctness of these language groupings (though this does not invalidate Nietzsche's main point concerning the relation between philosophical ideas and the grammar of a language).

24 It should also be noted that Nietzsche here does not seem to make a clear distinction between 'language' and 'ideas', and in fact implies that the limits of our language *are* the limits of our ideas (this is something that the twentieth-century German philosopher Ludwig Wittgenstein would have agreed with, and may be considered an aspect of *idealism*).

25 *BGE*, section 21, p. 51.

26 Here Nietzsche is showing himself to be what we might term an *anti-realist* in terms of our view of the world. That is, he is arguing that the concepts which we use to describe the world are themselves independent of the world, and therefore might conceivably be different. This is different to a *realist* position, which would argue that our concepts explain and accurately describe the world and – though we may occasionally be mistaken – there is no element of 'choice' in establishing them. I will return to this topic in a later section.

27 As Lampert points out, "once again" would seem to imply that philosophy and the sciences *were* once on the right road to answers to these questions (i.e. avoiding dogma and practising a sort of psychological analysis). Lampert suggests that this period was that of the "Greek enlightenment and the philosophers of the tragic age of the Greeks", which was ended by "Platonic dogmatism". See *Nietzsche's Task*, p. 60.

28 *BGE*, section 23, p. 53.

29 In different commentaries on Nietzsche, and in different translations, different terms are sometimes used to refer to these three stages (e.g. 'ultramoral' for 'extra-moral').

30 *BGE*, Hollingdale's translation, note to section 35, p. 228.

31 It should be noted that 'idealism' can mean different things, and that Berkeley and Schopenhauer are different types of idealists.

32 *BGE*, Hollingdale's translation, note to section 39, p. 229.

33 *BGE*, section 46, p. 75.

34 So, in seeking to prove that the mind existed, could exist separately from the body, etc., Descartes was arguably looking to provide philosophical support to Christian religious doctrine.

35 In the original edition of *BGE*, the numbering of two sections (65 and 73) was duplicated. In modern editions, the two later sections have therefore been renumbered '65a' and '73a' respectively.

36 Section 150 is not actually about religion (as you might think), but rather about what should be the free spirit's attitude to life; if he were a God, then all that surrounds him would be a . . . *comedy*, Lampert suggests (p. 142).

37 In section 181, Nietzsche suggests that, "It is inhuman to bless where one is cursed", implying that the new philosopher may occasionally do just that (i.e. value negative experiences).

38 *BGE*, section 186, p. 109.

39 See, for example, *Twilight of the Idols*, 'The Problem of Socrates', where Socrates is presented as "ugly", a "buffoon" and "rabble", and far from Plato's portrayal.

40 *BGE*, section 213, p. 146.

41 It is important to note that, whilst here and elsewhere I sometimes use such phrases as 'unconscious attitudes', Nietzsche himself did not speak in this way. So, whilst his ideas do seem to suggest something similar to our modern, popular usage of the term, it is debatable as to how similar his concept of irrational influences is to, for instance, Freud's concept of the unconscious.

42 *Thus Spoke Zarathustra*, Book I, 'On Reading and Writing', from *A Nietzsche Reader* (London: Penguin, 1977), translated by R. J. Hollingdale, p. 6.

43 *BGE*, section 225, p. 155.

44 I follow Lampert's threefold division here (see pp. 226–31), though it is possible to subdivide the drives in different ways. However, I don't think Nietzsche is aiming at a clear categorisation (seeing as the tendency to seek clear categorisations is in fact one of the tendencies he is criticising).

45 This is a difficult point to make clearly, but I think it is one of the most important and central concerns in the whole of *BGE* – and, in fact, in Nietzsche's philosophy. Basically, the problem lies in Nietzsche having denied that we can seek truth for its own sake. However, having shown how various philosophies are merely subconscious expressions of fundamental drives, he is left with a problem: what is the purpose of his own philosophy? How is he different? For either his philosophy fulfils some sort of drive, or else he would seem to be proposing that he is different in some way. However, this is a subtle point, and one which Nietzsche recognises, I think. Furthermore, I think the problem points the way to Nietzsche's conception of freedom and free thinking, for it is only when we are presented with such truly difficult problems that we are truly free. So, perhaps the answer lies in not being able to find a clear motivation for truth, because to find one would be to *fix* human nature, and, according to Aristotle (whom Nietzsche seems to have quoted favourably – see section 62, p. 88), "man is the animal whose nature has not yet been fixed" – or, potentially, *never can be.*

46 *BGE*, section 238, p. 166.

47 *BGE*, section 239, p. 167.

48 Hercules is the archetypal hero of Greek myth who was raised to the status of a demi-god after the completion of twelve tasks.

49 *BGE*, section 251, p. 181.

50 Lampert, *Nietzsche's Task*, pp. 255–6.

51 Obviously, Hume is Scottish, but I think Nietzsche is characterising British philosophy generally.

52 *BGE*, section 259, p. 194.

53 See Plato, *Gorgias* (London: Penguin Classics, 1960), section 470, pp. 55 and following.

54 *BGE*, section 260, p. 197.

55 See *BGE*, note to section 264 in the Hollingdale translation, p. 237.

56 Lampert, *Nietzsche's Task*, p. 279.

57 This point is made by Lampert, p. 281.

58 See, for example, the preface to the *Meditations*. Obviously, this is only an interpretation of Descartes's purposes, but it does serve to illustrate the point.

59 Johann Wolfgang Goethe, *Faust*, part II, final scene. Compare this also with Nietzsche's earlier discussion of another phrase from *Faust* in section 236: "the eternal womanly draws us upward". Here, once again, the ideal is 'up'.

3 Critical Themes

1 For general introductions to Nietzsche, see 'Bibliography and Suggested Reading'.

2   *BGE*, section 5, p. 37.
3   Incidentally, Hume's scepticism here is not to do with the existence of necessary cause and effect relationships – as is sometimes thought – but rather concerning *our knowledge* of them. So, in all other respects, Hume seems to have held the same beliefs regarding causation as most people.
4   *BGE*, section 11, p. 42.
5   *The Will to Power*, section 481 (1883–8).
6   William R. Schroeder, *Continental Philosophy: A Critical Approach* (Oxford: Blackwell Publishing, 2005), pp. 360–1.
7   John Gribbin, *In Search of Schrödinger's Cat* (London: Black Swan, 1984), pp. 19–22. The final proof came in 1905, with Einstein's paper on Brownian motion (see Gribbin, pp. 22-4).
8   *BGE*, section 12, p. 43.
9   Gribbin, *In Search of Schrödinger's Cat*, p. 34.
10 Gilbert Ryle, *The Concept of Mind* (London: Penguin, 1949), pp. 17–18.
11 See, for instance, Hume's *An Enquiry Concerning Human Understanding*, Section XI.
12 It should be noted here that Darwin himself did not think in terms of 'genetics', but simply in terms of inherited traits. The modern notion of genetic inheritance is a later synthesis of Darwinism with subsequent discoveries.
13 Robert C. Solomon and Kathleen M. Higgins, *What Nietzsche Really Said* (New York: Random House, 2000), p. 172.
14 Solomon and Higgins, *What Nietzsche Really Said*, pp. 171–2.
15 *BGE*, section 17, p. 47.
16 For the understanding of Kant outlined here, I am indebted to Sebastian Gardner's excellent *Kant and the Critique of Pure Reason* (London: Routledge, 1999), pp. 51–63.
17 *BGE*, section 11, p. 42.
18 This example is borrowed from Adam Morton's *A Guide through the Theory of Knowledge* (Oxford: Blackwell Publishing, 2003), p. 30 ('Experiment 4: Wise Babies'), where it is discussed in more detail than I have provided here.
19 Steven Pinker, *The Language Instinct* (London: Penguin Books, 1994), p. 19.
20 Wilfrid Sellars, *Empiricism and the Philosophy of Mind* (Cambridge, MA: Harvard University Press, 1997), p. 33.
21 William P. Alston, 'Sellars and the "Myth of the Given"', *Philosophy and Phenomenological Research*, 65 (2002), pp. 69–86.
22 *BGE*, section 21, p. 51.
23 Actually, in relation to the idea of the creation of the world, the problem does not simply go away if we adopt atheism, for we still have to account for the fact that either (a) the world has always existed (and there would be an infinite string of causation), or (b) the world appeared out of nothing. Either way, the situation is quite difficult to conceptualise. Incidentally, Kant cited this type of problem

as concerning things that were 'transcendental', and therefore beyond the under-standing of the human intellect.

24 Laplace conjectured that if a mind existed that could know all the forces and laws that governed events, and the actual constitution of the world, then such a mind could predict the future exactly. This scenario is often referred to as 'Laplace's demon' (because, obviously, such a mind would need to be superhuman).

25 According to the so-called 'Copenhagen interpretation' put forward by physicists Niels Bohr and Werner Heisenberg, there is a limit to what we can know about subatomic particles (the famous 'uncertainty principle'). So, for instance, at any one time we may only be able to know with relative certainty the position of a particle, but not its momentum (or its momentum, but not its position). See Gribbin, *In Search of Schrödinger's Cat*, pp. 119–20.

26 *BGE*, section 21, p. 51.

27 *BGE*, section 21, p. 51.

28 *BGE*, section 19, p. 49.

29 *BGE*, section 19, p. 49.

30 Richard Schacht, *The Arguments of the Philosophers: Nietzsche* (London: Routledge & Kegan Paul, 1983), pp. 304–9.

31 It may not be too fanciful to compare Nietzsche's attitude to certain strands of Buddhism, where the overcoming of desire is seen as a means to liberation or 'enlightenment'.

32 Nietzsche actually speaks of our tendency to "naturalize", but I have used 'reify' and 'reification' instead so as not to create a confusion with Nietzsche's *naturalism*.

33 Notice, here, that I say '*mind-independent* reality'. This is an important term, because – traditionally – the role played by the mind in understanding reality is occasionally a distorting one: we interpret reality, and we sometimes get things wrong. However, some philosophers argue that it is impossible for us to *get things right*. For such people (e.g. Kant), even though reality exists, we will not ever be able to comprehend it fully. For Nietzsche, however, there only exist interpretations.

34 *The Concise Routledge Encyclopaedia of Philosophy* (London: Routledge, 2000), entry on 'Gorgias', pp. 322–3.

35 Nietzsche, *Twilight of the Idols* (London: Penguin Books, 1990), 'How the "Real World" at Last Became a Myth', pp. 50–1.

36 *Twilight of the Idols*, 'How the "Real World" at Last Became a Myth', p. 51.

37 *BGE*, section 231, pp. 162–3.

38 *BGE*, section 249, p. 180.

39 Schacht, *The Arguments of the Philosophers: Nietzsche*, p. 125.

40 Curiously, Frazer himself was a Christian, so his rejection of superstition was merely restricted to primitive belief and magic. Also, since the work was first

published in 1890 (the year following Nietzsche's descent into madness), Nietzsche can certainly be said to have formed his opinions on this matter independently of Frazer.

41   Schacht, *The Arguments of the Philosophers: Nietzsche*, p. 126.

42   Schacht, *The Arguments of the Philosophers: Nietzsche*, p. 126. It should be noted that this has nothing to do with genes in the biological sense.

43   Ludwig Wittgenstein, *Remarks on Frazer's Golden Bough* (Retford: Brynmill Press, 1993).

44   See, for example, D. Z. Phillips, *Wittgenstein and Religion* (New York: St. Martin's Press, 1993).

45   I Peter 2.2.

46   The words come from 'Guide me, Oh thou Great Redeemer', an English translation by Peter Williams (1727–96) of the Welsh hymn, '*Arglwydd, arwain trwy'r anialwch*', by William Williams (1717–91). It is usually sung to the tune 'Cwm Rhondda', composed by John Hughes (1873–1932), and is therefore usually known by this title; however, since it is a favourite of Welsh rugby supporters – who can mostly only remember the refrain of the first verse – it is also commonly known as 'Bread of Heaven'.

47   William James, *The Varieties of Religious Experience* (London: Signet Classic, 2003), n. 1, p. 13.

48   *BGE*, section 175, p. 106.

49   Matthew 5.3.

50   Matthew 5.5.

51   Matthew 5.38–39.

52   Matthew 5.44.

53   *BGE*, section 10, p. 40.

54   Nietzsche, *The Gay Science* (New York: Random House, 1974), translated by Walter Kaufmann, section 125, p. 181.

55   The term 'paganism' is perhaps not the best one, but I use it here to refer to those indigenous religious practices which pre-date Christianity, and which therefore were marginalised and denigrated in the rise of monotheism generally.

56   *The Gay Science*, section 341, p. 273.

57   *The Gay Science*, section 341, p. 274.

58   *The Gay Science*, section 108, p. 167, quoted in Schacht, *The Arguments of the Philosophers: Nietzsche*, p. 119.

59   *The Gay Science*, section 125, p. 181.

60   There has been much debate about the exact translation of *Übermensch* into English. 'Superman' was the first English translation, but has been criticised for its distortion of the meaning of the word, and for its association with the comic book character. Walter Kaufmann's 1950's translation was 'Overman', and whilst some translators prefer this, others (e.g. Hollingdale) simply use the original German term instead.

61   Nietzsche's work by that name is sometimes translated as *The Anti-Christ*, which, I feel, gives it a misleading significance for some readers.

62   Nietzsche is not alone in adopting this type of stance to Christianity. For instance, the occultist Aleister Crowley (1875–1947) styled himself 'the Great Beast 666' to express his opposition to Christianity and what he saw as its life-denying influence. Incidentally, Crowley, like many other religious thinkers of that time (see the discussion of Theosophy below), may have been influenced by Nietzsche's ideas.

63   *Thus Spoke Zarathustra*, section 4.

64   Aryel Sanat, *The Inner Life of Krishnamurti* (Wheaton, IL: Quest Books, 1999), pp. 11–14. Interestingly, just to reinforce the point of the extent of Nietzsche's influence in these circles, one of the foremost Theosophists, Rudolf Steiner (who founded the Steiner schools, among other things), met Nietzsche (albeit after his collapse), and wrote a book (translated as *Nietzsche: Fighter for Freedom*) and some articles about him (Sanat, p. 14). Steiner seems to have been hugely impressed by Nietzsche, although he said he did not wholly share Nietzsche's world view.

65   Sartre's ideas owe much to Nietzsche and to Martin Heidegger (who was himself much influenced by Nietzsche).

66   Colin Wilson, *The Outsider* (London: Orion Books, 1967), p. 122. Wilson dedicates half of Chapter 5 to a discussion of Nietzsche (pp. 121–46).

67   Wilson, *The Outsider*, pp. 126–7.

68   *BGE*, section 295, p. 220.

69   I-hsüan, *The Zen Teachings of Master Lin-Chi: A Translation of the Lin-chi lu*, translated by Burton Watson (New York: Columbia University Press, 1999), Section 19, p. 52.

70   Wilson, *The Outsider*, p. 135.

71   Wilson, *The Outsider*, p. 135.

72   Lesley Chamberlain, *Nietzsche in Turin* (London: Quartet Books, 1996), p. 9.

73   John Gray, *Straw Dogs* (London: Granta, 2002), p. 45. Gray dedicates a short section to Nietzsche (see pp. 44–8).

74   Gray, *Straw Dogs*, p. 48.

75   I'm sorry, I couldn't resist the pun. A 'straw man' argument is where a view is misrepresented or distorted in order to find fault with it. I am not, of course, arguing that Gray has done this deliberately, but merely questioning his view of Nietzsche. By the way, *Straw Dogs* is a fascinating, well-argued and provocative book, and highly recommended.

76   Nietzsche, *On the Genealogy of Morals* (New York: Vintage Books, 1967), translated by Walter Kaufmann and R. J. Hollingdale, 'First Essay: "Good and Evil", "Good and Bad"', Section 13, pp. 44–5.

77   *On the Genealogy of Morals*, 'First Essay: "Good and Evil", "Good and Bad"', Section 13, p. 45.

78   William Blake, *The Marriage of Heaven and Hell*, 'A Memorable Fancy'.

79   Barbara Von Eckardt, 'Can Intuitive Proof Suffice?', from *Unauthorized Freud*, edited by Frederick Crews (London: Penguin, 1998), Chapter 9, p. 109.

80   *BGE*, section 13, p. 44.

81   Solomon and Higgins, *What Nietzsche Really Said*, pp. 77–8.

82   H. James Birx, 'Nietzsche, Darwin & Evolution', Hawai'i International Conference on Arts and Humanities, 12–15 January 2003, p. 5.

83   John S. Moore, 'Nietzsche's Anti-Darwin', 11th annual conference of the Friedrich Nietzsche Society, Emmanuel College Cambridge, 8 September 2001.

84   For a discussion of Nietzsche, Darwin and Lamarck, see Nickolas Pappas, *The Nietzsche Disappointment: Reckoning with Nietzsche's Unkept Promises on Origins and Outcomes* (Oxford: Rowman and Littlefield, 2005), chapter 4, pp. 181–216.

85   From the first edition of *Origin of Species*, quoted in Moore, 'Nietzsche's Anti-Darwin'.

86   From the first edition of *Origin of Species*, quoted in Moore, 'Nietzsche's Anti-Darwin'.

87   This is not to say that Nietzsche's views have not been influential, and there is a growing interest in the application of his ideas to philosophy of science. See, for instance, Babette Babich and Robert S. Cohen (eds), *Nietzsche, Epistemology, and Philosophy of Science: Nietzsche and the Sciences II* (Dordrecht: Springer, 1999). For studies of influences of scientific and other contemporary thinkers upon Nietzsche, see Robin Small, *Nietzsche in Context* (Aldershot: Ashgate, 2001), and Gregory Moore and Thomas H. Brobjer (eds), *Nietzsche and Science* (Aldershot: Ashgate, 2004).

Glossary

1   The cosmological argument can take a number of different forms, but essentially argues that 'nothing can come from nothing' and that there cannot exist a string of infinite cause-and-effect relationships. Therefore, the 'first cause' of everything was God Himself.

2   Nietzsche, *The Birth of Tragedy*, see sections 13 and 14.

Glossary

I have tried here to define most of the terms in this book that may be unfamiliar to readers, or else are in some way difficult, and whose meaning may need to be checked occasionally. I have also included brief sketches of the philosophers and key thinkers mentioned (listed by surname), important ideas, philosophies and historical events. Words and phrases which appear in the definition in *italics* indicate a cross-reference to another definition. Finally, next to most of the definitions, I have tried to list the sections in Nietzsche's text where those things are discussed. However, I haven't included any sections from Part Four ('Maxims and Interludes') in these lists, partly because I have already grouped these aphorisms according to theme in my summary of that chapter, but also because I felt it would clutter up the lists too much. Lastly, where the word or phrase begins with 'the', this does not affect the alphabetical order (so *the religious neurosis* can be found after *relativism*).

Word or phrase	Definition
a posteriori	From the Latin, 'that which comes after', referring to statements or truths which are based on experience, and which therefore may prove otherwise.
a priori	From the Latin, 'that which comes before', referring to statements or truths which are true independent of experience, and which it would be self-contradictory to deny.
ad hominem argument	A type of critical argument where the attack is aimed at the person himself rather than the views he holds. Therefore, it is commonly considered an invalid form of reasoning (though Nietzsche uses it for specific purposes).

amor fati	Latin: 'love of fate'. Nietzsche uses this term to describe the most life-affirming attitude that one can hold (i.e. to say 'Yes' to everything without wishing to change it). See also *eternal return*.
analytic	*Kant*'s term for statements which are true by virtue of the meaning of the terms involved (e.g. 'all bachelors are unmarried men'). See also *Kant*, *synthetic* and *synthetic a priori*.
anarchy	The political view that an ideal society could be achieved if there were an absence of state control. More loosely, the term is also often used as a synonym for chaos or lawlessness. See sections 202 and 242.
anthropomorphism	The tendency to depict non-human things (gods, animals, nature, etc.) as having human characteristics. More generally, the tendency to understand things in human-centred terms.
the Anti-Christian	Nietzsche's term for himself and his views as seen in opposition to Christianity, and an alternative translation of the title of his later work *The Anti-Christ*).
anti-realism	A general term for the view that *realism* is in some way false, and that there is no independently existing, absolutely objective reality (a form of which is held by Nietzsche).
appearance and reality	The 3rd philosophical prejudice. Nietzsche's criticism of the idea that we can clearly distinguish between what 'appears' to be the case (our experience) and what 'actually' is the case (reality). Associated with such philosophers as *Kant* and *Plato*. See sections 10–11, 14–15, and also *positivism*, *realism*, *anti-realism*, *naive realism* and *representative realism*.
Apollonian	Nietzsche's term for the tendency in human nature to measure, control and order experience. As such it is primarily rational. See *Dionysian*.
atomism	The 4th philosophical prejudice. The theory that everything which exists in the universe is actually composed of minute particles, or 'atoms' (from the Greek *atomos*, meaning 'that which cannot be divided'). The theory is generally traced back to the Greek philosopher Democritus (*c.*460–*c.*370 BC). However, Nietzsche argues that this idea is not only confined to science, and that there is a tendency amongst philosophers – and people in

182

general – to think *atomistically* (i.e. as if there is a centre or cause to every thing or event). This is also reflected in the way our language is structured. See sections 12, 17, 20, 32 and 34.

Ayer
Alfred Jules Ayer (1910–89), English philosopher who, in his early career, was associated with the *logical positivist* movement. In his most famous work, *Language, Truth and Logic*, he sets out his criteria for meaning (the verification principle), one of the consequences of which is to render most philosophical discussion in the fields of ethics, metaphysics and aesthetics (as well as other areas of philosophy) as having no real logical significance. See also *positivism*.

Bacon
Sir Francis Bacon (1561–1626), English empiricist philosopher, essayist and statesman. Bacon is seen as a foremost influence upon the scientific revolution. Nietzsche considers him typical of English philosophers, who have had a formative influence upon *modern ideas*. See sections 252 and 283 and *empiricism*.

Beethoven
Ludwig van Beethoven (1770–1827), German composer. Nietzsche sees him as representing a transition from the classical age to the modern, and believes that appreciation of his music will not last as long as that of *Mozart*. See section 245.

Bentham
See *utilitarianism*.

Bizet
Georges Bizet (1838–75), French romantic composer. Nietzsche considers him to provide an ideal synthesis between passion and intellect – between northern (*Apollonian*) and southern (*Dionysian*) traits – and held his opera *Carmen* in high esteem. See section 254.

Boscovich
Roger Joseph Boscovich (1711–87) was actually born in what would now be Croatia (and not Poland, as Nietzsche thinks). He had a wide range of interests, including physics, astronomy, mathematics, philosophy and poetry, but is now mostly remembered for the atomic theory which Nietzsche refers to in *BGE*. Boscovich's theory moved away from traditional atomistic thinking by describing atomic structure in terms of 'forces', allowing for a picture that did not rely on the search for minute, indivisible particles. See section 12, and also *atomism*.

Bruno	Giordano Bruno (1548–1600), Renaissance Italian philosopher. He was burnt at the stake by the Catholic Church (the Inquisition) for holding views that they considered heretical. Nietzsche sees him, along with Spinoza, as a type of philosophical recluse, whose philosophy is a sort of revenge upon a world that has rejected him. See section 25.
Buddhism	Nietzsche sees in Buddhist religion the same life-denying tendency that is to be found in Christianity and Judaism. See section 56.
causa sui	The 7th philosophical prejudice. From the Latin phrase meaning 'cause of itself', this is a concept used to argue that free will is possible if we accept the existence of an 'uncaused cause' (a concept which is also used in the *cosmological argument* for the existence of God).[1] However, for Nietzsche, as with the notion of *immediate certainty*, the concept is a 'myth' which has been created by philosophers who feel threatened by the idea of determinism (i.e. that all our actions are caused) and the possibility that there is no such thing as free will. See section 21.
the Cogito	From the Latin phrase *cogito ergo sum*, 'I think, therefore I am'. Refers to the argument first put forward by *Descartes*, who argued that it must be at least certain that I exist, because even to be deceived about that fact, one must be thinking, and something that is thinking must at least exist. As such, it is a type of *immediate certainty*. See sections 16–17, and also *Descartes* and *foundationalism*.
compatibilism	The view, held by such as David Hume (and arguably Nietzsche himself), that free will is in some way compatible with the idea that all our actions are caused. See sections 18–19, and also *determinism*, *libertarianism* and *causa sui*.
consequentialism	A general term for moral theories which hold that the consequences of an action are what give them moral significance (e.g. *utilitarianism*). Nietzsche sees this as a defining characteristic of the *pre-moral* stage of human ethical development. See section 32, *pre-moral, moral and extra-moral* and *intentionalism*.
Copernicus	Nicolaus Copernicus (1473–1543), Polish astronomer who formulated the first modern theory proposing that the

184

Earth orbited the Sun (heliocentrism), and not vice versa, as the Ptolemaic system pictured it (geocentrism). See section 12.

cosmological argument
A general term for various forms of argument that seek to prove the existence of God by argument from effect to cause (e.g. that the universe must have been caused by something, and that must be an uncaused cause – i.e. God). See also *causa sui*.

the critic
Nietzsche uses the term to characterise an aspect of the new philosopher (*free spirit*). The critic has clear ideas of what is 'good' and 'bad', and will not be afraid to pass judgement on things. However, unlike the critic, the free spirit will also be critical of his own values. See section 210.

cruelty
Nietzsche sees cruelty (slavery, domination, hardness of heart) as an essential component of civilisation – and of the true philosopher himself. Ultimately, such cruelty is the basis of discipline, and is used by the philosopher against himself. See sections 229–30 and 260, and also *pathos of distance*, *suffering* and *self-overcoming*.

cynicism
Historically, 'Cynic' is a term generally used to describe one of a number of early Greek philosophers who rejected social values and proposed that we can live more ethically – and truthfully – by returning to a simpler, more natural state. So, the Cynic considered most pleasures and social refinements as means whereby our true nature – as human animals – was corrupted. So, in a similar way, but in the modern sense, someone who is 'cynical' about something is usually arguing that what appear to be high, moral motives are in fact driven by baser, more selfish desires. See section 26.

Darwin
Sir Charles Darwin (1809–1882), English scientist and joint originator (with Alfred Russel Wallace, 1823–1913) of the theory of evolution by *natural selection* (*survival of the fittest*). The theory proposes that, because different environments will favour some kinds of creatures over others, through breeding and variation of inherited traits, some creatures will be more suited ('fit') than others for that environment, and so will survive. Moreover, 'fitness' is not necessarily to do with strength or dominance, but simply whether a creature's qualities will enable it to

	survive in a certain place. Nietzsche is in sympathy with some of Darwin's theory, but ultimately sees it as a mechanistic view of nature. See sections 13, 62, 213 and 253, and also *mechanism* and *survival of the fittest*.
Descartes	René Descartes (1596–1650), French rationalist philosopher, most famous for his counter-sceptical arguments, and the observation, 'I think, therefore I am' (see *the Cogito*). Nietzsche sees his philosophy as embodying certain philosophical prejudices, notably that of *immediate certainty* and *atomism*. See sections 16–17, 34, 54, 191 and 283, and *rationalism*.
design argument	A general term for an argument for the existence of God which argues that certain features of the universe imply that it was created or designed, and that therefore there must exist a 'designer' (i.e. God). Also known as the 'teleological argument'.
determinism	The view that we do not possess free will, and that our actions, attitudes, behaviour, etc. are all determined by physical factors (such as biological inheritance – or genes). See sections 18–19, and also *libertarianism* and *compatibilism*.
Dionysian	Nietzsche's term for the human tendency to embrace experience and lose oneself in participation. As such, it is primarily irrational, emotional and instinctive. See section 295, and also *Apollonian*.
dogmatism	Nietzsche's characterisation of past philosophers as basing their philosophies on unexplored (and sometimes unconscious) beliefs. These take the form of *philosophical prejudices*. See especially Part One (sections 1–23).
empiricism	The general philosophical view that all our ideas can be traced back to sense experience. So, in contrast to *rationalism*, empiricism generally denies that there are such things as innate ideas, or *a priori* truths which tell us something new about the world (as *Descartes* thought); rather, the mind is a *tabula rasa* or 'blank slate', upon which experience 'writes'. See also *Bacon, Hume, Locke, modern ideas* and *positivism*.
the Enlightenment	The so-called Age of Enlightenment was a period spanning from the middle of the seventeenth century to the beginning of the nineteenth. It was characterised by an emphasis upon the importance of rational thought (as

	opposed to faith), and principles of equality and freedom. Nietzsche sees it as a formative period for *modern ideas*. Note: this is not to be confused with the Buddhist use of the term 'enlightenment' to signify a state of spiritual realisation. See also *Voltaire*.
Epicurus	Epicurus (341 BC–270 BC), ancient Greek philosopher and founder of Epicureanism. He advocated the attainment of a happy, peaceful life through moderation. Nietzsche sees in him a non-dogmatic kindred spirit. See sections 7–8 and 270.
eternal return/ recurrence	This is Nietzsche's ideal attitude to life, which imagines that we were to discover that our life was to be repeated, exact in every detail, over and over again for all eternity. What, he asks, would the reaction be to this of the most life-affirming optimist? His answer is that such a person would not seek to change any aspect of their experience, but would rather ask for it again *exactly as it was*. See section 56, and also *suffering* and *tragedy and comedy*.
ethical naturalism	See *naturalism*.
eugenics	The name commonly given to the belief that our character, intelligence, etc. are linked to our genes, and that therefore to produce 'higher' forms of human being (e.g. more moral, intelligent, etc.), we must breed the best ones together (as we might breed race horses to produce a Derby winner). As such, Nietzsche's views would seem to fit with this view. Incidentally, Plato is also considered a eugenicist in that he believed breeding to be more important than education. See sections 190, 213, 219, 251 and 262.
existentialism	Philosophical movement which came to prominence in the mid-twentieth century, characterised by the assertions that life is essentially absurd, there is no inherent meaning, and that we must create our own authentic morality. Foremost existentialists include Jean-Paul Sartre (1905–80), Albert Camus (1913–60) and Karl Jaspers (1883–1969). For the above reasons, Nietzsche is often considered a forerunner of existentialism, along with the Danish philosopher Søren Kierkegaard (1813–55).
faith in antithetical values	The 2nd philosophical prejudice. Nietzsche's term for the belief that a great many philosophers and religious thinkers seem to hold that certain important ideas have no

187

relation to their opposites (antitheses), and therefore must have some separate origin. See sections 2, 3 and 47.

foundationalism The belief that knowledge must rely on more primitive beliefs or experiences. However, unless these 'foundational beliefs' are certain, then the knowledge which is based on them may be doubted. See also *Descartes, the Cogito* and *immediate certainty*.

Frederick the Great Frederick II (1712–86), later known as Frederick the Great, ruled Prussia from 1740 until his death in 1786. From his youth, he seemed an unlikely ruler, preferring literature and the arts to politics (to the consternation of his stern and authoritarian father, who was renowned as a great soldier). However, on coming to power he surprised many by proving a great military leader – though he also became known as a great patron of the arts (being a friend and correspondent of the French philosopher *Voltaire*). Nietzsche sees in him a combination of *scepticism* and courage, which are essential characteristics for the new philosopher. See section 209.

free spirit Nietzsche's term for the new type of philosopher, characterised by lack of *dogmatism*, a desire to explore and create new values, and the courage to go beyond traditional morality and philosophy. He is therefore part *critic*, part *sceptic* and part *scholar*, but is also more than the sum of these parts. See the Preface, and sections 23, 24–44 (Part Two), 62, 203, 207, 210–11, 213–14, 224–7, 250, 253 and 280. See also *master morality, masks* and *suffering*.

French Revolution The French Revolution (1789–99) saw the abolition of the monarchy and the execution of many members of the aristocracy – including the then King and Queen. For Nietzsche, the event represents "the last great slave revolt", and he considered it one more step in the process of inverting noble values. See sections 38, 46, 239 and 258, and also *slave revolt in morals*.

Freud See *psychoanalysis*.

gai saber A phrase used by the French medieval Provençal poets (the 'troubadours') to describe the art of love poetry (literally, 'joyful knowledge'). It is used by Nietzsche to refer to the ideal attitude to life and philosophy, a blend of knowledge and life-affirmation. It also forms the basis for the title of his book, *The Gay Science*. See section 293.

genetic fallacy	An invalid form of argument in which a view or idea is held to be incorrect because of its origins. For example, Nietzsche's view that religious ideas are a form of *projection* (which, even if true, does not conclusively prove that God doesn't exist).
the given	The idea that certain ideas are given to us as the basis of our experience of life (e.g. as *immediate certainties*, or even just as basic possibilities of experience – such as *Kant*'s notion of categories). This idea has been criticised by, among others, the American philosopher Wilfrid Sellars (1912–89), who called it the 'myth of the given'.
Goethe	Johann Wolfgang Goethe (1749–1832), German poet, dramatist and author. Nietzsche's attitude towards Goethe is slightly ambivalent: he mostly recognises him as a great man, a creative and life-affirming genius, and moreover a *good European*. However, he also recognises that Goethe is not an example of the new philosopher, and – like Wagner, and other great men – is the highest expression of traditional values which must be transcended. See sections 256 and 266.
good European	Nietzsche's characterisation of the new philosopher's attitude to politics and nationalism – i.e. one where patriotism is replaced by a broader European unity. See sections 241 and 256.
Hegel	Georg Wilhelm Friedrich Hegel (1770–1831), German philosopher. Nietzsche sees him, along with Kant, as an example of the type of philosopher who seeks to reduce truth to a series of formulas. See section 211.
herd morality	Nietzsche's term for the moral code of the common people. Furthermore, with the rise of democracy and other *modern ideas*, herd morality has become the norm. See also *slave revolt in morals*, *slave morality*, *master morality* and *modern ideas*, and also sections 62 and 199–203.
Hobbes	Thomas Hobbes (1588–1679), English political philosopher. In a small way, Nietzsche and Hobbes are quite close: they both see human actions as determined by self-interest. However, whilst Hobbes proposed traditional Christian morality to keep this self-interest in check, Nietzsche sees morality as stemming *from* it (the *will to power*). See section 294.

Hume	David Hume (1711–76), Scottish empiricist philosopher. Along with *Locke* and *Bacon*, Nietzsche sees Hume as an example of practical, unimaginative 'English' philosophy. See section 252 and *empiricism*.
idealism	Generally, the range of philosophical positions that consider knowledge of reality to rest on the perception of ideas (e.g. Plato and Kant). In extreme cases – such as the idealism of Irish philosopher George Berkeley (1685–1753) – it is even argued that ideas are the *only* things which exist. See sections 11 and 15.
immediate certainty	The 6th philosophical prejudice. Because it is always possible to question *why* something is true, a great many philosophers have sought to defend themselves against sceptical arguments by seeking to establish certain things which are beyond doubt. However, the only way this can be achieved is if these truths do not in turn rely on anything else for their being true – that is, they are 'immediate certainties'. However, Nietzsche points out that, far from being absolutely or necessarily true, even these 'certainties' can be doubted and shown to rely on prior assumptions and beliefs (and which in turn could be otherwise). See sections 16–17, 34 and 281. See *the Cogito, Descartes, foundationalism* and *causa sui*.
intentionalism	A general term for moral theories which hold that the intentions behind an action are what give them moral significance (e.g. *Kant*'s moral theory). Nietzsche sees this as a defining characteristic of the *moral* (current) stage of human ethical development. See section 32, *pre-moral, moral and extra-moral* and *consequentialism*.
the Jesuits	The Society of Jesus, a Roman Catholic religious order founded by St Ignatius de Loyola (1491–1556). The Jesuits tried to reconcile changes in moral values in society (a move away from Christianity) with continued religious faith. Therefore, Nietzsche sees them as attempting to 'relax the tension' between reason and belief. See the Preface.
Julius Caesar	Julius Caesar (*c.*100 BC–44 BC), Roman general and first Emperor of Rome after the Roman Republic (sixth century BC to first century BC); assassinated by a group of political conspirators. Nietzsche sees in him an example of the man of "mixed inheritance" whose instincts are at war with one

another, but who through discipline and *self-overcoming* becomes a great man (see also *Leonardo da Vinci*) and section 200.

Kant Immanuel Kant (1724–1804), hugely influential German philosopher. Kant attempted to show that many types of judgement – including moral ones – were defined by the limits of human reason. As such, Nietzsche sees his philosophy as a prime example of the disguised *will to power*, based on *dogmatism*. See *synthetic a priori* and sections 10–11, 15, 54, 187 and 211.

the ladder of sacrifice The ladder of sacrifice is a consequence of the *religious neurosis*, where a person is driven to sacrifice more and more that they hold dear. Ultimately, Nietzsche argues, this results in atheism – the sacrifice of the idea of God itself. See *nihilism* and section 55.

Lamarckism This refers to the ideas of Jean-Baptiste Lamarck (1744–1829), a French naturalist, whose version of evolution posited that an organism's behaviour could affect the traits that it passed on – e.g. giraffes stretching their necks to reach leaves (as opposed to *Darwin*, who thought that physical traits were fixed, and unaffected by behaviour). Interestingly, Nietzsche seems closer to Lamarck than he does to Darwin – see sections 213 and 264.

Leonardo da Vinci Leonardo da Vinci (1452–1519), Italian Renaissance artist, often considered a genius for his wide-ranging interests and abilities. Considered by Nietzsche to be a man of "mixed inheritance" – see section 200, *Julius Caesar* and *self-overcoming*.

libertarianism The view that we have free will and that our decisions are not wholly determined by outside causes. See sections 18–19, and also *determinism*, *compatibilism* and *causa sui*.

Locke John Locke (1632–1704), English empiricist philosopher. In Nietzsche's eyes, grouped together with *Bacon* and *Hume* and seen as a formative influence on *modern ideas*. See section 252 and *empiricism*.

logical positivism The philosophical movement, begun in early twentieth-century Vienna, which sought to provide a logical basis for meaning (thus excluding such things as ethics, theology, etc.). See also *Ayer* and *positivism*.

Lutherism Refers to the movement associated with Martin Luther (1483–1546), German Christian theologian, whose writings inspired the Reformation, where the Protestant faith was formed by a breakaway from the main Catholic Church. See sections 46 and 247.

Madame de Guyon Jeanne-Marie Bouvier de la Motte-Guyon, most commonly known as Madame de Guyon (1648–1717), French Christian mystic and advocate of Quietism, a doctrine which proposes that the best approach to spiritual perfection is through passivity and intellectual submission. See section 50.

masks Nietzsche's idea that there exists a necessary 'mask' between the philosopher and the common man, and more generally between each individual and their true self. The higher man, Nietzsche argues, by the very fact that he is different, and has different tastes, to the common man, must wear a disguise in the face of people who cannot understand him. However, *because* they cannot understand him, he will have a mask anyway – whether created by himself, or provided by their misunderstanding. See sections 25, 40–1, 223, 244, 270, 278–9, 283–4 and 288–90, and *tragedy and comedy*.

master morality Nietzsche's term for the values which stem from the ruling class and aristocratic society in general. As such, it is characterised by pride, love of wealth, power, health and dominance. See sections 46, 242, 257–67, and also *slave morality*, *slave revolt in morals*, *order of rank* and *pathos of distance*.

mechanism The idea, associated with such philosophers as *Descartes* and *Hobbes*, and the scientist Isaac Newton, that nature (and the physical world in general) runs much like a machine (or mechanism). This may be contrasted with *vitalism*, which Nietzsche holds to, and which favours the idea that the world is in some way alive and 'vital'. See section 213.

Mendelssohn Felix Mendelssohn (1809–47), German Romantic composer, praised by Nietzsche for his light, uplifting music. See section 245.

metaphysics The term *metaphysics* actually comes from a description of the works of Aristotle, which were traditionally arranged by later commentators so that his works on natural science and physics (the *Physics*) came first, and his works dealing with such things as the existence and composition of the

soul, ethics, and so on, came after. These works (and
therefore the topics they described) were therefore known
as *ta meta ta physika* (Greek, 'after the physics').
Therefore, all discussions of morality, aesthetics
(philosophy of art and beauty) and theory of knowledge
are in a sense *metaphysical*. More specifically, metaphysical
ideas are those which assume that some sort of reality
exists separately from the physical world. In general,
Nietzsche is critical of metaphysical notions because they
are both unverifiable and *dogmatic*. See, for instance,
section 15, and *realism* and *anti-realism*.

Mill
John Stuart Mill (1806–73), English philosopher and
utilitarian. Refined the ideas of Jeremy Bentham (1748–32)
to allow for higher and lower forms of pleasure (called
'two-level utilitarianism'). Nietzsche classes him, along
with *Darwin* and *Spencer*, as representative of "respectable
but mediocre Englishmen", who may provide useful ideas,
but are not themselves men of genius. See section 253.

modern ideas
The collection of philosophies, movements and attitudes
that drove social change in Nietzsche's time (such as
positivism, *empiricism*, democracy, equal rights, and so
on). Nietzsche generally considered their influence to be
harmful, and to spring from the values of the common
man (*herd morality*). See sections 10, 58, 224, 239, 242,
252–4, 260, 262, and also *the scholar*, *positivism* and *herd
morality*.

morality as
timidity
Nietzsche's term for the tendency of temperate, mild-
mannered people to use morality to justify these qualities
– and to condemn and control those who do not follow it
(such as the "man of prey"). See sections 5, 197–8 and
260, and also *slave morality* and *slave revolt in morals*.

Mozart
Wolfgang Amadeus Mozart (1756–91), Austrian
composer. Considered by Nietzsche to represent the
flowering of the classical period, appreciation of whose
music would outlast that of *Beethoven*. See section 245.

naive realism
A general term for the view that we experience the world
as it really is. However, since this is difficult to defend, it is
often thought of as an uncritical or *naive* position. See also
realism, *anti-realism* and *appearance and reality*.

Napoleon
Napoleon Bonaparte (1769–1821), a general during the
French Revolution, conquered and united much of Europe,

ruled France as a republic, and later become Napoleon I, Emperor of the French; was deposed and exiled after defeat at the Battle of Waterloo. Considered by Nietzsche, along with *Wagner, Goethe* and *Schopenhauer,* to represent "great Europeans" – but of a type soon to be surpassed by the *free spirit.* See sections 199 and 256.

natural selection   The idea, stemming from *Darwin,* that creatures are 'selected' by natural factors to survive according to the possession of certain traits. So, for instance, on long flat plains, the faster creature will survive over the slower one (it will be selected to survive). This is also known as the *survival of the fittest* (thought 'fittest' here means 'most fit for their environment'). See also *Darwin, teleological explanation* and *will to power.*

naturalism   The general notion that human values and perspectives can best be understood in terms of biological and natural forces (as opposed to *metaphysical* reality). In this sense, Nietzsche's *will to power* may be seen as a naturalist account of morality (ethical naturalism).

the naturalistic fallacy   A term coined by the English philosopher G. E. Moore (1873–1958) to refer to the type of ethical mistake that he considered *ethical naturalists* often made (e.g. *utilitarianism*). Moore argued that we cannot define 'good' by reference to natural properties of actions (e.g. pleasure), because we can always ask whether certain pleasures are good (thus proving that good is a more fundamental concept). See also *naturalism.*

nihilism   The philosophical position that human life, and the world in which we live, has no inherent meaning, purpose or value (from the Latin *nihil,* 'nothing'). See section 31, and also *pessimism, scepticism* and *modern ideas.*

noumena   *Kant's* term for those aspects of a thing that exist beyond sense experience, and which cannot by definition be directly perceived. In other words, the 'thing in itself', as opposed to relative perceptions of it. See also *phenomena* and *appearance and redlity.*

objectivity   Because of his *perspectivism,* Nietzsche does not hold that complete objectivity is possible. However, in a limited way, he believes that we may achieve a kind of objectivity by becoming aware of our drives and instincts. Furthermore, he points out that certain types of individual

	are fitted for such objectivity in a limited way by the fact that their studies are not driven by any strong motive. See sections 1, 3, 5–6, 33, 39 and 206–7, *the scholar*, *will to ignorance* and *will to truth*.
Occam's razor	Also known as the 'principle of parsimony'. The idea, stemming from the fourteenth-century English philosopher William of Occam (*c*.1288–*c*.1347), that we should favour explanations that make as few assumptions as possible (are 'simpler').
order of rank	Nietzsche's idea that society has a natural order determined by the character of its members, where some are born to lead, and others to follow (to different degrees). See sections 219 and 228, and also *master morality* and *pathos of distance*.
the Overman	See *the Übermensch*
Pascal	Blaise Pascal (1623–62), seventeenth-century French philosopher and mathematician, best known for his collection of philosophical essays (the *Pensées*), and for various contributions to science and mathematics. Pascal is also famous for turning his back on his intellectual gifts following a religious experience, fearful that they would lead to sinful pride in his own knowledge. Nietzsche therefore sees him as representative of the "suicide of reason", which is the basis of a particular type of religious faith (an aspect of the *religious neurosis*). See section 46.
pathos of distance	Nietzsche's idea that the more sophisticated, higher type of man experiences his superiority as a feeling of distance between himself and those who are inferior to him. It is this feeling which therefore gives rise to the possibility of self-improvement or *self-overcoming* (as Nietzsche calls it). See section 257 and also *order of rank*.
perspectivism	The term generally given to Nietzsche's view that any notion of truth is only ultimately a *perspective*, and that, just as there can be no 'ultimate perspective', so there can be no absolute, objective truth. See the Preface, sections 3, 24, 34, and also *objectivity* and *relativism*.
pessimism	Generally, pessimism consists in the tendency to view life negatively and to emphasise the worst in human nature. However, in a philosophical sense – where it is often associated with *Schopenhauer* – it is the belief that an understanding of the true nature of the world is not one

that can ever make us happy. So, for example, the fact that humans are mortal, that there is pain and suffering, that individuals are really motivated by instinct instead of reason, etc., all suggest that the world has not been made for humanity (as many religious believers hold), but rather has a purpose of its own (if it has one at all) which is at odds with human interest. See sections 39, 56, 186, 207–8, 222, 254 and 260.

phenomena   *Kant's* term for those aspects of a thing that can be directly experienced and known, and which are therefore relative to human perception (and not the 'thing in itself'). See also *noumena* and *appearance and reality*.

philosophical prejudice   Nietzsche's idea that philosophers frequently rely upon unproven assumptions. In Part One, Nietzsche outlines eight of these: *the will to truth, faith in antithetical values,* distinction between *appearance and reality, atomism, teleological explanation, immediate certainty, causa sui* and *reification* (these are all listed in this glossary). See also *dogmatism.*

Plato   Plato (427 BC–347 BC), ancient Greek philosopher who believed that we could arrive at knowledge of the true nature of reality through direct apprehension of pre-existing ideas, which he called 'forms'. For Nietzsche, Plato is an example of the type of philosopher who distinguishes between *appearance and reality* in order to create a *metaphysical* basis for his own views. See the Preface, sections 7–10, 14, 28, 186 and 190–1, and also *idealism, realism* and *Socrates.*

positivism   The doctrine (based on *empiricism*) that true knowledge is only achievable through scientific method and the evidence of the senses. Positivism has its beginnings with Auguste Comte (1798–1857), a French thinker who first coined the term 'sociology'. Comte's positivism was mainly aimed at the study of social phenomena, but it has since been applied more generally to the scientific approach to knowledge. See sections 10, 14, 204 and also *modern ideas* and *sensualism.*

pragmatism   Specifically, a philosophical movement associated with the American philosophers William James (1842–1910), John Dewey (1859–1952) and C. S. Peirce (1839–1914). More generally, it is an attitude to truth, and philosophical and scientific enquiry which emphasises the importance of a theory's practical consequences. So, for instance, pragmatists might favour a theory based on whether it seems to 'work', and not because it can be shown to be absolutely certain.

pre-moral, moral and extra-moral Nietzsche's threefold classification of the history of morality: in the pre-moral stage, actions are good or bad depending on their consequences; in the moral stage, depending on their origin; but in the extra-moral stage – which Nietzsche argues we are entering – actions will be based on a conscious analysis and revaluation of our values. See section 32.

projection Generally, the process whereby psychological qualities (feelings, emotions, desires, etc.) are projected outwards onto some external thing. In Nietzsche's case, he sees most religious belief as a psychological projection. More specifically, in psychoanalysis, the theory that a person will project his own undesirable qualities onto another, externalising qualities that he fails to recognise in himself. (Note: 'projection' is not really a term that Nietzsche uses, and I am merely using it to describe his approach.)

psychoanalysis Psychoanalysis was a psychological movement which began in Vienna in the late part of the nineteenth century, coming to prominence shortly after Nietzsche's death. It is now generally associated with the writings of Sigmund Freud (1856–1939) and his followers, though many of its doctrines – such as the notion of the *unconscious mind* – are common also to other psychological schools. A psychoanalytic interpretation of motivation would look at the 'real', unconscious forces that govern our choices – in this way, whilst Nietzsche was not a psychoanalyst, some of his views are similar (and may even have influenced Freud).

rationalism The general philosophical view that true knowledge is based in some way upon rational certainty, and that it is reason that plays the primary role in philosophical enquiry. Unlike *empiricism*, rationalism therefore argues that we need some sort of rational guarantee for knowledge which is independent of experience – such as innate ideas or *a priori* principles. See also *Spinoza*, *Descartes* and *immediate certainty*.

realism	The view that there is a 'real' world which exists objectively behind our perceptions of it. Furthermore, because we do not (or cannot) perceive it directly (and *naive realism* is false), then we must rely on 'representations' of it (*representative realism*). See also *anti-realism* and *appearance and reality*.
reductio ad absurdum	From the Latin, 'reduction to the absurd'. A form of argument that attempts to show that the consequences of following a line of reasoning to its conclusion will eventually lead to an absurdity (i.e. a self-contradiction). See, for instance, section 15.
reification	The 8th philosophical prejudice. Nietzsche is critical of the scientific tendency to "naturalise" abstract concepts, and to treat them as if they are physical events. This tendency, he argues, is based on an ignorance of the fact that such concepts have actually been *created* by human beings, and that there would exist no 'causes' or 'effects' without our existence. See sections 21–2.
relativism	A general term for any philosophical position that holds that there is no absolute, objective truth, and that our views are only ever true 'relative' to other beliefs (which are themselves relative). Hence, Nietzsche may be considered a relativist in regard to morality and truth.
the religious neurosis	This term is used by Nietzsche to refer to what we generally think of as a common religious attitude (embodied in the persona of *the saint*). It is generally associated with fasting, solitude and celibacy, and – Nietzsche argues – promotes a negative, life-denying attitude to life (a "denial of the will"). See sections 47, 53, 55, and also *ladder of sacrifice*.
representative realism	See *realism*.
ressentiment	Nietzsche uses this term (from the French, 'resentment, jealousy') to describe the tendency of those who feel inferior or jealous of others to attribute the cause of those feelings to the unjust actions of others (e.g. 'slaves' considering their 'masters' evil). More generally, Nietzsche sees it as the basis for *slave morality*. See sections 187 and 219.
Romanticism	A general movement, spanning the end of the eighteenth century and the beginning of the nineteenth, characterised

	by a reaction against the *Enlightenment* emphasis on rationality in favour of emotional expression and a celebration of nature. See section 245.
the saint	Nietzsche sees the archetypal figure of the saint as an embodiment of the life-denying principles of Christianity and other religions. The saint gains power over himself and impresses others with his self-denial, but his ultimate attitude is unhealthy, and springs from *ressentiment* and the *slave morality*. See sections 47, 51, 55 and 271, and also *the ladder of sacrifice* and *the religious neurosis*.
St Augustine	St Augustine (354–430), Algerian-born Christian theologian, very influential in the formation of the early Christian church, and well known for his religious autobiography, *The Confessions*. See sections 50 and 200.
scepticism	The philosophical attitude that questions the possibility of knowledge and certainty. Nietzsche uses sceptical arguments as a means of criticising philosophical *dogmatism*, and he considers scepticism to play an essential role in the makeup of the new philosopher. However, it is not an end in itself, and can lead to "paralysis of will". See sections 31 and 208–10.
Schelling	Friedrich Wilhelm Joseph Schelling (1775–1854), German philosopher who is generally associated with German *Idealism* (which itself developed through the influence of *Kant*'s philosophy). Nietzsche sees him as being misled by Kantianism. See section 11.
the scholar	Nietzsche sees modern academic scholars as products of the *herd morality* and *modern ideas*. As such, they are generally atheistic and unsophisticated. Occasionally, where they are objective, then their ideas and discoveries can be useful (e.g. *Darwin*). However, it takes a true philosopher to make use of such knowledge. See also *objectivity*, *free spirit*, *critic* and sections 6, 58, and most of Part Six (sections 204–13).
Schopenhauer	Arthur Schopenhauer (1788–1860), a German pessimist philosopher whose ideas were very influential upon the young Nietzsche. However, Nietzsche is later critical of him for his negative evaluation of the value of life, and for maintaining a traditional moral perspective in the face of his own *pessimism*. See sections 10, 36, 56, 186, 254 and 256.

Schumann	Robert Schumann (1810–56), German composer and music critic. Nietzsche considers him to have "petty taste", and compares him unfavourably with *Mendelssohn.* See section 245.
self-overcoming	Nietzsche's idea that, by struggle, discipline and *suffering,* we can 'overcome' our own lower natures and create ourselves anew. This is the importance of *cruelty* in the creative process, but turned against oneself. See sections 32, 200, 222–4, 257, 273, 277, and also *pathos of distance.*
sensualism	Nietzsche's term for the tendency of modern science to only give credit to the evidence of the senses. See also *positivism* and sections 11 and 15.
slave morality	The moral outlook of the lower classes and common people – generally, the ruled and powerless. Nietzsche sees this as springing from *ressentiment,* and the desire of the ruled to have power over the rulers. However, since they cannot have more power in worldly terms (they cannot be more powerful than their 'masters'), they create a way in which they are simply more deserving ('the meek shall inherit the Earth'). Slave morality therefore proposes 'harmless' qualities: brotherhood, friendship, love, peace, etc. See also *master morality, slave revolt in morals,* and sections 22, 46, 62, 195, 221–2, 225 and 260–1.
slave revolt in morals	The general inversion of values in Western society which has seen *slave morality* become dominant and in turn define *master morality* as evil. See *slave morality* and sections 46 and 62.
social Darwinism	The idea that *Darwin*'s ideas of natural selection can be applied to society. So, social Darwinism might argue that the weakest in society should not be helped so that 'nature may take its course' (i.e. they will eventually die). Nietzsche is often accused of social Darwinism because he criticises Christianity and modern morality not only for preserving the weakest, but also for holding up pity as an ideal. However, the case is debateable. See also Herbert *Spencer* and section 62.
Socrates	Socrates (470–399), Ancient Greek philosopher and teacher of *Plato.* Sentenced to death for allegedly 'corrupting the youth of Athens'. Nietzsche sees Socrates as a degenerative influence upon noble values because of

his *rationalism*, and his equation of 'the Good' with truth. See sections 190 and 212.

Spencer — Herbert Spencer (1820–1903), English social and political philosopher. Classed by Nietzsche along with Darwin and Mill as one of the "mediocre Englishmen" who have provided useful ideas to the modern age, but who in themselves are limited. Spencer is now mostly remembered for his *social Darwinism* (though, in fact, his application of the theory of evolution is more in line with *Lamarckism* – though he did coin the phrase 'survival of the fittest' to describe *natural selection*). See sections 62 and 253.

Spinoza — Baruch de Spinoza (1632–77) was a Jewish Dutch philosopher in the tradition of *rationalism*. His main work, the *Ethics*, advocates a form of 'monism' (that the world is one substance) and the whole work is set out in short, mathematical-like propositions. His personal problems, which Nietzsche seems to be aware of and hints at, stemmed mainly from his excommunication from the Jewish community for his heretical beliefs. See sections 5, 25 and 198.

Stendhal — The pen-name of Henri Beyle (1783–1842), nineteenth-century French writer, admired by Nietzsche for the psychological portrayal of character in his novels. See section 46.

stoicism — A school of Greek philosophy founded in the third century BC by Zeno of Citium (334 BC–262 BC). It flourished in both Greece and Rome, and can be characterised by belief in *determinism* (or, more generally, a belief in fate), indifference to misfortune and a call to align one's will with nature (it is this last piece of advice that Nietzsche mocks in section 9). See also section 189 for the possible usefulness of stoicism and puritanism.

straw man argument — An invalid form of argument which uses a misrepresentation of a certain position in order to criticise it.

suffering — Nietzsche sees the ability to suffer as a vital quality. Suffering leads to self-development and a strengthening of will, and is vital in the evolution of the higher type of man. This is linked to his idea that we should measure an individual by how much reality they can stand. See also *cruelty*, *self-overcoming* and sections 39, 225 and 270.

	However, this should not be confused with the "cult of suffering" and pity represented by slave morality (see sections 260 and 293).
the Superman	See *Übermensch*.
survival of the fittest	See *natural selection*.
synthetic	*Kant*'s term for types of statement where something is added to the original meaning of the term (e.g. 'all bachelors have brown hair'). See also *analytic* and *synthetic a priori*.
the synthetic a priori	*Kant*'s doctrine that certain judgements can be both *a priori* (independent of experience and necessarily true) and synthetic (provide new knowledge – i.e. are not simply true by definition, such as 'all bachelors are unmarried men'). This is a somewhat complicated topic which I discuss in more detail in Chapter 3, 'Immediate Certainty'. See section 11, and also *synthetic* and *analytic*.
teleological argument	See *design argument*.
teleological explanation	The 5th philosophical prejudice. To explain something teleologically is to identify a purpose as the reason for the action or event. For instance, in philosophy of religion the 'teleological argument' (or 'argument from design') proposes that God must exist because the world shows evidence of design and purpose (e.g. the purpose of the eye is to allow our brains to interpret light waves as information). However, as *Darwin* held, it is arguably possible to account for things which appear to have an inbuilt purpose ('teleology') purely in terms of blind mechanical processes (e.g. inheritance of physical traits) and their relation to the environment, where the 'fittest' – that is, most fitted to its environment – will survive (this is known as the process of *natural selection*). Nietzsche is therefore pointing out that teleological explanations are another example of the 'false beliefs' that human beings employ for their *own* purposes. See section 13.
tragedy and comedy	Nietzsche quite often uses the metaphor of drama in *BGE*, and together with his talk of *masks*, it can have various meanings. Firstly, the difference between the true philosopher and the common man is such that the latter cannot truly understand the former; also, since they hold

such different values, what is comic to one may be tragic to the other, and vice versa. Furthermore, the philosopher may reach a point where his understanding allows him to transcend what others think of as tragic. See sections 30, 150 and also *masks*.

Secondly, Nietzsche a number of times refers to philosophers as "play actors". By this he not only means that they are dishonest, but also that they create a world around themselves which is 'made up'. Their philosophy is therefore an act, a drama which they play so seriously that they start to believe it. Nietzsche's antidote to this is therefore to mock them; he looks at the tragic poses they strike and notes how such attitudes are in fact not necessary. See sections 7–8 and 25.

A final point to make about tragedy is its redemptive role. In *The Birth of Tragedy*, tragic drama is seen as providing the individual with a means to experience the whole of life without being destroyed by it. This idea is the basis of the idea of the *eternal return*, because the greatest attitude we can have is to accept everything, good and bad, painful and pleasurable, without desiring to change or rationalise it (which would be the *Apollonian* tendency), because that way we celebrate the totality of life. In this sense, tragedy allows us to experience this truth (it is *Dionysian*): we 'enjoy' tragic stories, and in doing so we partake in the irrational. In this sense, Nietzsche sees *Socrates* as bringing about the "death of tragedy"[2] through his attempt to rationalise morality. See section 295 and *suffering*.

the Übermensch   Nietzsche's concept of the new man or *free spirit*. It is sometimes translated as 'Overman' or 'Superman', but Nietzsche's basic intention here is to suggest a progression beyond the current concept of 'man'. The *Übermensch* will therefore go 'beyond good and evil' and establish a new set of values and a new philosophy. See also *free spirit*.

the unconscious   The theory, possibly current over centuries, but developed
mind   by Austrian psychologist Sigmund Freud (1856–1939), that there are non-conscious motives and reasoning which influence our conscious behaviour. Nietzsche's conception of such a thing is not explicitly set out, but his notions of *philosophical prejudice* and *will to power*, as well as his general comments on character and motivation, all suggest

that he believed in some form of unconscious. See also
psychoanalysis and sections 3, 53, 55, 188, 193 and
215–16.

utilitarianism The theory, first developed by Jeremy Bentham (1748–32),
that pleasure or happiness is the basis of all moral action,
and that the best action is that which brings the most
happiness to the greatest number of people (this is called
'classical utilitarianism'). See also *Mill* and section 228.

vitalism The idea, held by such thinkers as Jean Baptiste *Lamarck*
and Teilhard de Chardin (and of course Nietzsche), that
nature is not just a mechanical system (*mechanism*), but is
in some sense 'alive'. Vitalists may suggest that a living
being is alive because it consists of something more than
its physical or chemical processes, or that some life force
plays an active part in determining these processes.
Nietzsche seems at least to have held to the latter view. See
also *mechanism, Darwin, will to power*, and section 36.

Voltaire Voltaire or, to give him his true name, François-Marie
Arouet (1694–1778), was a French philosopher and writer
known for his satirical wit, for his defence of civil liberties,
and his championing of freedom of religious worship. As
such, he was a key figure in the *Enlightenment*. See section
35.

Wagner Wilhelm Richard Wagner (1813–83), German composer.
Wagner was much admired by Nietzsche, and his first
book, *The Birth of Tragedy*, was written very much with
the composer in mind. Wagner later adopted a more
Christian outlook (e.g. *Parsifal*) and was increasingly anti-
Semitic, which – amid other factors – eventually led
Nietzsche to break the friendship. *The Wagner Case* and
Nietzsche Contra Wagner represent Nietzsche's account of
the split and an assessment of Wagner and his music. See
sections 240–1, 251, 254 and 256.

will to ignorance The idea that the tendency to distort and simplify reality is
a fundamental drive. This may be opposed to the *will to
knowledge* (our desire to increase what we know).
However, both drives are aspects of the more fundamental
will to power. This should not be confused with the *will to
truth*, which is Nietzsche's term for the philosophical
prejudice that we can approach absolute truth in an
unbiased fashion. See sections 230–1.

will to knowledge   This is the opposite drive to the *will to ignorance*, and represents our desire to amass information and experience in order better to control our environment. In this sense, the will to knowledge is closely allied to the *will to ignorance*, in that we must necessarily simplify things in order to understand them (which allows for *oversimplification* and the desire for the world to be simpler than it is). See sections 230–1.

will to power   Nietzsche's idea that all creatures are driven by a desire to express their essential nature, seek dominance over others, and perpetuate the expression of their own 'type'. This may take a physical form (such as the dominance of stronger animals over weaker ones), or an intellectual form (such as the attempt of philosophers and founders of religions to control the way others see the world through systems of thought). *Will to truth* is therefore, for Nietzsche, merely a form of will to power in disguise. See sections 9, 13, 18–19, 22, 36–7, 51, 211, 230–1, 259, and *master morality*.

will to truth   This is the first of the so-called 'prejudices of philosophers' that Nietzsche considers have misled philosophers in the past. The 'will to truth' is therefore Nietzsche's phrase for the assumption, associated with most philosophers to date, that 'truth' exists separately from all human self-interest. He also posits it as a competing drive with the *will to ignorance*. See sections 1, 6, 177, 191, 211 and 230–1, *will to power*, *dogmatism* and *philosophical prejudice*.

Bibliography and Suggested Reading

Having diligently worked your way to the end of this guide, the keen among you will no doubt now be eager to scuttle off in search of further reading. So, being the helpful chap that I am, I typed 'Nietzsche books' into Google and came up with the following.

As with my previous guide to Descartes's *Meditations*, I have tried to give some indication of how useful the following books will be for different purposes and levels of interest. Accordingly, I have used the following code:

L = Layperson (a beginner – no specific knowledge)
A = British A-level student/US Freshman (intermediate – some knowledge)
U = Undergraduate (introduction at university, A-level detailed study)
D = Degree (suited for intensive study at university level)

By the way, I have only just noticed that the code spells out 'LAUD', which – I swear – was not deliberate. However, I suppose it does fit.

This is not an exhaustive list, but merely a useful one. Also, as I find new and useful books, I will add them to the website (www.philosophyonline.co.uk).

So, here are the books which I LAUD.

Nietzsche's Works

Beyond Good and Evil, translated by R. J. Hollingdale with an introduction by Michael Tanner (London: Penguin Classics, 1990). [This is an excellent translation, and the one that I have quoted from. However, there are a number of other good translations out there, and I would not wish to suggest that some of them are not equally good. My main purpose for favouring this edition was that it is the one used by AQA for the A-level syllabus.]

A Nietzsche Reader, selected and translated by R. J. Hollingdale (London: Penguin Classics, 1977). [This is a selection of passages from the range of Nietzsche's work, and provides a useful means of expanding your understanding of his philosophy. The sections are set out according to various themes (e.g. 'Morality', 'Will to Power', 'Religion'), which lends itself to comparative study of his different works. Furthermore, since Nietzsche frequently wrote in short passages of text, his philosophy is not really distorted by being presented as short selections. Once again, there are a number of different editions of this type of work, but I just happen to be familiar with this one.]

As regards other works by Nietzsche, the best thing is probably to begin with those which are closest to *BGE* in terms of date of composition. So, *The Genealogy of Morals*, his next published book, is probably a good place to start as it expands upon a number of the central themes in *BGE*. Similarly, *The Gay Science* was written just before, so there will also be a number of links between the two works which will provide fruitful study. Apart from that, Nietzsche's later works provide an increasingly punchy presentation of his views on a wide range of topics: *The Twilight of the Idols*, in a similar way to *BGE*, provides a sort of drive-by-criticism of various philosophical targets, whilst *The Anti-Christ* focuses on Nietzsche's views on Christianity.

Books on Nietzsche/*Beyond Good and Evil*

As regards other books about Nietzsche, there are many. These are ones that I have found particularly useful.

Laurence Lampert, *Nietzsche's Task: An Interpretation of 'Beyond Good and Evil'* (New Haven: Yale University Press, 2001) [**UD:** A very thorough and detailed, section-by-section account of *BGE* (the one I consulted when I got stuck!). It is, however, not ideally suited for the beginner or A-level student, and accordingly, I would only recommend it to those studying at a higher level.]

Robert Solomon and Kathleen Higgins, *What Nietzsche Really Said* (New York: Schocken Books, 2000) [**LAUD:** This is a wonderful book, and I cannot recommend it highly enough. It provides a handy overview of what Nietzsche said on certain topics, whilst also dispelling some misconceptions and myths that have grown up around him. Essential reading.]

Shelley O'Hara, *Nietzsche Within Your Grasp: The First Step to Understanding Nietzsche* (Hoboken, NJ: Wiley Publishing, 2004) [**LAU:** This is a handy little book (less than 80 pages) which provides a useful overview of the man and his philosophy. It gives a brief biography, accounts of his works, and lays out his main ideas in plain terms. An ideal introduction if you just need an overview.]

R. J. Hollingdale, *Nietzsche: The Man and His Philosophy* (London: Ark Paperbacks, 1985) [**LAU:** A well-written and readable biography by a trusted Nietzsche scholar. Sufficiently detailed to be informative, yet also with a general appeal.]

Rüdiger Safranski, *Nietzsche: A Philosophical Biography* (London: Granta Books, 2002) [**UD:** A detailed, insightful and fascinating account of Nietzsche and his philosophy (focusing on the latter). Not ideal for beginners, but excellent for those wishing to get deeper into the relationship of the man to his ideas.]

Lesley Chamberlain, *Nietzsche in Turin* (London: Quartet Books, 1996) [**LUD:** Once again, this is not particularly suitable for beginners, but it is a great read, and so may provide a way in to Nietzsche for those who enjoy biography, history, or even travel writing. It concerns Nietzsche's last sane part of his life spent in Turin, Italy, and gives us a detailed picture of his day-to-day life as he was composing his last works.]

Keith Ansell Pearson, *How to Read Nietzsche* (London: Granta Books, 2005) [**LU:** An interesting introduction to Nietzsche's works based on discussion of various extracts. Not really a beginner's guide, but intelligent and well-written, providing a useful bridge between a discussion of Nietzsche and the texts themselves.]

Peter R. Sedgwick (ed.), *Nietzsche: A Critical Reader* (Oxford: Blackwell, 1995) [**D:** A useful collection of critical essays. Only really suitable for degree-level study, but a good basis for identifying different theoretical approaches to Nietzsche's thought.]

Background and Wider Reference

Peter R. Sedgwick, *Descartes to Derrida* (Oxford: Blackwell, 2001) [**LAUD:** Something here for everyone, though not something that everyone would read cover to cover. A sufficiently detailed and readable account of the main European philosophical trends and philosophers from Descartes to modern times. This helps to put Nietzsche in context, and the treatments of Kant, Descartes, Hegel, etc. provide useful reference for Nietzsche's views on these philosophers, whilst later sections provide a picture of his influence on modern philosophers. These latter sections are more challenging, and not so useful for A-level students and the layperson, but such a book would be a good reference for anyone interested in the development of modern European philosophy.]

Roger Scruton, Peter Singer, Christopher Janaway and Michael Tanner, *German Philosophers: Kant, Hegel, Schopenhauer, and Nietzsche* (Oxford: Oxford University Press, 1997) [**UD:** A collection of introductions rather than a unified book, but nevertheless useful to have all this in one place. Each of the studies is written by an eminent philosopher, and the Nietzsche one alone is worth reading. However, this would be an excellent read for anyone who needed to relate Nietzsche's thought to these near-contemporaries and the times themselves.]

Colin Wilson, *The Outsider* (London: Orion Books, 1967) [**LAUD:** Wilson's classic study of the intellectual and artistic outsider has a whole chapter dedicated to Nietzsche. However, it also helps to identify certain of Nietzsche's concerns as common themes of a particular creative type. Recommended for everyone for its general readability and interest.]

John Gray, *Straw Dogs* (London: Granta Books, 2002) [**LAUD:** Such books as these prove that philosophy is still alive and well and relevant to today's society. Gray is a modern-day pessimist, and his views – whether you agree with them or not – are provocative and interesting. Furthermore, aside from an interesting but short section on Nietzsche himself, readers will recognise in the book many of the same themes and concerns that run through *BGE*.]

Index

Note: page numbers in *italics* refer to illustrations or tables; 'Nietzsche' is usually abbreviated to 'N'.

ad hominem argument (N's use of)
    107–8
    problems with   107
Alston, William P. (and non-conceptual
    perception)   128–9
amor fati see eternal return, the
analytic/synthetic distinction *see* Kant,
    Immanuel (synthetic *a priori*)
anarchy   63
Anaximenes   115
anti-realism (in N's philosophy)   114–15,
    135–7
anti-semitism   x, 5, 7, 86
Appollo (the Appolonian)   5, 103
a priori/a posteriori distinction   124–7;
    see also prejudice, philosophical
    (immediate certainty)
Archelaus of Macedonia   92
aristocracy *see* nobility
Aristophanes (and Plato)   36, 58, 102
Aristotle   57, 61
    four causes   120–1, *121*
    four elements   115
    law of excluded middle   111
atheism   136
    N's   137–8, 144–9; investigated
    146–9

Augustine, St   47, 62
Avogadro, Amadeo   116
Ayer, A. J.   64

Bacon, Sir Francis   87, 100
Beethoven, Ludwig van   9, 84
Bentham, Jeremy   8, 150
Bergson, Henri   156
Berkeley, Bishop George   41, 135
Berlioz, Hector   9
Birx, James H.   156
Bismarck, Otto von (and *Realpolitik* of)
    12
Bizet, George   88
Blake, William (*Marriage of Heaven and
    Hell*)   104, 153
Boscovich, Roger Joseph   25, 116
Boyle, Robert   115
Bruno, Giordano   35
Buddhism (the Buddha)   11, 49–50, 142,
    144, 147
Byron, Lord George Gordon   9

Caesar, Julius   62
capitalism   152
Chamberlain, Lesley   148
Charlemagne   11

Christianity (and Christian values) 15,
   44–5, 47–8, 52, 60–3, 76, 87–91,
   97, 100, 111, 114, 135, 140, 142,
   144, 146–9, 152–5; *see also*
   religion
Cicero 120
Coleridge, Samuel Taylor 9
comedy 35
communism 152
compatibilism 130; *see also* free will,
   problem of
consequentialism 151; *see also* morality,
   history of
Constable, John 9
Copernicus 25
Cromwell, Oliver 44
cruelty/exploitation (as basis of all culture
   and knowledge) 76–8, 89–90
cynicism 36

Dalton, John 116
Dante Alighieri 58
Darwin, Charles (Darwinism) 26, 52, 68,
   87, *122*, 122–4, 155–60
   difference/similarity with N's
      views 123–4, 155–60
   natural selection (survival of the
      fittest) 52, 122–4, 155–60
   self-preservation in 155–7, 160
   social Darwinism 52
da Vinci, Leonardo 62
Delacroix, Eugene 9
democracy/democratic spirit 15–16, 32,
   80–1, 94; *see also* modern ideas
Democritus 115
Dennett, Daniel 134
Derrida, Jacques 13
Descartes, René 8, 48, 100, 108–9, 130,
   135
   Cogito, the (N's critique of) 28–9,
      108–9, 117–18, 124–5, 127, 133
   dualism 134
determinism 29–30, 32, 68, 129–32, 134;
   see also free will, problem of

biological 129, 132
   theological 130
Dionysus (the Dionysian) 5, 103, 147
diversified descent, man of 62, 70; *see
   also* free spirit (role of
   self-overcoming)
dogmatism 14–16; *see also* prejudice,
   philosophical
dualism *see* Descartes
duck-rabbit illusion 127, *128*

Eckardt, Barbara Von 155
empiricism 8, 68, 87, 127; *see also*
   modern ideas; positivism; science
England (and English character) 87
Enlightenment, Age of 8–9
Epicurus 21
eternal return, the 35, 41, 50, 133, 145
eugenics (heredity) 68, 71, 86, 94, 132
existentialism 146

falsification (as condition of life) *see* will
   to ignorance
feudalism 152
Fichte, Johann Gottlieb 9
foundationalism 127
Förster, Bernhard (N's brother-in-law) 7
France
   decline due to modern ideas 87–9
   French Revolution 8; as slave revolt in
      morals 80, 89
Frazer, Sir James (*The Golden
   Bough*) 138
free spirit/higher man 15, 34–44, 54
   ability to face truth as sign of strength
      in 42, 51, 109
   as 'attempters' of new values/
      knowledge 43, 70
   as critic 66–7
   as good European, the 82–3, 88
   as sceptic 39, 66
   as *Übermensch* 145–6
   'bad' qualities necessary for 39, 42, 67,
      75, 104

free spirit/higher man (*cont'd*)
  difference with common man   37, 71,
    95–8, 100
  different from 'free thinker'   43–4
  distinguished from scholar, men of
    science   67–8
  necessary isolation of/difficulties faced
    by   36–7, 42, 95–103; *see also* masks
  self-overcoming, role of   38, 62, 73, 89,
    132–3
  suffering, value of for   74–8
  traps to be avoided by   42–3, 75
  uses of religion for   51–2
free will, problem of the   29–32, *30*,
    129–3
  N's solution to   130–2
  response to N's views   132–3
Freud, Sigmund   138, *139*, 140–1
  problems with method   154–5
Friedrich, Caspar David   9
Fritzsch, Ernst Wilhelm   6–7

gai saber (joyful wisdom/gay
    science)   57–8, 92, 102
Gast, Peter   6
Germany
  as 'active' culture   85
  German character   81–5, 87; in
    literature   84–5; in music   81–3, 88
  patriotism as symptom of
    'indigestion'   82–4, 86
given, the (myth of)   127–9
God *see also* religion
  as metaphysical error   138–42
  as projection   138–42
  cosmological argument for existence
    of   129; *see also* prejudice,
    philosophical (*causa sui*)
  genetic fallacy, N accused of   139–40
  teleological argument for existence
    of   120; *see also* prejudice,
    philosophical (teleological
    explanation)
Goethe, Johann Wolfgang   9, 88, 95, 101

Gorgias of Leontini   135–6
Gothic movement, the   9
Gray, John (*Straw Dogs*)   148–9
Guyon, Madame de   47

Hegel, Georg Wilhelm Friedrich   9, 67
Heidegger, Martin   13
Heraclitus   115
herd morality   61–3, 67, 71–2, 83, 94,
    146; *see also* morality as timidity;
    slave morality
history, N's critique of progressive view
    of   41
Hitler, Adolf (influenced by N)   x, 7
Hobbes, Thomas   103, 130
Holmes, Sherlock   121
Homer   73
Horace   94
Hume, David   8, 87, 127, 130, 137
  on cause and effect   108
  on teleological argument   121

idealism   9, 41; *see also* Berkeley, Bishop
    George
  German idealism   9
  N's refutation of   *27*, 27–8
  transcendental idealism *see* Kant,
    Immanuel
illusion, argument from   112
Industrial Revolution, the   8–9
intentionalism   151; *see also* morality,
    history of
intuitionism, moral   150

James, William (*The Varieties of Religious
    Experience*)   141–2
Jesuitism   15, 147
Jesus   21, 54, 96
Judaism/Jewish culture   47–8, 60, 85–6,
    142, 144, 153; *see also* anti-Semitism;
    slave morality

Kant, Immanuel   10, 27, 40, 48, *49*, 56, 67
  and moral duty   150

noumena and phenomena   9, 113, 119
synthethic *a priori* 125–6; N's critique
of   24–5, 126–7
transcendental idealism of   9, 24, 113,
135
Kaufmann, Walter   xiv

Lamarck, Jean-Baptiste (Lamarckism)   68,
69, 156–7
language (role in formation of thought/
limitations of)   31, 36, 84–5, 103,
117–18, 130–1, 133, 141–2
Laplace, Pierre-Simon   130
Lavoisier, Antoine   115
Leibniz, Gottfried Wilhelm   10, 135
Leo III, Pope   11
Leucippus   115
libertarianism   29–30, 130–2; *see also* free
will, problem of
Locke, John   8, 87, 127
logical positivism   64
Luther, Martin   44, 47, 85

'man of prey'   61–2, 92
Marx, Karl   152
masks   35, 42, 73, 77, 84, 97, 99–102
master morality   32, 45, 60, 83, 90–3, 138,
142, 153–5; *see also* free spirit; pagan
(noble) values
materialism   133–4
Maxwell, James Clerk   116
mechanism   68, 157–9
Mendelssohn, Felix   84
metaphysics   26–7, 108–11, 127, 149–50
Mill, John Stuart   8, 87
modern ideas   24, 50–1, 76, 80–1, 87, 94
man of, lacks 'taste'   73–4
Moore, G. E.   150
morality
as arbitrary discipline   56–8
as timidity   61–2, 92
history of (pre-moral, moral and extra
moral)   38, 151–2
science of   55, 76

Mozart, Wolfgang Amadeus   84
multi-valued (fuzzy) logic   111–12

Napoleon, Emperor   11, 62, 88
naturalization *see* prejudice, philosophical
(reification)
naturalism
ethical   111, 149–51; problems with
(naturalistic fallacy)   150–1
ethical non-naturalism   150–1
in epistemology   108–10, 112, 136–7,
139; problems with   109–10
Naumann, C. G.   6–7
Newton, Sir Isaac   8, 115, 130
Nietzsche, Carl (father)
as possible source of N's illness   3
death of   1
Nietzsche, Elisabeth (sister)
anti-Semitism of   x, 7
role in presenting N's work   x, 7
marriage to Bernhard Förster (as source
of quarrel with N)   7
Nietzsche, Franziska (mother)   1, 7
Nietzsche, Friedrich   *2, 17*
approach to philosophy   xi–xii
life   1–7
madness   x, 7
myths surrounding, anti-Semitism   x,
86; Nazism (N's influence upon)   x,
7, 13
Will to Power (Revaluation of all
Values) project   12–13
writing style (difficulties of)
xii–xiii
works:
Anti-Christ, The   7, 13, 148
Beyond Good and Evil, history and
purpose of text   7, 12–13
Birth of Tragedy, The   4–5, 103, 147
Ecce Homo   7, 13
Gay Science, The   6
Genealogy of Morals, The   7, 13, 45,
152–3
Human, All Too Human   5, 13

Nietzsche, Friedrich (*cont'd*)
    Thus Spoke Zarathustra 6, 13, 98–9,
      103
    Twilight of the Idols, The xi, 7, 135
    Untimely Meditations 5
    Wagner Case, The 7
Nietzsche, Ludwig Joseph (brother) 1
nihilism 24, 37, 144–6
nobility
    as expression of will to power 90
    as purpose of society 89
    as source of positive values 90–3
    attitude to vanity/self-estimation 93,
      95, 101
    linked to 'pathos of distance' 88–9; *see
      also* order of rank
    noble society, stages of decay in 89,
      93–4
    reverence as sign of 94, 101
    see also master morality; pagan (noble)
      values

objectivity, possibility of 20–1, 65, 71–2,
    108–9, 137; *see also* prejudice,
    philosophical (will to truth)
Occam's razor (principle of
    parsimony) 157–9
order of rank 71, 89
Overbeck, Franz 4, 6

pagan (noble) values 44, 62, 76, 88–103,
    114, 144; *see also* master morality;
    nobility
Paine, Thomas 8
Paley, William (teleological argument
    of) 120; *see also* prejudice,
    philosophical (teleological
    explanation)
Pascal, Blaise 44
pathos of distance *see* nobility
perspectivism (N's) 15, 19, 110, 113–15,
    136–7; problems with 114–15
pessimism 49, 65–6, 73, 87, 88, 144–5;
    see also Schopenhauer, Arthur

Phillips, D. Z. 140
Pinker, Steven 127–8
pity/compassion, Christian virtue of (N's
    critique of) 45, 52, 63, 65, 73–5,
    102
Plato 10, 23, 26–7, 40, 135
    and Aristophanes 36, 58, 102
    and Socrates 58–9
    contrast with Epicurus 21
    forms, doctrine of 113, 150
    Gorgias, The 92
    Platonism 15, 24, 36, 135, 144
positivism 24, 64, 68, 134–5
pragmatism 110
prejudice, philosophical xi–xii, 14–16,
    33–4, 53–4, 77, 106–8, 148
    appearance and reality 23–4, 112–15
    atomism 25–6, 38, 115–20, 133;
      response to N's views 119–20, 139
    causa sui 30, 31–2, 129–33, 139
    faith in antithetical values 16–17, *18*,
      46, 85–6, 104, 110–12, 150–1;
      response to N's views 111–12
    immediate certainty 28–9, 39–40, 99,
      124–9
    reification 31–3, 133–4, 136
    teleological explanation 26, 120–4;
      response to N's views 124, 160
    will to truth 14–16, 20, 38–40, 42, 59,
      71–2, 108–10, 136–7
pre-moral, moral and extra moral (N's
    distinction between) *see* morality,
    history of
psychological approach (N's use of) 33–
    4, 44, 60, 71, 102
puritanism 57

quantum physics 130

rationalism 8–9
realism 135; N's critique of *see*
    anti-realism
    naive (direct) 112
    non-reductive 134, 159

representative (indirect)   112–14, *113*, 135

reductio ad absurdum (N's use of)   27–8

Rée, Paul   5–6

relativism (and N's philosophy)   114–15

religion   54; *see also* Christianity; God

'anti-Christian', N as   146

faith as 'suicide of reason'   44

linked to environment and culture   44, 46, 47

in pagan (noble) cultures   45–7

religious language as anthropomorphic   140–2

religious neurosis, the   44–6, 142–4, 148; and ladder of sacrifice   48–9, 143; response to N's views   143–4; and saint, figure of   46–7, 97, 143; and science   49, 143

soul, notion of   48, 146–7, 158

uses of for free spirit   51–2

will to ignorance in   49, 51

ressentiment   56, 138, 152–5; response to N's views   154–5; *see also* slave morality

Ritschl, Professor Friedrich Wilhelm   4

Romanticism   9, 84, 136

Rousseau, Jean Jacques   8, 9

Russell, Bertrand   135

Rutherford, Ernest (model of the atom)   116–17, *117*

Ryle, Gilbert (and category mistake)   117–18

Salomé, Lou (N's proposal of marriage to)   6

Sartre, Jean-Paul   13

scepticism

as a 'sickness'/negative influence   37, 65–6

positive use of *see* free spirit/higher man

Schelling, Friedrich Wilhelm Joseph   9

scholar, the (as herd animal)   64–5, 76; *see also* free spirit, distinguished from

Schopenhauer, Arthur   *10*, 41, 88

influence on Nietzsche   5, 9–11, 49–50, 106

pessimistic philosophy of   5, 9–11, 24, 35, 49, 55–6, 144, 148

Schumann, Robert   84

science (N's view of)   26, 31–3, 41, 116, 157–9, 160; *see also* positivism

supplanting philosophy   63–4

Searle, John   134

Sellars, Wilfrid (myth of the given)   128–9

sense data (sense impressions)   127–9

sensualism   25; *see also* positivism

Shakespeare, William   73

slave morality   32, 45, 56, 83, 90–3, 138, 153–5

slave revolt in morals   45, 52, 60, 72, 89, 104, 114, 142–3, 153–4

Socrates   58–9, 92

Spencer, Herbert   87, 156

Spinoza, Baruch de   8, 20, 35, 61, 107

stoicism   21–2, 57, 61

'straw man' argument   149

synthetic *a priori see* Kant, Immanuel

Teilhard de Chardin, Pierre   156

teleological argument (for existence of God) *see* God

Thales   115

theosophy   146

tragedy (N's conception of)   35

troubadour poets   58; *see also gai saber*

truth, N's view of *see* prejudice, philosophical (will to truth); objectivity; free spirit (ability to face truth as sign of strength in)

Turner, Joseph Mallord William   9

Übermensch (superman)   144–7; *see also* free spirit

unconscious

influence of instincts upon opinions and morals   18–19, 58–9, 70, 78, 103, 106

unconscious (*cont'd*)
  psychoanalysis   20; *see also* Freud,
    Sigmund
utilitarianism   8, 76, 150

vitalism   68, 134, 157–9
Voltaire   8, 40

Wagner, Cosima   4–5
Wagner, Richard   *82*
  anti-Semitism of   5, 86
  as forerunner of 'good European'   88
  influence of Schopenhauer upon   5,
    10
  music of   81–3, 88
  N's friendship and quarrel with   4–5

Wilhelm I, Kaiser   12
will to ignorance   19–20, 34, 37, 39–40,
  49, 51, 77–8, 102, 111
will to knowledge   77–8
will to power   23, 26, 33, 40–1, 47, 67,
  77–8, 90, 109–10, 114, 120, 124,
  131–2, 134, 143, 153–60; critique of
  155–60
  in inorganic matter   40–1, 134, 157–9
will to truth *see* prejudice, philosophical
Wilson, Colin (*The Outsider*)   146–8
Wittgenstein, Ludwig   140
women, N's views on   54, 78–81
Wordsworth, William   9

Zoroaster (relation to N's *Zarathustra*)   6